HOW TO RUN SEMINARS & WORKSHOPS

FOURTH
EDITION

HOW TO RUN SEMINARS & WORKSHOPS

PRESENTATION SKILLS
FOR **CONSULTANTS, TRAINERS,**
TEACHERS, AND **SALESPEOPLE**

ROBERT L. JOLLES

WILEY

For general information about our other products and services, please contact our Customer Care Department within the United States at (800) 762-2974, outside the United States at (317) 572-3993 or fax (317) 572-4002.

Wiley publishes in a variety of print and electronic formats and by print-on-demand. Some material included with standard print versions of this book may not be included in e-books or in print-on-demand. If this book refers to media such as a CD or DVD that is not included in the version you purchased, you may download this material at http://booksupport.wiley.com. For more information about Wiley products, visit www.wiley.com.

Library of Congress Cataloging-in-Publication Data:

Names: Jolles, Robert L., 1957- author.
Title: How to run seminars and workshops : presentation skills for
    consultants, trainers, teachers, and salespeople / Robert Jolles.
Description: Fourth edition. | Hoboken, NJ : John Wiley & Sons, Inc., [2017]
    | Includes bibliographical references.
Identifiers: LCCN 2016054282| ISBN 9781119374343 (pbk.) | ISBN 9781119374336
    (epub) | ISBN 9781119374282 (ePDF)
Subjects: LCSH: Seminars–Handbooks, manuals, etc. | Workshops (Adult
    education)–Handbooks, manuals, etc. | Meetings–Handbooks, manuals, etc.
Classification: LCC AS6 .J65 2017 | DDC 658.4/56–dc23 LC record available
    at https://lccn.loc.gov/2016054282

Printed in the United States of America

10 9 8 7 6 5 4 3 2 1

*This book is dedicated to my wife, Ronni, who supported,
assisted, and endured the trials of this most unusual profession;
to the tens of thousands of participants who allowed a struggling
professional speaker learn his trade and ultimately learn
his lessons in humility and compassion; and to the memory
of my dear friend Tony Fox.*

Contents

Preface

About 25 years ago, I wrote the first edition of this book and invited you into the world of seminars and workshops. Whether you are a professional speaker, trainer, seminar leader, guest speaker, or just someone who occasionally must deliver an idea by addressing a group of people, this book was created for you. From marketing and preparation to all aspects of delivery, this book will guide you through the many nuances that will allow you to direct a group of strangers so that they come together as a team and accomplish a common goal.

A lot has changed over the years. More and more people are tasked with presenting information to others. These presentations are often delivered to a green dot on the top of a monitor and seen by others many miles, and sometimes continents, away.

A lot has stayed the same. The need to gain the attention of others and hold that attention, whether on a stage, in a classroom, on a conference call, on a podcast, in an online video, and more, still challenges us all. In this fourth edition, I hope to address some of the new challenges that come with the changes in technology, and how we give and receive information. The communication process hasn't changed as much as the speed with which we communicate.

There are many misunderstandings surrounding the professional speaking profession. I hope to address many of those misunderstandings. There are many opinions regarding right and wrong. As a former corporate trainer and professional speaker, I hope to give you definitive answers based on my experiences. As with any presentation I deliver, I hope you find the book both informative and fun. I hope also that you will find support and motivation within these pages. That is one of the true values of a good Presentation Skills program, and that is what this book is about.

After I had finished school at the University of Maryland, my first job was for the New York Life Insurance Company. In four days, I was taught how to be an insurance salesman. I was taught the difference between term and whole life insurance. I was taught about preexisting conditions and other key areas of health insurance. I was even taught about disability insurance and the "curse of the living death." Very scary! Four days later, when they were all through teaching me about insurance, I was shown the door and told, "Two apps a week, ten apps a month. Go get 'em, tiger!" I was trained. But my training failed me. I was taught about my product, but no one ever told me how to sell it.

Most people who become trainers or presenters fall into the same trap. *They are taught what to teach but rarely* how *to teach it.* They appear in front of their audiences as ill prepared as I was initially selling insurance. Customers want more than product knowledge, and so do trainees. Therein lies the importance of having information not just on what to teach but on how to teach it.

I have been teaching presentation programs for over 35 years. Thirty-five years of active stand-up delivery training is kind of like dog years—that is, about 245 years of professional speaking to you and me. I have delivered these courses while employed by three major corporations as well as for myself as an entrepreneur. In those years, I have developed a love–hate relationship with a topic that I find fascinating. The love portion of training others to speak like a professional is connected to seeing thousands of presenters just like me—groping for new methods, validating and replacing old ideas, and sometimes just hanging around to get their batteries recharged. The hate portion of training others to speak like professionals centers around its unforgiving nature. In just about any program taught, it is more than acceptable to misplace a handout, forget a trainee's name, or even lose your train of thought. When teaching someone "how it is done," however, there is very little forgiveness for errors. It is a challenge. It will also age you a bit.

I view this book, as I do a good Presentations Skills program, as a kind of vitamin. When you take a vitamin, your body absorbs only what it needs. In this book, my intention is to give you too many ideas. Each may be appropriate depending on your topic, seminar size, personality, style, and any number of other factors. Take what you need and disregard what is not suitable to your situation.

You will be reading and relating to real-world situations and solutions. Let me give you a quick taste of real world in the life of a presenter. Recently I was asked to speak in front of about 100 managers for one of the largest insurance companies in the country. This presentation was set to last for six hours. The individual who coordinated the presentation on behalf of the insurance company had come to me only weeks before the presentation date, telling me the presentation was "no big deal," and to just "walk the group through some simple sales skills." Well, as a professional trainer, I have learned that all presentations are a "big deal," and I've spent 35 years guarding against the temptation to not take presentations as seriously as they need to be taken. My preparation was thorough and disciplined, following the techniques taught in this book. Minutes before the presentation was set to begin, my contact person informed me that there would be a couple of visitors in the room. These visitors each happened to be senior vice presidents. At that time, I was also informed that instead of six hours, they would like to stretch the presentation to eight hours. "No problem" was my response. The reserve material that I always have on hand took care of the time, and my mental preparation took care of the senior vice presidents. By the way, senior vice presidents rarely sit for seminars without a motive. As I suspected, that presentation acted as an audition for my company and its training capabilities. The results? As of this writing, we have received somewhere in the neighborhood of a half million dollars in training revenue from this company.

That story is a microcosm of what it is to be a professional speaker and why throughout this book you will see references to the term "under fire." Whether you are speaking in front of senior vice presidents or senior citizens, 150 customers or 15 customers, the pressure is always there. The potential for triumph or trouble is always there. The opportunity for success or failure is always there. Each room is a puzzle that you need to figure out. As a professional trainer, you can die from the pressure or thrive under it. One other reference you will also see from time to time is a reference to the "pit." This is the area in front of the lectern that separates the presenter from the participants. Depending on the size of the audience, this is where presenters (with the help of a wireless microphone or a booming voice) need to live to stay connected with their audiences. This book is dedicated to teaching you how to understand the pressure of going under fire and thrive in the pit.

One last point before you read what awaits you. Please remember that in no way do I wish you to walk away from what you are about to read with a desire to change your style. The greatest lesson I ever learned about style came mercifully early in my career. There are many who claim to be the greatest salespeople who ever lived. You can pick from any number who have written books, put out tapes, or delivered seminars. Each is good in his or her own way, and far be it from me to knock what others do.

For example, I consider a man named Ben Feldman the greatest salesperson who ever lived. In 1979, while I was with New York Life, Ben led the industry in sales. That is in all the insurance companies, not just mine. Actually, it is unfair to say he led the industry; he *dominated* it. The top nine agents were all fairly close to each other. Ben Feldman tripled the next closest competitor. What a legend! From the metropolis of Youngstown, Ohio, this man was rewriting the record books in sales. I had never seen a picture of Ben, but I imagined what he looked like. Tall, aggressive, good looking. I sensed he looked a lot like me (okay, minus some of those attributes). One day we received a tape of Ben Feldman in the office. I got dressed up the day I was scheduled to watch the tape, and my life changed. The Ben Feldman on the tape was about five foot four, somewhat overweight, balding, and spoke with a lisp. Not quite what I had expected; however, I watched on. Within seconds, I was drawn to the techniques Ben Feldman was using. It was then and there I learned the most valuable lesson I would ever receive in my life regarding style: I could not be Ben Feldman; I could, however, focus on his techniques and continue to ask myself "How can I do that so it sounds like Rob Jolles?" Rob Jolles cannot do Ben Feldman, and Ben Feldman cannot do Rob Jolles.

As you read this book, continue to ask yourself: "How do I implement these ideas so they sound like me?" If you commit to your own style and implement some of the ideas and techniques recommended in the following pages, I believe you will do just fine. Who is actually attending your presentation, their jobs, their positions within the company, the health of the organization, and more affects how you will apply what you will be learning. In an attempt to connect this information with as many of you as possible, I will refer to you as professional speakers, presenters, and trainers. As for those you are speaking to, I will refer to them as participants, audience members, and trainees. With that in mind, sit back and remember that what is presented in the pages to follow, the good, the bad, and the occasionally ugly, is real world. So, what are we waiting for? Let's get ready to rumble!

Rob "The Rocket" Jolles

Acknowledgments

I would like to acknowledge the following people:
Bill "Scooter" Leathwood who introduced me to the training profession and whose actions inspired me to become a trainer.

Robert C. Camp, author of *Benchmarking,* for showing me that a project of this nature can be done.

Mary Ellen Silk for her careful maneuvering around my "fragile writer's ego" and providing the editing assistance I so badly needed.

Decades of Wiley editors who have each had a piece of this book, my most recent being Liz Gildea. I'm beyond grateful for your continuing guidance, support, and belief in this book.

Emmett Reagan and Larry Domonkos for graciously filling the roles of mentor and role model, showing me what it is to be a Xerox trainer.

Xerox Corporation for putting their faith and trust in me as a trainer, allowing me to touch so many wonderful trainees inside and outside the company.

And you, the reader. It isn't often a book survives over 25 years on the bookshelf. I'll keep trying to get better, if you keep coming back for more.

Part I

Getting Started

Chapter 1

Creating a Seminar Business

When I first wrote this book, I was a senior trainer for Xerox Corporation. In that capacity, I felt I had created a program that taught individuals everything they needed to know about corporate training. In fact, that might have been the case for a corporate trainer whose audiences came from within the corporation. However, it has now been over 25 years since I left Xerox to open my own training business. In those years I have certainly learned one simple fact about how to run seminars and workshops. If you can't populate a room with participants, you don't stay in business.

In the following chapters you will learn everything you need to know about how to grab an audience and take them for one terrific ride. In this chapter you will learn how to run a seminar business. Every speaking professional has his or her own way of doing things, and I'm a creature of habit as well. My goal is to provide you with choices and opinions that go along with those choices and then ultimately equip you with enough knowledge to let you decide how to run your own seminar business.

Branding Yourself

Before we start working on putting participants into the seats, referred to as "populating the room," you must figure out what these participants are coming to hear. The concept of branding yourself sounds a little rough, but not to worry. It isn't as bad as it sounds. You see, rarely are you the only person on the face of the earth who will be talking about the subject you profess to be an expert in. The term "branding" refers to how you will differentiate yourself within your industry.

For instance, there are many who lecture on selling, one of the topics I lecture on. Go to the bookstore and you will notice that there are a few people who claim to know as much, if not more, than I do. However, my branding has been threefold:

1. I teach a classic Xerox sales approach.
2. I teach from "repeatable, predictable processes."
3. I teach the art of creating urgency.

This becomes my branding, or my niche. It allows clients to differentiate what I do from what others do. It might differentiate me into a job, or it might differentiate me out of a job. Clients can decipher what makes me unique.

What will be your branding? It may be one of the most important questions you ask yourself. Do not rush into a quick answer. In a sense, you may be married to this concept for quite some time. Whatever you decide, I suggest you follow a couple of simple rules.

RULE #1—THINK OUTSIDE OF THE BOX

That can be a tired phrase, but the fact of the matter is that many geniuses of today are working with ideas that have been around for quite some time. What initially makes them different and employed is the creativity they use to attract their clients.

One of my colleagues, Eric Hargens, works with salespeople as well. He's spent time as a consultant and sales manager, and he struggled with this for a while. He wanted to focus on the initial conversation that goes on between client and salesperson. That doesn't sound much like a branding, now does it? After a few long walks and a couple of cigars, he came up with a different way of articulating this concept. He calls it "the art of chitchat." Now he has a simple way of explaining what makes what he does unique. That's what I call thinking out of the box.

RULE #2—KEEP IT SIMPLE

I hear from many people working on their consulting businesses who are trying to brand themselves. When I ask them what they speak on, often the next sentence out of their mouths tells me all I need to know.

When I hear someone take five minutes to answer the question, there is a problem. If you can't explain it, how in the world are you going to sell it? Most people are not interested in hearing a dissertation or pieces of your seminar. They just want to know what you are going to teach them. My rule of thumb is simple: If it takes you more than five words to say it, it's not simple enough.

Please understand that "simple" doesn't mean "obvious." "Simple" means "easy to understand." My suggestion is to write out and practice little sound bites that would interest prospective clients.

RULE #3—DON'T UNDERESTIMATE THE BASICS . . . JUST DON'T ADVERTISE IT!

Now that you will be thinking out of the box and trying to keep the concept simple, you are probably asking yourself, "How do I come up with the next hula hoop?" You don't have to. You need to put your own slant on your topic and surround it with solid presentation skills that you will learn in abundance as you read through this book. If it were me, I'd start with the basics.

When I left Xerox and started my consulting business, I felt I was on the cutting edge of every process that related to selling. During one of my seminars an individual came up and complimented me on how I was defining the art of selling. I wasn't that surprised because I felt this was one of the most unique definitions I had created.

He then told me he had seen a similar definition in a book he had read. I was flabbergasted and immediately challenged him to give me the name of the book. I had read plenty of books and had never seen anything close to my definition. The book he was quoting was *Salesmanship and Sales Management*, written by John G. Jones from the Alexander Hamilton Institute. Jones's definition of selling went this way:

> *Salesmanship, in its broadest sense, is essentially the selling of one's point of view—the ability to start with the other fellow's point of view and to lead his mind to the viewpoint of the seller.*

I must apologize for the indifference to gender within Jones's definition, but that is how they referred to many things in 1917, when this passage was written. You see, this is not new information; this is information that *has* been around . . . it has simply been forgotten.

RULE #4—BE PASSIONATE

The quickest way out of the seminar business is to lack passion for the topic you are building your business around. Experience is very important, but experience can be attained. Passion cannot be attained. It must be felt.

What do you truly love to study and talk about? You and your topic are going to be together for quite some time; my suggestion is to think long and hard about this. You and your audiences will be a lot happier if you do!

General versus Closed Seminars

Now that you are branded, you have a second major decision to make. Will your seminar business run general sessions, or will you run closed seminars? The answer to this question will go a long way to determining how you go about marketing yourself. Let's spend a moment or two looking at the pros and cons of each.

GENERAL SESSIONS

A general session seminar is one that is put on for a mixed audience. Such seminars typically are attended by multiple companies and accommodate large audiences. If you have ever attended one, you'd know it. Frequently these seminars are held in hotels or facilities that hold large audiences.

The biggest strength of building a seminar business with general sessions in mind is profit. When I decided to go into the seminar business, one of the contributing factors was my attendance in a general session seminar. The program I attended was a one-day coping-with-conflict seminar, and the cost was a measly $175. Of course, I wasn't the only one attending. My guess is there were more than 500 people in attendance. I'm not a math major, but I believe that represents a one-day total of $87,500. There were other costs, like renting of the room, marketing of the seminar, snacks, and coffee, but any way you stack it, that was one heck of a day in the seminar business.

These types of seminars are typically marketed by utilizing key elements of social media, email blasts, and mass mailing flyers sent to selected mailing list clients. This list is determined by the topic. For instance, the session I just described was marketed to human resources professionals. In the sales industry where many of my sessions are delivered, if I were to mass market, I'd aim for a mailing list of sales managers. If I were to put on a general session for training professionals, I'd mass mail to training managers and possibly human resources professionals where training often resides.

If the profit is so high, why would anyone ever want to create a seminar business with any other marketing approach in mind? The answer lies in the topic and the techniques you choose to deliver that topic. As you lean back and decide if this is an approach that you want to consider, ask yourself these questions:

1. Is my topic generic enough to deliver competently to multiple customers?

    When conducting a general session seminar, you may have well over 100 different companies represented in the room. Your topic has to be generic enough to provide examples that will be pertinent to all. Sometimes this isn't possible, and speakers begin to move to multiple industry examples. This is done by highlighting various industries represented by participants in the room, and providing direct examples that relate to them. Once you begin to do this, just be careful to have a wide range of examples to include as many different industries as possible.

2. Will my message be lost in a large audience seminar format?

    Delivering seminars to large audiences requires more lecture than many speakers would like. This doesn't mean there can't be small-group activities sprinkled throughout. However, some topics don't lend themselves to smaller group activities. I'm a little stubborn regarding this topic because I believe any size audience can participate in certain types of activities. However, your exercise has to be conducive to the topic. There's nothing worse than attending a seminar where a forced group exercise is inserted that doesn't add any value to the session.

3. Are you prepared to dedicate your business to this marketing approach?

    Populating a room of up to 300 strangers requires a lot of work and expense. If this is the type of business you will choose, then prepare to be committed to it. This is a year-round marketing approach that will place you in large cities all across the country. Each year in business will allow you to reap the rewards of return customers and word-of-mouth attendees. It is essential that a professional handle the marketing. Personally, I wouldn't skimp one penny on professional marketing, because they are the ones who will get those rooms populated with attendees.

Listen and learn from the professionals.

The costs to put on open sessions can creep up on you. When you look at up-front costs that can include the marketing, mailing lists, hotel, travel, breaks, and AV support, it's not unusual to see a breakeven cost hovering around $10,000 a seminar.

The profit is high, and it's an exciting way to conduct business. If you do choose to conduct your seminar business this way, you will have a head start in providing closed sessions based on specific requests from clients. You see, general sessions always have the potential to create leads toward closed sessions; however, closed sessions never create the potential for general sessions.

CLOSED SESSIONS

For many professional speakers like myself, general sessions can be a challenge because the application of what we teach is specific. My topic is not generic enough to deliver competently to multiple customers. When I teach people to sell, I need to know exactly what they sell to provide real-world examples. My techniques do not work generically. I also need to role-play clients on the techniques I teach. Although multiple role-plays can be conducted in larger sessions, if the participants don't understand each other's businesses, the exercise is useless. That's where the closed session approach to the seminar business comes in.

A closed session seminar is a program delivered to a singular client. This doesn't necessarily mean a singular environment, just a client. When I started my business, I quickly started accumulating clients in the financial industry. This both thrilled and worried me at the same time. I was thrilled because I began to quickly create a following within a specific industry. I was worried because I was concerned I might get typecast, much like an actor, and lose my credibility in any other industry.

Closed session seminars generally are not marketed through mass marketing approaches. They are marketed slowly and methodically to specific clients. The sales cycle can often be years; however, the sale to a single client can easily represent a six-figure consulting fee. This is because these clients aren't looking for a generic message. These clients want someone to understand what they are doing and specifically to tailor the message to fit their industry and niche within that industry. In other words, they are looking for exactly what they cannot get from a general session.

The fees can be high because rarely are these companies looking for a one-day session with 300 strangers. They want to create a cultural change within their organization. To do this, they want a consultant who can map out a complete training program for all employees within their organization.

There is no set formula for this, but as your guide through the seminar world, I'd be happy to give you one man's approach. In its most simple form, my definition of truly training an organization consists of three basic programs.

1. **Initial Training.** For most people who put on seminars, this is their bread-and-butter program. Depending on the client's commitment, this program can take various lengths of time to deliver. It typically runs between one to three days. Allow me to make one more recommendation. Clients request closed sessions to receive the direct feedback from the speaker. This means that these programs need to be highly interactive with exercises tightly monitored. For that reason, I rarely recommend a training session with more than 20 participants.

2. **Follow-up Training.** Gone are the days when consulting companies could survive by delivering initial training programs and moving on. It's unfair to clients who have difficulties implementing the information they are learning in the programs they purchase. It's also foolish for the consultant who is clearly leaving money on the table. Follow-up training is not a repeat of the training that was initially offered but instead a program delivered to add on to whatever was initially taught. Sadly,

many companies never make it to the follow-up training because it was never implemented. That's where the third basic program comes in.

3. **Implementation Training.** One of the most common questions I'm asked when I complete the initial training for a company is "When will you be back to follow up?" My answer is "Tomorrow if you would like. As a matter of fact, I'd be happy to come back on a weekly basis. However, I don't think that's a very good cost-effective solution." I then add, "Why don't I spend some time teaching you how to implement this program? That way you can protect your investment. Then, when I come back in six months to a year, we won't have to conduct the same seminar. We can simply add to what has already been implemented." My suggestion is when you put together a seminar or a workshop program, make sure you are putting a program together that will help management use job aids, feedback models, and implementation benchmarking. That way you'll be creating a client for life.

Another important decision that anyone who speaks for a living needs to make is how long he or she intends to speak. Let's take a moment and look at the two most common types of presentations.

Keynotes

When people think of professional speakers, often they think of keynote speakers, who give presentations that are typically delivered in an hour-or-less time frame, and often to larger audiences. With larger audiences and that short of a delivery time, it's pretty difficult to create change on a deep, cultural level. Often the expectations of these types of audiences typically can be summed up this way: "If I can learn one or two good ideas from this presentation, I'll be happy."

When I first left Xerox, I swore I would never conduct a keynote presentation. After all, I came from what I had always felt was the Green Berets of speakers, Xerox—the greatest trainers on earth. We didn't necessarily walk into a room to speak to teach you one or two good ideas to motivate or make you feel better. We taught repeatable, predictable techniques that required fairly lengthy workshops. To talk to a group for an hour and call it training was ridiculous in our eyes.

My first year in business, I frequently was asked to deliver keynote-type presentations. I declined. There was no way I was going to give in and compromise my materials. Then one day a new client successfully persuaded me to deliver such a presentation by asking me what I normally got paid and offering to double it. A keynote speaker was born.

It didn't take me long to fall in love with this style of delivery. Not only was the money good, but the wear and tear on my body was a lot less. Which would you prefer: spending a couple of days on the road and speaking for eight or more hours, or getting up early, blowing into town, taking a limo to and from your speaking site, and making it home for dinner? I fell in love with this rock star existence, and who wouldn't? Then in 2002, the stock market corrected, the economy turned, and the speaking industry changed with it.

Those speakers who made a living giving keynotes and *motivating* audiences for an hour suffered, with many going out of business. In a sense, the herd was thinned a bit. Those speakers who remained in business were forced to adapt to a new way of working with clients, and keynote-type deliveries fell out of vogue. Within a few years the industry crawled back to life, and in 2008, as the market dropped, the herd thinned once again. The industry came back to life once again within a few years, and so it goes.

Does that mean you should never deliver a keynote? Of course not! Just understand what a keynote is and is not. A keynote is not a seminar. It's not a workshop, and it will not create the cultural change many companies are looking for. However, keynotes will do something else that makes them very valuable. They sell seminars.

My clients call the one-hour speaking engagements that I deliver "keynotes." I call them "sales calls." When I introduce myself to an organization and the company also gets to know my company and my services, I can add value to that company. That's a home run. In my mind, the keynote becomes the appetizer to creating a more realistic approach to training and to establishing a long-term relationship.

Seminars and Workshops

When you move away from the keynotes and toward a longer delivery, with fewer participants, you are now delivering a seminar or workshop.

Whether the delivery lasts three hours or three days, you are no longer there to motivate, inspire, or introduce people to your services. You are there to teach.

Personally, I try not to deliver a seminar to more than 20 people at a time. This size limit allows you to circulate among the small groups you create, listen to role-plays, monitor case studies, provide individual coaching and feedback, and bond with your participants. If a client wants to put more than 20 participants in a seminar, I often bring a second trainer with me to make sure we get the coverage we need. This obviously affects the pricing of the seminar.

Most speakers in the seminar industry seem to commit to one type of delivery or the other—either general or closed. I'm of the opinion that anyone who enters into the seminar business should never deliver in only one format and exclude the other. It might mean a little more development work, but it will be well worth it.

Seminar Materials

Regardless of the type of presentation you deliver, the seminar materials you provide in your sessions will say a lot about who you are and the work you do. Often keynote presentations provide little to no handouts, and I can't figure out why. Your materials add credibility to your message and help participants follow your presentation. From a marketing standpoint, materials provide participants with a way to contact you.

For keynote presentations, I do not recommend building a participant guide, but I do recommend a handout. Most people use Power-Point presentations during their delivery. My recommendation is to keep it simple. Provide the notes and tools available within the Power-Point program. There are two approaches that I like. The first is fairly simple and requires that you insert text below each slide you deliver. Audience members see the slide on the screen in front of them but have a smaller slide in their handout, with the text you provide. They will look something like what is shown in Figure 1.1.

This approach requires some development from your end. If you want to distinguish yourself from other speakers, these handouts certainly will go a long way toward doing just that.

If you prefer to let your clients take more notes, the second option would be to simply print your slides using the Handouts section of the

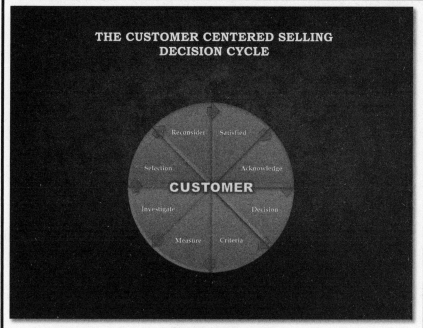

The Decision Cycle

1. **Satisfied Stage:** The customer is totally content perceiving no problems with his or her current situation.
2. **Acknowledge Stage:** The customer is aware that problems exist within his or her current situation, but feels no sense of urgency to do anything about it.
3. **Decision Stage:** The customer, feeling "fed up", resolves to fix his or her existing problems.
4. **Criteria Stage:** The customer shifts the focus away from problems and attempts to determine what his or her buying criteria will be.
5. **Measure Stage:** The customer better defines his or her list of criteria.
6. **Investigate Stage:** The customer begins to compare various solutions to address his or her criteria.
7. **Selection Stage:** The customer chooses the solutions that best addresses his or her criteria.
8. **Reconsider Stage:** The customer reevaluates the decisions that were made.

With a few variations, this repeatable and predictable process is the same from customer to customer, product to product, and industry to industry. Therefore, sales success is not solely determined by the salesperson's ability to convince the customer, but rather, relies on the salesperson's facilitation of this decision process.

FIGURE 1.1   Sample slide and handout

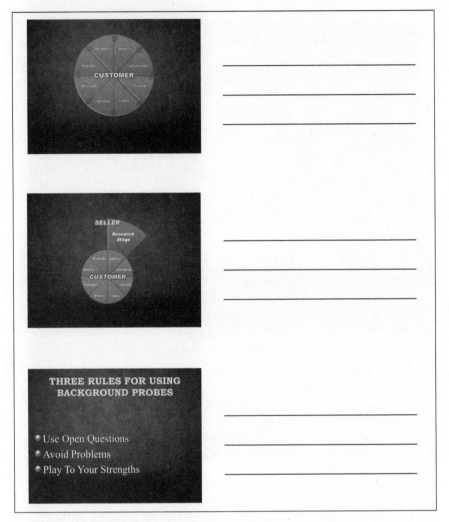

FIGURE **1.2**   Presentation software slides with notes page

print screen within your presentation software. Then go to the section marked "Slider per page" and select "3." By doing this, you will provide your participants with both copies of your slides and a convenient place to take notes. The resulting handout will look something like Figure 1.2.

For seminars and workshops, the materials change dramatically. The intent is no longer to allow participants to follow along or to take some stray notes. The intent is to teach, and the document you provide needs to be created with that intent in mind. Here are a couple of guidelines to think about as you develop your participant materials.

1. Remember that the materials you provide are participant guides, not books. The guides should be created not as teaching tools but as participant tools. That means the materials should be designed with directions on various exercises you intend to cover, worksheets that will allow participants to become involved in your material, and plenty of room to take notes. As far as text is concerned, just list the facts. Remember, it's not a teaching guide. It's a *participant* guide.

Individual Exercise:
——————— Closed and Open Questions ———————

Instructions

Read the following questions. After each, try to determine if it's a closed or an open question and circle the appropriate response. If it's a closed question, use the space below it to rewrite it as an open question. If it's open, leave it alone.

1. Do you have any major problems?	Open	Closed
	(Circle	(Rewrite
	one)	below)

_____

---

2. Move your font size up to 13 or 14. The guide should be easy to read and easy to follow. A larger font not only accomplishes this task, but once again, it moves the text away from looking like a book and toward looking like a participant guide.

3. Put a copyright symbol on every page you produce. This symbol will remind anyone who sees it that your materials are not to be reproduced without your permission. Unethical people will do strange things, but the key here is to not allow that unethical behavior to be justified or to go unnoticed.

---

4. Make sure you have your contact information in the guide. Be sure to put your contact information behind the cover page and on the last page of the participant guide. I can't count how many times I've been contacted by a participant who took a program from me years ago, held onto the participant guide, and used the guide to track me down.

This material has been prepared for the participant's use only. It may not be reproduced without written permission from:
Jolles Associates, Inc.
Email: Training@Jolles.com
www.Jolles.com
(703) 759-7767

AFTER THE SEMINAR

I used to think that I had the perfect system for finishing a seminar. I'd make myself available for hours before a session, but after the session, if you blinked, you would miss me. During more seminars than I would like to mention, I would start packing my laptop bag during the last five minutes of delivery. That meant I could finish and catch a flight booked with a tight connection.

Gone are the days when professional speakers could take to the stage, wow an audience, shake a few hands, sign a couple of books, and leave. The days of flying clients to beautiful locations, sending in internal speakers to educate the clients, sprinkling in a couple of professional speakers to hold the meeting together, and marching clients to golf courses after lunch no longer exist. Remind yourself that each delivery is a blessing.

My suggestion is a simple one. Book the later flight, and do not run out of the room when you've finished your delivery. Quite possibly the best selling time for additional seminars takes place the moment you finish that seminar. You owe it to your client and yourself to spend as much time as necessary to sign books, answer questions, and let the audience get to know you.

Marketing Your Programs

Whether you conduct open session seminars or closed session seminars, keynotes or actual seminars, you still will need to market your services.

Nothing else matters if no one attends your seminar. We call the populating of programs BITS, or "butts in the seats!" Fortunately, regardless of which type of program you choose to deliver, the marketing basics will not change. It all starts with your book.

WRITING THE BOOK

Like it or not, books build credibility. It might not seem fair, but that's the way it is. That means if you are going to run seminars and workshops, you better start working on that book now. I suppose all authors create their masterpieces differently. However, you're stuck with me as your mentor, and I'm going to tell you how I do it.

Step 1. Create an Outline. The most brutal moment for any author is the day the first word goes into that computer. It's brutal because it's a little like starting to run up a mountain path that's 100 miles long. The first couple of miles seem as hopeless as the first couple of words—that is, unless you've created an outline. That's the first step in this process.

A book outline allows you to create a blueprint for the work you will be creating. It would be rather hard emotionally to put your hands on a keyboard and start typing away without an outline. When I create my book outlines, I usually try to wait until I have a nice environment to be inspired. It may very well be one or two hours of the most critical time of the project, so I recommend you pick your environment carefully.

In 1992, when I started to create the first edition of this book, I'll never forget where that outline came from. I was traveling to Cairo, Egypt, to conduct a Train-the-Trainer course for Xerox Egypt. It was the first of many trips I would take to that wonderful city, but I knew I was going to want to come back with an outline. I checked into a hotel called El Gezirah Sheraton Hotel. When I got to my room, I stepped out on my balcony and nearly lost my breath. Fifteen stories below was the Nile River calmly breaking around the small island my hotel was on. I could look up the river for miles. Between the melodic calls for prayer from the mosques, the boats, and the beauty, I was entranced and inspired. With my trusty notebook and pen in hand, and in what was probably less than 30 minutes, I had a 15-page outline in front of me.

Each page represented a chapter. Each chapter consisted of bulleted points. When you are outlining, you are in what I call "expansion mode." This means that this is not the time to evaluate what you are writing. Rather it is the time to simply write . . . and keep writing. While you are writing, make sure you leave some space in between those bullets of yours, because you will fill in the space shortly.

I'm assuming you will be writing about something you've spoken about before. At first, these bullets should flow in a logical sequence. However, information can be moved at any time, anywhere. Don't obsess too much about sequence. In between those bullets should be one- or two-word reminders of the stories, analogies, or other creative ideas you intend to make a part of your chapter.

Before you know it, phase one of the outline is complete, and you have yourself a loose skeleton of a 12- to 15-page outline. Never underestimate the empowering feeling of holding that outline in your hand. Along with it will be the first sensation that you actually have enough information and really can write this book!

Step 2. Adding to the Outline.   With your trusty outline in hand or on your computer screen, you're on your way to the next step, which is to add to your outline. The idea now is to allow your mind to wander morning, noon, and night. Keep adding thoughts to that outline. These thoughts might be a story, a better way to explain a concept, a creative way to display something, or countless other ideas. Just turn your mind loose.

My suggestion is to use the record feature on your smartphone or invest in a small digital recorder.

Remind yourself, no matter how obscure the idea or how positive you are that you will remember it, to put it on the recorder. This is particularly important at night. I can't tell you how many times I've fallen asleep swearing I'll remember a certain idea in the morning, only to wake up remembering one thing. I'll say to myself, "I had an idea. Now what the heck was it?" It's a lot like trying to remember a dream; sadly, most of the time you just won't remember.

Step 3. Writing.   Now, it's time to get started writing. The first couple of pages are the toughest. You might want to prepare this writing around an event; maybe you have a long train ride, you are flying cross-country, or you have a vacation planned. What you are looking for is three to five hours of uninterrupted time alone.

Personally, I've always loved to write on planes. It doesn't hurt that I travel a lot, but the planes create an environment that suits me to a tee. There are no phones ringing, and the humming engines create a type of white noise that works wonders for me. The few minutes of waiting to load, waiting to push back, waiting to take off, and waiting to reach 10,000 feet and open that laptop allow me to focus on my topic at hand.

I've never actually seen what I look like, but you'll recognize me if you ever see me travel. I'm the guy who usually appears somewhere between being lost in thought and daydreaming before the flight begins. Then I look like I was shot out of a cannon once the flight attendant makes the "cell phones and laptops can now be used" announcement. I'm also the guy who sends absolutely no signals to the person sitting next to him regarding the remote possibility of a conversation. Let me apologize in advance. My time at home is for conversation with family and friends. My time on the road is to write.

Wherever you choose to write, my suggestion is to try to do it consistently. If you want to get up and write early in the morning, do it every day. If you want to put the kids to bed and write from 9:00 p.m. to 10:00 p.m., do it every day. The key is consistency. The longer you adhere to a consistent writing schedule, the easier it is to fight off the doubts that will haunt you.

I've always treated my writing projects like training for a long race. As a former triathlete and marathoner, I used to train pretty hard. I wasn't crazy, but I was consistent. I used to set distances to run not by the day but by the week. For instance, I might set a month or two of training with a goal of 30 miles a week. In a sense, I didn't really care how I got to those 30 miles. I'd log my daily workouts and plan my normal daily activities to ensure I got them in.

Some weeks were much easier than other weeks. I might have some free time and take a few long 10-mile runs. That certainly took the pressure off the rest of the week. I never liked running in the rain much. If you ever saw me slogging by, it was usually later in the week. That meant I did not have my miles in, and I had no choice but to get wet.

Have you got the analogy yet? I recommend you handle your writing the same way. Set a weekly goal. I like 10 pages, but it's up to you. If you are like me and have a trip planned, you might do your writing then. You may not need to write at home at all. Maybe it's a short trip week, so there will be a little writing on the road and a little writing at home. Maybe you won't be traveling at all, so there will be a week of writing at home.

As for slogging away, running in the rain, occasionally you might have to cancel plans and be a little miserable on a Sunday getting those last couple of pages in. The most important thing is, once you start, you mustn't allow yourself to miss a week's total. Perhaps it's just my way of thinking, but once you let your mind get away with justifying failure, the next failure becomes infinitely easier to accept and justify.

With every new book I write, and I've written six, I strategically buy an old-school calendar. Once the project begins, almost ceremoniously on Sunday night I write in my page total for the week. Ten pages a week is my goal, but I almost always try to get a couple of extra pages in. This allows me a little cushion in case I have a week of rain. It also introduces a little bit of mystery. After a month or two, I don't really know how many pages I've written in total, and I like it that way. That is a reward I allow myself at the end of each month. At that time I add that month up and the other month or two that precedes it to the total. It's a terrific feeling when the number crosses over the first 100-page barrier.

Allow me one last suggestion that will help you to get to that first 10-page barrier. Don't micromanage your writing. That means don't edit your work. That's for another stage, but not right now. Your job is to write. There will be a time and a place to edit and fix. That's not happening until you bring this writing project in for a landing. That "landing" used to be around 215 pages, but this too has changed over the years. Most business publishers are looking for books in the 150- to 175-page range, with many looking for even fewer pages.

Step 4. Editing Your Book.   Want to know one of the best feelings in the world? It's the first time you print out your manuscript and actually hold it in your hands. I'm not much of a cigar smoker, but I usually keep a cigar somewhere near my computer while the typing is going on. Once I hold that manuscript (and I mean the whole thing), I usually light up that cigar. Often it's a bit dried out from sitting by my computer for so long, but it tastes great to me.

There are two editing options now for you to consider. The first is to edit the manuscript yourself, and if you can do that, you are a better person than I. I have a real problem reading my own words for any significant length of time. What's more, I'm a bit sloppy because I know what I'm trying to say and will assume anyone can follow me. You'll save some money here by doing the editing yourself, but personally I don't think it's worth the possible savings.

The editing option I recommend is to find a third party to do this for you. I usually find a retired English teacher or someone who edits material for a living. The costs are usually around $500 and well worth it. You'll have to train your editor, but most of them know what to do. Their job is not to agree or disagree with what you've written. You are the expert, and that's why you've written the book. Their job is to concentrate on grammar and syntax. I know for me, my editor needs to look for a repeated story here or there. Remember, this project may well have been written over a four- or five-month period of time. It's very easy to tell the same story or to use the same analogy two or three times.

Keep in mind that whoever decides to publish your book will have their own editor look over your book and suggest changes. The goal here is to have not only a great book but a well-written book as well. With a small investment in an editor, that's just what you'll have.

Step 5. Getting Published. With manuscript in hand, it's time to get a publisher. Once again, there are two ways to go here. You can try to find a publisher or publish yourself. There are books written on this subject alone, but allow me to cut through the rhetoric a bit and lay out both sides of this equation for you. If you want to avoid self-publishing your book, you can lay out the ideas you have for your book, write a sample chapter, get that proposal together, and see what happens. Not me.

Many speakers—and by many I've heard numbers as high as 95 percent of professional speakers—self-publish their books. Self-publishing means the authors pay the publisher to publish their work. Their books are printed and bound beautifully. The publishers they use leave no trace of the fact they were paid to do the work. Companies like Amazon now self-publish for no charge, and e-books obviously require no binding.

You can spare yourself the time and trouble of creating a proposal because the self-publishing companies will be selling *you* to allow them to do the work. Why not? They are not taking any risk whatsoever. It is purely business. Most print on demand, and some will save you a few extra dollars and print as many as you would like.

Wait. There's more. For each book you sell, you now stand to make five to six times more money. More money per sale, no begging a publisher, not detectable by your average reader, and quicker to market are some pretty powerful selling points for self-publishing. So, what's the catch?

The catch has to do with distribution. With conventional publishers, you become partners with their marketing team. By self-publishing you are your own marketing team. Some self-publishing companies offer a marketing program, copyediting, graphics, and other options, but if you avail yourself of these services, your costs will rise dramatically.

There are wonderful stories of authors who could not get published, self-published their manuscripts, sold a lot of books, and then got picked up by publishers. Those are wonderful stories. Unfortunately, they are few and far between.

If your goal is simply to make money and gain credibility within your seminars, self-publishing may be the way to go. However, if you want to tough it out and take a shot at creating a book that can find its way into anyone's hands, the traditional publishing route may be for you.

Whatever decision you make, my suggestion is to write the book— now. The sample chapter and proposal idea is a good one. I just think it's the primary reason why 99 percent of the people who want to write a book never do. Once you write that sample chapter and send off that proposal, guess what usually happens? The publishing business chews it up, and you never write the book.

Write the book. In fairness to the publishing industry to which I personally owe so much, it's not all its fault. Imagine being an editor sitting in an office and having dozens of book proposals land on your desk on a daily basis. Tunneling through, here comes another proposal. It looks interesting, and then you get to the experience part: "Never written a book before and has 18 pages written for a 200-page book. Next."

Write the book. When I wrote my first book, I decided to treat the book proposal much like a real estate proposal. It's not the price that holds up so many of these contracts. In fact, it's the contingencies. Sometimes it's a home inspection. Sometimes it's a contingency on the sale of the buyer's house, but one thing is for sure. The more contingencies that are attached to the contract, the worse your chances are of closing the deal.

Write the book. My theory is a simple one. When it comes to writing and selling your book, get rid of the contingencies. The first one to get rid of is the contingency that dogs both you and your publisher. "This person has never written a book before, and I've got to try to believe that with no track record, this person can hit every writing deadline and get me another 125 pages. Hmm . . ."

Write the book. If you do this, you get rid of the biggest objection and contingency your publisher may have. It's easier for you to sell and easier for your publisher to buy. The only negative might be that your publisher will want the book but will want you to change certain things. It might mean more rewrites than you would like. However, if you have a publisher that wants your book, nothing else really matters.

The most important thing to do is to write! Nothing else matters if you don't write! That's why when I work with new authors, I always have them print out this quote and place it where they intend to do most of their writing. It reads like this:

> *Planning to write is not writing. Thinking about writing is not writing. Talking about writing is not writing.*
>
> *Researching to write, outlining to write—none of this is writing.*
>
> Writing *is writing.*
>
> —E. L. Doctorow

What happens if you write a great book and can't find a publisher to take it on? Simple, you publish it yourself. There are those in the seminar business who swear by this approach to publishing. Their arguments are good.

Royalties   Publishing a book yourself can allow you to move from a 7.5 to 15 percent royalty, to a 90 to 100 percent royalty. Remember, you are paying to publish your own book, so most of the sales belong to you.

Distribution   To me, distribution is the biggest downfall of publishing a book yourself. You will be able to get your book on a bunch of Internet sites, including Amazon.com, but the rest of your distribution is up to you. Self-publishers are working their way through this problem by offering their marketing services to you . . . for a price. It's not inexpensive, but the larger self-publishing companies have effective marketing departments. If I were to go the self-publishing route, I would engage their marketing programs. Remember, if you write a book and no one sees it, the book is not doing you any good other than establishing a perceived sense of credibility.

Pride   Funny that I should include the word "pride" as a factor to consider, but in fact I have a lot of pride surrounding the publishing of my books. I sold them myself and affectionately refer to them as my children. In theory, anyone can have a book self-published, but not everyone can find a publisher.

I have gotten into some pretty interesting debates with others in the industry over this publishing argument, so let's settle it this way. If you think you can sell more than 1,000 books a year yourself within your seminars, it might be cost effective to self-publish your book. You will certainly make more money that way. Of course, remember this: If within your proposal you can commit to selling more than 1,000 books a year by yourself, plenty of conventional publishers will sit up and listen.

Step 6. Selling Books.   So how do you go about selling 1,000 books a year? Well, there are two schools of thought. The first is to deliver seminars and to offer books at the back of the room at the end of your seminar. That's the conventional approach, and, boy, do I dislike it!

To me this says to your audience, "I hope you enjoyed our work together. Now, if you really liked what I had to say, for a few dollars more, I'll help you learn it." If you are conducting general sessions, it might make sense to do this. Personally, I'd add the cost of your book to the tuition and make it a part of their seminar package.

If you are conducting closed-session seminars, it's a little tougher but well worth your effort to make the sale of books a part of your training routine as well. In seminars that are a half day or longer, it should not even be a topic of discussion. Any client who wants a half-day program or longer is saying to you, "Help us to make the cultural change you are teaching us." That means the client needs participant guides and books—period.

For keynote deliveries, it's a little bit tougher. When you are speaking to 500 people for an hour, it's tough to add the cost of 500 books to the proposal without the client protesting. However, let me tell you a quick story of how I recently sold 650 books for a one-hour keynote presentation.

When I first approached the client with the idea, they immediately said, "No." I mentioned I *never* charge a client more than the cost that I pay for the book. Even at $9.10 a book, the answer was still "No."

My contracts typically allow me to fly business class. My next move was to offer to bump that $2,000 ticket down to an $800 coach ticket. I now had the books down to about $7.25 each, but the answer was still "No." Finally, I offered to pick up the airline ticket myself. When you are in the seminar business, you accumulate airline miles. With more than 1 million miles in my United Airlines account alone, this was an easy thing to do. This brought the cost to about $6.00 a book. Most companies that bring in large groups of clients to meetings often put gifts in the hotel rooms each night. One of those nights became Rob Jolles Night, and the attendees found an autographed book of mine waiting for them in their room.

Six other professional speakers spoke at the meeting I'm writing about. Each set up a little table in the back of the room and hawked books at the end of their seminar. From what I could see, each sold five or six books.

One last comment on buying books and selling them to clients. I strongly recommend that you find a distributor you like, develop a relationship, and set up a distribution channel. The reason for this is a simple one but often is overlooked by those who conduct seminars.

It's wonderful to be published but even more wonderful to make your book a best seller. If you buy your books directly from your publisher, your discount will be deep. Depending on quantity, it could be as large as 50 percent. However, every single book that you buy will not be counted toward any best-seller list.

If you buy your books from a distributor, your discount usually will not go higher than 45 percent. So why use a distributor? Use a distributor because book sales can count toward these best-seller lists.

Let me tell you how these lists work. When a book makes a best-seller list, it doesn't necessarily mean it has sold more than any book of its kind. It means it has sold more than any book of its kind *from the major book chains that make up the count*. It's almost like watching television from a TV with a Nielsen box on top of it. Those ratings don't track how many TVs are watching a certain program. They track how many TVs with Nielsen boxes on them are watching a certain program.

What you potentially give up in book sales, you make up in seminar fees. When a book hits the *Business* Best-Seller List or the *New York Times* Best-Seller List, it is the equivalent of receiving an Academy Award. When an actor is nominated, the cost of hiring that actor goes up. When an actor wins the award, the cost goes up even higher. You do the math. When you are marketing your services, which sounds better, "Please welcome author Glenn Faulkner" or "Please welcome best-selling author Glenn Faulkner"?

Write the book. Ultimately, it's your decision whom to sell your book to and whom you buy your books from. For me it's an easy decision. I strongly recommend you try to sell your book to a publisher. If your selling is unsuccessful, you can always move to self-publishing. There are plenty of stories of those who self-published their book, had it sell well, and then had a publisher offer to publish and distribute their book.

Most important, write the book.

Speakers' Bureaus

Once you have your book in hand, another marketing approach you might want to consider is establishing a relationship with various speakers' bureaus. You won't be the only speaker they represent. However, the easier you make it for them to sell your services, the more seminars they will sell for you.

The speakers' bureaus will want that book of yours, and they'll want a clear sense of your particular branding. There's also one other thing they will want, and that's a speaker's tape. They will want that tape because it will be their primary tool to help sell your services.

For years I avoided creating a speaker's tape because I felt it was a terrible way for me to sell my services. Eleven years later I still believe this. Almost all the seminars I sell for myself are sold based on an existing relationship, someone who has seen a seminar I've delivered, or on a referral.

However, in the world of the speakers' bureaus, almost all their sales of speakers go to clients who have no idea who you are. That means they have to see you in action. Clients who call speakers' bureaus looking for speakers are already prepared to receive links and watch YouTube videos of the speakers they intend to contract.

Speaker's tapes are not inexpensive. They often cost between $10,000 to $15,000. Just remember this: The first sale made as a result of the first-class video your client sees pays for your video. This is not an expense you want to try to avoid or skimp on. Speakers' bureaus tend to move collectively in similar directions regarding the types of materials they are looking for, and this has created a slight change in what they want to see on speaker's tapes. Currently bureaus are frowning on overproduced tapes with voiceovers, flying graphics, music, and more. Instead they are looking instead for 10 to 15 minutes of uninterrupted speaking for an actual event. You still will need at least two cameras on these shoots—one of you and one on the audience—but the cost of production has come down a bit.

My suggestion is to find the most reputable speakers' bureau in the marketplace and ask it for help. The big ones have their own departments that create speaker's tapes. Again, they are not inexpensive, but they are worthwhile. With a turn-key approach to delivery, the bureau will contract and organize live videotaping of your presentation, graphics, editing, and packaging of your video. Remember, speakers' bureaus are in the business of selling speakers. They know what sells on a speaker's tape.

Third-Party Marketing

My final suggestion regarding the marketing of your seminars is a little out of the ordinary but has worked well for me over the years. Often you will find that you are delivering seminars to an industry that is competing for business the same way you are. For example, the financial industry is famous for lavishing amazing gifts on its prospective clients. When watching an NBA game, have you ever wondered who those people at courtside are and what lottery they won to be privileged enough to get those seats? Often the answer is that they are someone's clients, and they are there as a "value-added incentive" to do more business with whomever bought those tickets.

Tickets and tee times were very popular approaches to generating new business in the 1990s, but we are living in a new era now. Most companies that are being courted would rather pass on the courtside tickets. Instead, they would prefer doing business with a company that can take care not only of their immediate needs but can help in other ways to make them successful.

This is where you come in. In many situations, you will find that the seminars you offer may fit beautifully with your client's customers. Now you become the value-added incentive that your client can offer, and that means you have just adopted a new sales team that can offer your services. I'd venture to guess that, over the years, this might very well be the most successful approach for me since I went into the consulting business.

Summary

Whatever type of seminar or workshop you deliver, and whatever type of audience you deliver to, it's my hope that you now have a clearer understanding of how to run your seminar business. From branding to book writing, and from marketing to material development, you now have a bird's-eye view of the decisions you need to make. Armed with this information, it's time to look at the delivery side of this most wonderful occupation.

Chapter 2

Working with Adult Audiences

When I was about six years old, I wanted very badly to grow up and be a basketball player. I was totally hooked on the sport and longed to be tall and famous. As I grew, so did my aspirations of adulthood. I passed through various stages of wanting to be a football player, an astronaut, a doctor, a lawyer, even the President of the United States. In fourth grade, however, these dreams took on a more serious focus.

I wanted to be a teacher. I had a fourth-grade teacher named Ms. Tuttweiler. She was everything a teacher should be. She was compassionate, she was kind, and she was sensitive to the needs of your typical 10-year-old. She had a spunky side too! If you were caught chewing gum, Ms. Tuttweiler made you wear it on your nose. If you talked too much, she made you talk to yourself for a few minutes back in the coat closet. She even discouraged note passing by reading that private little message in front of the class. The funny thing is, even with all those punishments, everybody loved good old Ms. Tuttweiler. I liked her so much that I actually felt an inspiration to teach. Unfortunately, for most of us who are drawn to corporate training, this harmless role model often can expose us to some potentially dangerous situations.

The first, and most important, point that you have to understand is that what worked with a child will not work with mature audiences. When asked to conduct training, the first instinct new presenters have is to draw on their previous experiences in the classroom. It is not that most of us do not have corporate training experiences to utilize. It is just that for every hour of adult training, there have been about 500 hours of other schooling. Assuming a schedule that allows for five to seven hours of schooling in a day, an approximate number of hours of schooling from kindergarten through four years of college would be about 21,420. In a corporate environment, having structured training for 40 hours in a year can be viewed as excessive. Not only do those early schooling years represent numerous hours, but as a child, you are more vulnerable to change.

With this in mind, try asking an adult to put a piece of gum on his nose if you do not allow gum chewing. Read aloud a message that an adult is passing to another adult in the seminar. Needless to say, these ideas would backfire horribly in a training environment. For most presenters, though, what other experiences do they have to draw on?

Adults must be dealt with in a mature manner, and with that in mind, I would like to show you some basic needs that adults have that are different from those of children. It should be noted, however, that these are ideas that I would like to see implemented with the way my children currently are being taught. Unfortunately, as you will read, there are certain things we can get away with when teaching children that we cannot get away with when training adults.

This chapter illustrates the differences in working with adults as opposed to children. I will point out these differences and why they are important. I will not go over the solutions to some of these problems in this chapter. Later on, when the creation of effective training is covered, we also cover a process that speaks to these differences with concrete solutions in mind.

Create an Atmosphere Conducive to Training

One of the first major differences between teaching a child and training an adult is the necessity of attention to surroundings. Children are really exceptional when it comes to the atmosphere in which they learn. If you drive past most schools, you will notice a rather peculiar sight. It looks as if the larger buildings have actually spawned some children of their own. Those odd structures are referred to as "temporary class-rooms." Speak to children about the difficulties of learning in a small, cramped environment, typically too warm in the summer and too cold in the winter, and they will respond by telling you "It's neat."

Not so for an adult. For whatever reason you choose, adults come to training with a different attitude. Anything less than first class becomes an immediate knock of the training itself. You can have the best curriculum, the best presenter, and the best combination of students. Often, if the surroundings are not appropriate, your message will fall on deaf (or distracted) ears.

A classic example of inappropriate atmosphere is the case of on-site training conducted in a field office. Thousands of dollars are being spent for participant guides, trainees' time out of the field, and a presenter's time and travel expense, but to save those last few pennies, the training is conducted on-site. Typically, you can count on physically losing every student in your training session at least once for an extended period of time. Training is constantly interrupted for emergency phone calls and with students coming back from breaks and lunch late because of important problems. The distractions are endless. For a few more dollars, the training could be moved across the street (although I would suggest across town), eliminating this problem.

Try to establish an atmosphere that is relaxed yet businesslike. If this sounds like walking a rather precarious tightrope, you are right! For an inexperienced presenter, the desire is often to create that relaxed atmosphere at all costs. What can start off being an attempt for a relaxed atmosphere can often wind up turning into a total lack of discipline. I can remember early in my career a time when I was asked to step out in the hallway by an observer who had just watched my seminar. I had worked extremely hard to create an atmosphere that was relaxed. I had done such a good job that, as the observer was going over his evaluation, the students could be heard in the other room tossing things about, ringing bells and buzzers, and playing with any other objects I had left behind. I sheepishly looked at the observer and muttered, "Perhaps I did too good a job creating a relaxed atmosphere."

I have also observed instructors who lean too heavily to the opposite extreme. In an attempt to create a businesslike atmosphere, the seminar room takes on the look of a prison. The presenter creates a threatening environment. Students do not speak unless spoken to; the presenter's word is all that matters, and little interaction occurs. Not only does the seminar not benefit from other experiences and points of view from the participants, but there is an air of resentment among the students.

The presenter's role is to walk the tightrope between relaxed and businesslike. This can often mean crossing back and forth depending on the situation. I often refer to the role of a presenter as more of a

"Teflon" position. For example, sometimes the joke that is told by a student can and should be laughed at by the presenter. Other times, depending on its appropriateness, despite the punch line, it cannot be laughed at. I am not suggesting that presenters should not be human, merely that they constantly must exercise careful judgment.

You are the role model; you are the one who must keep the seminar on an even keel. As the presenter, it is your responsibility to use your best judgment to create the kind of atmosphere most conducive to good learning. When in doubt, leave it out!

Build and Maintain Interest

When a child is not kept interested in school, the mischief that child can get into is generally containable. Sometimes it may mean a trip to the principal's office or some other threat. The mischief an adult can get into can be a lot more damaging to the training that is being conducted.

As I mentioned earlier, threats are not an effective way to maintain an adult's interest. As a matter of fact, the only effectiveness threats may have within your training is to initiate contact between student and presenter. Additionally, adults can be more openly hostile about their lack of interest within the training. With the potential for a full range of audience emotions playing a part within your training, it is important to try to keep the trainees' interest any way you can. Unfortunately, this can sometimes result in an unfair level of stress on the presenter.

One rule of thumb I usually follow, when working with a new group of trainees, is not to worry about being instantly interesting. It is unrealistic and can contribute to the type of stress that burns out so many presenters so quickly. I have often fantasized about walking into a room of trainees I have never met before, approaching the lectern, slowly opening the curriculum, and being met with a crescendo of applause. Good fantasy. The only thing lacking is reality. In fact, when a presenter walks into the room, the tension and anxiety of the trainees goes up a notch. There are a number of unknowns and other factors that will soon be touched upon contributing to this anxiety, but these issues are certainly not the stuff that fantasies are made of.

The goal I establish for myself, and suggest for others, is a little more modest. I assume that when a group of trainees first meet me, there will not be much interest. I will give them time to worry about what they are wearing, where they are sitting, what I look like, and so forth. By the first break, I would like to think that I have created a spark of interest. By lunchtime, maybe a couple of head nods of approval. By the end of the day, we have interest. By the end of the second day, we have a lot of interest. By the end of the third day, they cannot wait to start the next day. By the end of the program, it is my hope, they have just completed the best training they have ever attended.

A number of techniques can be used to get and maintain interest, which I will systematically outline in Chapter 8. The key point is simply this. If you are going to establish a goal regarding the interest you intend to generate within your training, let it be this: From the first minute to the last, at no time will you allow the interest you are working for to take a step backward. Forward, ho!

Capitalize on the Experience of Adult Trainees

One of the greatest aspects of working with adults is the abundance of experiences they bring to the training room. I am not, however, necessarily referring to their experiences with your given subject matter. Subject matter experience is definitely a positive in most situations, but it is the trainees' *other* experiences that can often be the diamond in the rough a lot of presenters miss out on. These experiences can be just the link that is needed to teach a difficult concept.

Let me provide you with an example. When I came out of college, the first job I ever had was as an insurance salesman for the New York Life Insurance Company. I had certain strengths and weaknesses as a salesman, but my ability to, as I used to call it, "teach the sale" served me well. An example of this was my ability to explain the difference between whole life insurance and term insurance. As an apprentice field underwriter, I watched intently as certain agents spent hours trying to explain the difference to customers who made the unfortunate mistake of asking. Like any good trainee, when the explanation became endless, customers would fake their best "Oh, now I get it," and the salesman would move on, mercifully putting that topic out of its misery. The reality is, these salesmen rarely made the sale. If a presenter does the same thing, the presenter will rarely get his or her point across.

An experienced salesman then told me to draw on the customer's experience to get the point across. He suggested using an example of purchasing a house. Many adults have either purchased or considered purchasing a home. Using that experience is what made the point easier to understand. My explanation sounded something like this:

The differences between whole life insurance and term insurance are similar to the differences between owning a home and renting a home. When you own a home, you pay more up front and your monthly payments are higher. As a trade-off, your payments remain consistent and although no one can guarantee exactly how much money you will make, chances are if you stay in the home for three to five years, you should make a significant profit. Whole life insurance is very similar in concept. Your monthly payments will be higher but never increase. No one can guarantee exactly how much cash value your policy will earn, but after three years it should be significant.

When you rent a home, the initial rent is usually considerably less than what a mortgage would be on a similar structure. However, rents are raised at various times, and when you leave, other than perhaps the repayment of a security deposit, you receive nothing. Term insurance is similar. Premiums are lower, but they can be raised through the years, and when you leave or quit the policy, you receive nothing.

Now, I am not claiming to have made anyone an insurance expert, but in the 30 seconds or so that it took you to read the example, you gained a basic understanding of the concept. When was the last time your insurance agent tried to explain the difference, how long did it take, and how well did you understand it?

Years ago, when computers were making their way into the workforce, I was on the front lines of teaching others how to use those computers. Many trainees forced to incorporate the computer into their lives at this time initially suffered from the dreaded illness referred to as "computerphobia." To soften this fearful device, my approach was to break it down into understandable experiences and terms they could all relate to:

See this computer keyboard? It is a lot like a typewriter keyboard that all of you have probably used at one time or another. The monitor is a lot like the television set you curl up with at night, and the central processing unit acts like the brain.

Once, while conducting a Train-the-Trainer course in Egypt, I was having a great deal of trouble communicating a difficult concept. Most Egyptians are clueless to many of our customs and sports, as I was to theirs. Finally, we found soccer (referred to as "football" by Egyptians), and I found myself happily clinging to soccer examples to illustrate key points for the remainder of the course.

Some trainees will exhibit mental blocks relating to certain information. It is the presenter's job not only to become aware of this but to find a way to communicate the information to the trainees. It may be your analogy of a golf swing, a reference to a book that you read, or maybe even a popular movie you have seen. Unlike a child, an adult has a wealth of experience you can relate your information to. It is that common ground of experiences that you must find to facilitate effective learning.

Structure Your Presentation Logically

To list logic as one of the key components to working with adult audiences may seem a bit obvious, but it is critical just the same. Curriculum developers often have limited experience in the subject they are writing about because they are sought after for their writing ability.

When curriculum is developed, subject matter experts are called on to help with the creation of a course. Their involvement is usually to get the writers up to speed as quickly as possible and then step aside. Even when the development is carefully monitored, reading curriculum is one thing; teaching it is a whole different story. This is why pilots exist. One of the intents of a pilot is to take what is technically correct and determine if it is being presented in a logical manner.

One of the first points I look for when handed a new course to study is whether I need more information than what is available to understand it. I have often said that the first emotions experienced by a presenter sitting through a seminar he or she is to teach can be the most valuable. Whatever emotions you perceive, the students most likely will feel, too, at the exact same spot. What's more, if while teaching the material you find yourself wishing you could refer to material that has yet to be taught, you probably are experiencing a clue that there may be a logic problem.

When trying to figure out curriculum logic, often a presenter can walk away unsure which came first, the chicken or the egg. Sometimes, despite consistent confusion among trainees, a presenter will become so out of touch with the fact that there has been constant trouble in one area (dating back to when he or she first taught the material), the presenter will mistakenly begin to believe his or her own excuses as to why certain messages are not working. Trust your initial instinct, and do not be afraid to try to reshuffle your curriculum to deliver a more logical message.

Use Activity to Promote Involvement

Not everyone in this world has a Type A (or slightly hyper) personality, but when it comes to training, one thing is certain among all personality types: Adults cringe at the thought of sitting for extended periods of time. Unfortunately, due to less-than-creative previous teachers or presenters, most of us assume that attendance at a training session will mean nonstop sitting. The truth is, successful training can be so much more.

There are three basic reasons to get adults involved in activities when you are conducting training. The first is *morale*. Let's face it: Hearing from a presenter that the course you are attending will be a 16-hour lecture is enough to make the strongest stomach weak. Remember: In the business of training, the presenter is guilty until proven innocent. In other words, if students previously had a bad experience with a similar course, they will assume they are in for the same treatment again. If the training previously dragged, had no interaction, or was boring, students naturally assume it will probably happen again. Morale is damaged before the presenter even opens his or her mouth.

The second reason for wanting to involve adults in activities is *to stimulate interest*. What are some of the most memorable and interesting courses you ever attended? What made them that way? I am willing to bet the success of these courses centered around some kind of activity.

An example of a successful activity-centered session involved a course that I started teaching for Xerox. I was reluctant to teach it because I had taken it as a student years before and disliked it. My memories of the class were that it was dull and that it was filled with hours of useless theory. What's more, everyone I knew who had taken this course shared my opinion. While being coaxed to teach the class, I was promised that some changes had been made. I was still skeptical, however, because I knew the curriculum content could not be drastically altered. Despite the course's poor reputation, when I finally taught it, it was a tremendous success due to a small but significant *delivery* change. Although the *curriculum* had not changed, a simulation had been added to the course, tying together the previous three days' material. The students loved the activity and loved the course. Even though the simulation did not begin until the third day of the program, the anticipation of the coming activity made the course far more exciting.

The third benefit of involving adults in activities is *to increase retention*. Again, think back on some of the lessons you learned and still remember from the classroom; I have a sneaking suspicion there was an activity run around that lesson. There is an old saying that goes something like this: "What people hear, they forget. What people see, they remember. What people do, they learn."

Activity to promote involvement within the curriculum is a technique used by many top curriculum writers and presenters. *Performing* a task, rather than being told about the task, benefits the trainee's morale, interest, and ability to retain the information taught.

Set Definite Goals

In any type of training, there is an overall goal involving what is being taught. This is sometimes referred to as "the big picture." What is it that you want the students to get out of the seminar? Adults demand to know this.

The issue really can be traced back to a simple fact about working with adults. For many, it has been a long time since they have attended a training seminar, and, frankly, many have forgotten how to learn. We are often not dealing with a college student who has been conditioned to follow and absorb a professor's lecture. We are dealing with possible confusion and anxiety relating to what is, and is not, important. The signs are often obvious early in a presentation. All the presenter needs to do is watch the trainees' note taking for the first clue. Often I start a seminar by passing out a participant package. Some trainees immediately uncap the highlighter like a drawn weapon. As I welcome the students to the course, I can spot trouble from trainees who have already highlighted the participant package cover to capture the course name and other housekeeping information, while quietly muttering to themselves:

"Glad to have us here, hope our trip was a good one; gotcha!"

Boy, I would hate to miss that critical information in my notes! Given a little time, the trainees' materials begin to turn the color of that poor, overworked highlighter. Even when I make eye contact with these individuals, there is a sense of note taking pride. This look is not much different from that of a young child's proud gaze, as he brought home that first clay pot made in school. Could there be a finer pot anywhere? The only difference is the trainee's eyes are saying, Is there a finer note taker anywhere? This overuse of note taking is no longer limited to a participant guide and highlighter. It's been extended to laptops, tablets, smartphones, and various recording apps as well.

I would like to think that in every seminar I teach, everything is critical information. In fact, that is unrealistic. In a well-written movie, some parts are filled with action and other parts are designed to let the audience collectively catch its breath. This also allows the audience to better focus on the key portions of the story. Curriculum is written in much the same way. There are what is referred to as "nice-to-knows" and "need-to-knows" within the material. This assists trainees in focusing in on critical information. By giving trainees the big picture and informing them of the goals of your training, you are in a better position to influence their perception of what is and is not as important.

Without a sense of the goal of your training, your trainees may experience problems focusing on the really important portions of the curriculum. Many of us just cannot maintain that level of concentration for long lengths of time, especially if it has been a long time since we attended school, where these skills were necessary. Clear the air and let students know you will be sure to emphasize the need-to-knows and share with them the overall goals of your training. While you are at it, have them give those electronic devices a rest, and pass the boxes of highlighters on to another seminar.

Use Repetition to Increase Retention of Critical Information

One of the most basic techniques used when working with adults, as well as with children, is to incorporate a steady diet of repetition. It probably is no mystery to you that the chances of increasing retention go up substantially the more you repeat a message. What a lot of presenters do not know, however, is there is an art to using repetition effectively within a seminar room. The mistake many presenters make is never reconnecting their curriculum with the experience. Eventually the trainees have to start using the presenter's terms and not their own.

To help clear this up, let's use an example I mentioned earlier relating to learning the names of certain pieces of computer hardware many years ago. After detecting some computerphobia among our students, we decided to simplify these terms a bit. One of the goals for this module may well have been for the trainees to be able to comfortably use the terms associated with computer hardware. Let's face it, although the trainees might now understand the various pieces of hardware, I would not be real keen for them to leave my seminar calling the central processing unit a "brain." Here is an area where you can rely on repetition to help you. Each time you have the.trainees repeat these terms, tighten up their explanations. What follows is a possible dialogue.

PRESENTER: Okay, now what is this called?
TRAINEE: The brain.
PRESENTER: Right, also referred to as the central processing unit.

Later:

PRESENTER: Now, what is this called again?
TRAINEE: The brain.
PRESENTER: Also referred to as?
TRAINEE: The central processing unit.
PRESENTER: Excellent.

Repetition allows the presenter to clean up the responses being provided by the trainees. The intent is to provide a bridge using the trainees' experiences. You can begin to remove that bridge using repetition and have the trainees using the terms and concepts that they need to keep the new material clear in their minds when they leave the seminar.

The advantages of repetition also relate to another concept previously covered. Repetition helps the adult learner focus on particular goals of the training. Repetition provides tremendous yet subtle assistance in guiding student thinking. When you keep repeating a message, it begins to unconsciously look like a need-to-know item. Make sure you carefully choose which pieces of curriculum you want to repeat so that the trainees better grasp the importance of the information.

Repetition is a powerful tool to assist in adult learning. It not only increases retention, but, selectively used, it allows you to fix areas of curriculum that need tightening and guide the trainees in learning critical information.

Tell Trainees What You Require of Them

If you listen carefully when working with adults, sometimes you might actually hear a faint ticking sound. That noise is a time bomb that could have been set as recently as the last training session the trainee attended or as long ago as a bad experience from this trainee's school days. It involves the element of surprise. A successful tactic in war. A miserable failure with the adult learner.

Remember how you felt being informed of a pop quiz? I can still hear the groans from my schoolmates and feel the knot in the pit of my stomach. After announcing a pop quiz to an adult learner, you may find that knot on the top of your head! Adults hate surprises. Frankly, if I felt surprises would assist your training in the least bit, I would not be so hard on this tactic. However, they do not.

Adults have much larger egos than children. Without carefully going over what trainees can anticipate within your training, you run the risk of badly embarrassing them. Embarrass a child, and that child may just tell his parents. Embarrass an adult, and you are looking at possible aggressive behavior either immediately or down the road within your training.

Although it may appear obvious that a presenter should avoid tests or quizzes without first telling trainees of his or her intentions, other requirements are less apparent and are just as upsetting to adults:

♦ Will there be any form of involvement during the seminar itself?
♦ If so, will your feedback be based on the trainees' level of participation?
♦ Do you want the trainees to take notes throughout?
♦ Will the seminar cover the same old stuff as last year's session?

Then there is the question of feedback:

♦ Will any formal or informal feedback be provided to the trainee's mentor or manager?
♦ What affects that level of feedback, either positively or negatively?

This factor has the potential to be a highly emotional issue.

The frustrating element to the issue of establishing requirements with adults is that most adults will not request this information. Therefore, it is easy for the presenter to skip over telling the trainees what is anticipated of them. In a perfect world, regardless of the last time the trainee attended a seminar, this information would be provided up front and fairly. The problem is, this is not a perfect world. This information is rarely provided up front, and trainees become scarred from these surprises. That is why I mentioned the ticking of a time bomb. It is hard to predict, but an adult is going to accept the unfair practices of attending courses without a clear set of requirements for only so long. Then the trainee is going to blow! The real kicker is that this explosion may come before the presenter barely opens his or her mouth. Bad luck? Bad trainee? Once again, the presenter simply becomes guilty until proven innocent.

Allowing the trainees to know, up front, the requirements of the course and what they can anticipate is an intelligent way to start a seminar. Not only does it give the trainees a road map of what to expect, it reduces the charges of aggressive behavior toward the presenter. Establishing requirements also allows you to guide the trainees' thinking from the nice-to-knows to the need-to-knows. If I know up front that I am going to be tested on certain pieces of information, it will be no coincidence that I focus a little harder when that information is discussed.

Motivate Adult Trainees to Learn

In my mind, perhaps one of the biggest differences between working with children and working with adults is the motivation to learn. With children, the motivation is rather typical. Do well, get good grades. Do poorly, get bad grades. All of us can remember the sickening depression of taking that long walk home with an occasional bad grade. I would like to believe that my children's teachers motivate them, but the fact of the matter is, they do not have to because the motivation is automatically built in. As children grow, the motivation shifts from having parents see the report cards to having college admission offices see the report cards.

With adults, there is rarely anything that even resembles a report card. Oh, yes, sometimes when written feedback is recorded, a copy is sent to the trainee's mentor, but more often it is not. In the instances where the feedback is sent to the mentor, I would still not recommend using it as the primary motivator. When working with adults, this issue usually boils down to one point. What type of motivation does the presenter bring into the training room? Techniques for establishing motivation in the beginning as well as throughout your presentation will be addressed later in this book when we look at a process to assist your training. For right now, let's agree that if you, the presenter, are upbeat and positive about the material you are asked to deliver, this has a strong effect on the motivation the trainees will feel.

The question of providing motivation to trainees becomes a question of technique and attitude. Both of these skills are controlled by the presenter. The most basic point is that it is a mistake to think the trainees will automatically be motivated by the value of the curriculum. It is not the responsibility of the trainee to attend the training motivated. It is the responsibility of the presenter to find a way to provide that motivation. The reward for you is a highly interactive, participative group of trainees who are eager to face the next challenge.

Make the Presentation Visual

When you are writing about adult learning, another critical factor to consider is how your message is designed to appeal to the senses of the trainees in the room. One- or two-hour lectures may be fine in a university setting, but they do not work well in the corporate training world.

How much do you still remember from those large lecture classes? What you do remember is often a result of the teacher's ability to affect more than one of your senses during the presentation. When examining how your senses affect what you learn, we must consider not only which senses are most critical but strategies for using these senses as well.

Let me pose a question to you. Which senses do you think are most critical in our learning process? A great deal of research has been done in this area, with some pretty interesting results. If you were able to ask an infant, he or she would tell you the sense of touch is critical. It does not take too many lessons in touching the stovetop for this infant to realize it is hot. As the child grows, everything begins to go into the mouth. The sense of taste becomes a critical factor. Finally, reaching adulthood, we become bombarded with different educators lecturing to us, appealing to the sense of sound. That would be all well and good, if our sense of sound were not such a poor sense to rely on.

Numerous studies have been conducted to try to pinpoint just what percentage of learning comes through which sense. Most break the numbers down approximately this way:

Taste	3 percent
Smell	3 percent
Touch	6 percent
Sound	13 percent
Sight	75 percent

The numbers are rather staggering when you consider how much time often is expended trying to get the words of a presentation together. I am not saying that the words we use will not influence what is going to be learned; I am merely interpreting these numbers to say that if you want people to remember your message, you had better be visual. Certainly, using the two senses of sight and sound together make for a very effective combination.

I also want to warn against overreacting to the sense of sight. One of the biggest mistakes made by inexperienced presenters is to attempt to be too visual. There is an old saying that pertains to the use of visuals: "If you emphasize everything, you emphasize nothing!"

Hopefully, now I have begun to make you a believer in visual presentations. Let me now suggest that you choose wisely not only the frequency of how many visuals you use but the variety as well. Later in this book, we look at the positives and negatives of various presentation aids. For now, simply understand that varying the presentation aids you choose will certainly enhance their effectiveness.

Appealing to the various senses to better communicate your message is a time-tested success story. At times, when teaching students this point in a seminar, I will purposely not be visual in certain areas and visual in others. When we review in the morning, guess which group has more trouble remembering the information taught. You got it; the group that was not exposed to any visual aids. Although in reading this book you are actually flooding only one sense, close the book and see if you can remember which percentage of learning comes through which sense. I am willing to bet you will be closer than you think. You would not do nearly as well if those numbers were recited to you in a lecture.

Satisfy the Information Needs of the Trainees

When I was growing up, I was one of those kids who saved the best part of his dinner for the end. (Truth be known, I still do.) When it comes to working with an adult learner, I have also saved the most important part for last. How often have you as a trainee heard someone groaning about why he or she really should not be in the seminar? Perhaps the person feels he or she already knows the material, or feels it will be a waste of time. A person may not want to be there for any number of reasons. Maybe that someone has been you. One thing is for certain. If someone feels he or she will not benefit in any way by attending your training, nothing else really matters. You can put together that best curriculum, recruit the best presenter, provide the best visuals, and attempt to satisfy all the other adult learning principles. The bottom line is there will not be anyone there who is listening. This also means a much higher chance of aggressive behavior from the trainee toward the presenter.

What needs to be accomplished is to answer one question that may or may not be asked out loud. You need to provide the trainees with a WIFM.

No, that is not a radio station's call letters, nor did I sneeze. The acronym WIFM stands for a question the majority of trainees ask themselves before attending any type of training: what's in it for me?

Does this point sound a little selfish to you? Ask yourself why you would want to attend training if you felt there was absolutely nothing in it for you. This sense of greed actually becomes a basic human need. This issue was brought out in a rather famous speech in one of my all-time favorite movies, *Wall Street*. In this movie, Michael Douglas delivers a presentation to a couple of hundred people at a shareholders' meeting. Douglas's character, Gordon Gekko, redefines being under fire in an apparently hopeless attempt to convince his audience that a buyout of their company is beneficial. As he starts his presentation, he is jeered and booed. The title of his presentation is, appropriately enough, "Greed Is Good." If you ever want to watch a master speaker give an effective WIFM, watch this movie. By reminding his audience that most of them are attempting to be as successful as possible, and connecting his message to their success, he convinces the audience that, in fact, greed is good! The audience ends up convinced, cheering his efforts and supporting his plan.

The question then becomes: Is this form of selfishness or greed a bad characteristic? I say no! I want trainees who are greedy and selfish. I want trainees who want to get the most possible out of training. Who would you rather do business with, someone who is greedy or someone who is not? I choose the greedy individual. I make that choice because as long as this individual is ethical, he or she is certainly easier to understand and satisfy. Most people who are successful in business have found a way to channel their greed professionally. If I can appeal to that sense of greed and show how my product can make them more successful, I too will be successful. It is a basic message that is accepted in the training field as well.

I believe that the people in my audience are in fact greedy. They want as much as they can get out of what I have to say. I do not believe they would be as successful if they did not have this goal. We are all greedy to a point. I would much rather have students attending my classes who are greedy and want to know "what's in it for me?" If I am able to answer that question, I will be in a better position to achieve my goals of providing the best training this individual has ever received.

With that said, and the point made that you must convince your trainees there is a need to learn, the question now becomes, How? Before entering the body of the curriculum, how do you hook trainees into your curriculum and give them a need to learn? Ah . . . pardon my own rather obvious hook, but the formula for that is carefully outlined in Chapter 7: The Secret of Success: Selling Your Presentation. I will give you a hint though: Remember the word "utility."

I hope this talk of selfishness and greed did not offend anyone. I assure you, I am both ethical and honest as a businessman. My intent was to point out a very basic need that most of us have regarding training or any other service. You must be able to answer the question "What's in it for me?" Hopefully, I have been able to provide a little bit of insight as to where that need comes from.

Summary

Working with adults can be a challenging and rewarding experience. The most basic point presenters must know is that their early school experiences are not as big a help as they may first appear. Studying some of the differences between children and adults will make your approach to working with adults more successful and satisfying. It will also provide a rationale for a structured process in the training of adults.

Chapter 3

Recognizing Trainees' Levels of Behavior

Probably the best place to begin would be to look at your trainees' current levels of behavior. In everything we do, including training, everyone's behavior falls within one of the four levels outlined in this chapter. Have you ever been taught a particular skill or idea and thought to yourself, "I have been doing that correctly all along"? One somewhat confusing aspect to training is that trainees come to seminars and workshops performing at various levels of behavior as well. What makes this issue potentially confusing is that these levels can change like the wind. It is therefore important to understand four basic levels of performance.

Level One—The Unconscious Incompetent

At this first level, the trainee is ineffective and unaware. I also refer to this level as the "blissfully ignorant stage." Often on the first day of training, a lot of trainees actually start at this level. The good news is that if you are at this stage right now, you would not even know about it. For example, all of us have known someone who got on everyone's nerves in the office and had absolutely no idea those around him or her felt this way.

One of the problems with individuals at this first level is that these people generally do not seek training as a solution. Why would you want to learn to do something you feel you already know how to do well? Presenters who see individuals at this stage have to be careful that they begin to move these people slowly to the next stage. It is difficult to accept suggestions about something you currently feel good about.

Some jobs have built-in safeguards that keep people from staying in this stage too long. In selling, you can convince yourself how well you are doing for only so long. When the commission checks are cut, reality often sets in. Presenters can operate at the Unconscious Incompetent stage also. A presenter at this first stage usually is difficult to work with. One reason I say this is the nature of a presenter's work. It is not a position where individuals who are unsure of themselves survive long. Also, presenters at this level have absolutely no idea there is even the hint of a problem. All I can say is thank goodness for evaluation forms!

Level Two—The Conscious Incompetent

At this level, things begin to get a little more interesting. The trainee is still ineffective; however, he or she is now aware of these deficiencies. If you have ever attended a training course, listened to the presenter, and thought to yourself, "Hey, I do that! I didn't know that was wrong," you were passing from the Unconscious Incompetent level to the Conscious Incompetent level.

If there is a problem with individuals at this level, it might be that sometimes there is resistance to moving on. Some people even revel in being consciously incompetent. Have you ever known individuals who seem to take pride in informing you that they do not do a particular task very well? There is no mention of wanting to improve, just the fact that they do not do this task particularly well. Many times, these individuals have preached about their ineffectiveness for so long and the impossibility of ever fixing it, their myth becomes a reality. They proudly remain consciously incompetent forever.

Fortunately, that problem is much more the exception to the rule than the norm. Training is typically created with the Conscious Incompetent in mind. Once individuals come in touch with their own deficiencies, they are much more receptive to the idea of training.

Many presenters whom I work with when I teach a Train-the-Trainer course start out with me at this stage. This is because we do not live in a perfect world, and the majority of new presenters are forced to conduct seminars before they have ever been taught anything about how to teach. It is often a case of product or curriculum knowledge without any training skills. This is another one of many reasons why I refer to the realities of training as being an under-fire position. After presenters take their lumps a few times in front of an audience, they are usually very much in touch with some of their incompetent areas. Practice, preparation, and confidence instilled by the presenter who is working with these individuals usually help a great deal to move them to the next level. If a participant is open to change, this level should not be visited for long.

Level Three—The Conscious Competent

Level Three indicates that an individual is both effective and aware of exactly what it is that is making him or her effective. There are a couple of different schools of thought as to whether this is the optimum level of performance. Remember, not only are you effective, you are keenly aware of everything you are doing to make you effective. Sounds about perfect . . . almost.

There is one issue that must be discussed when dealing with the Conscious Competent. Just how conscious do you really want to be when you are performing a given task? Think back on the last time you attended training and learned a new skill. When you left that training, you were the picture of conscious competency. You did not make a move without checking that manual or going through a given checklist. You were probably able to methodically produce what you were taught, step by step. No steps missed by you, no, sir. You were a machine! That, unfortunately, is where the weakness is on this level. One of the frustrations often experienced by new trainees is that while they feel good about the process they have just learned, they want to know when they will be able to implement it without using their notes or sounding like an encyclopedia. I have often felt that this level should be renamed the Mechanical Competent.

There is certainly nothing wrong with attempting to be effective and aware of what makes you that way. This is the Conscious Competent. When just starting out, or learning new curriculum, most presenters prefer to teach a couple of seminars before being observed. The reason for this is that by practicing and rehearsing, they are often attempting to push through Level Three and move to the next level.

Level Four—The Unconscious Competent

At this fourth and final level, people are effective but no longer aware of certain things they are doing right. They are quite simply producing the expected results without having to think about what they are doing to achieve these results. The mechanical part of what they have learned to do has given way to a more natural, relaxed ability.

The Unconscious Competent level does not necessarily mean we have achieved utopia. Some trainees actually arrive at training with many Unconscious Competent abilities. Have you ever attended a seminar and thought to yourself as the presenter was going over a new concept, "Hey, I do that. I didn't know you were supposed to. I must be pretty good!" This happens to be another basic reason for training, particularly in areas that involve subjective training.

Many trainees will show up ready to learn how to learn a new trade because they showed certain abilities as they were growing up. Someone probably patted them on the back and said, "You ought to be a ____ [fill in the blank], you are so good at ____ [fill in the blank]." When you hear this enough times, it does a couple of things. First, it instills a confidence that assists you in doing whatever the task is, and, second, these comments are probably a tip-off that you are showing some instinctive abilities in that area. Sometimes these trainees are referred to as "naturals." In sports, they are the natural athletes.

Natural Unconscious Competents would seem to have it made if it were not for one problem. Without ever being consciously aware of what it is they are doing correctly, they fall prey to second-guessing themselves when things do not go well. It is rare to find anyone whose position does not leave them susceptible to a slump of some kind. In selling, sales may drop off from time to time. In training, maybe a few extra-negative evaluations are received. We are all subject to ups and downs within our given occupations. A natural Unconscious Competent who has no idea what is causing the slump he or she is experiencing is often left second-guessing everything he or she is doing and ends up attempting to fix the wrong problems. It is certainly understandable to witness a panic when faced with poor performance he or she cannot explain. This is one of the reasons that even trainees who are performing at an optimum level should receive training up through conscious competency to teach them what it is they are doing right. Perhaps now, not only will they be better prepared in the event of a downturn in performance, but they will be better in touch with what it is they are doing right and maximize this strength. This may also be why historically, in the world of sports, natural athletes make poor coaches. To me, it is not much of a mystery at all.

Take the career of a natural baseball player as an example. Since he was a boy, he had a natural ability to play baseball. Some say that hitting a Major League baseball is one of the most difficult tasks to master, but to him, it was a piece of cake. The sport came easily to him from Little League on up. Ask him about the science of hitting a baseball, and he will tell you, "Swing and it will go." That is an unconscious competent. Years later, this baseball player retires and decides to take a crack at coaching.

A slumping hitter looks through the batting cage out at the new coach and asks, "Any tips, Coach?"

"Yeah," the coach replies. "Swing and it will go!"

Not much of a lesson. It is not surprising who typically make the finest coaches. It is usually the player who had a mediocre career at best. Oh, this player quite often played in the big leagues . . . for a week or two. Usually most of his or her career was spent struggling to make it. These players were not blessed with natural ability. Any success they experienced was due to kicking, biting, clawing, and bleeding to bring out every ounce of talent they possessed. They trained themselves to be Conscious Competents.

Ask this second new coach how to hit a baseball and he will tell you, "Get your bat back, keep your eye on the ball, and shift your weight," among other things. He has made a science out of hitting a baseball from struggling with his own limitations. Typically, being more in touch with his own abilities allows him to be better able to communicate these ideas to others. While there are exceptions to this rule, one point is clear: Learning what it is you do well and do not do well can only improve the natural abilities you possess.

The Four Levels of Behavior in Action

Now let's look at another example that will illustrate all four levels in action. The game of golf immediately comes to mind. After breaking my hand in two places a couple of years ago playing basketball, I decided to take up a safer, less physical sport, the game of golf. I chose golf for one other reason. After watching various golf tournaments on television, I was convinced that the game would be easy and fun. Now, that is what I call an Unconscious Incompetent. I had absolutely no idea how misguided I was. A friend of mine suggested I might want to take a few lessons, or at least hit a bucket of balls on a driving range, but I would have none of it. Until I stepped out on the golf course, I was totally unaware just how ineffective I was going to be.

I approached the first tee calmly and ready for action. There was a crowd of golfers building behind us as we waited our turn. Little did I know this would be the last time I approached the first tee without butterflies in my stomach. I believe it was the third time that I swung and missed the teed-up ball that I began to move to Level Two, the Conscious Incompetent. It became quite clear to me that I was not the natural I had thought I was going to be. All of a sudden, lessons did not sound like such a bad idea.

After what seemed like the three days it took me to finish that first humiliating round of golf, I signed up for a series of lessons. I was given the 500 or so necessary tips required to play the game at a beginner's level, and began to practice. As with most other people who are moving toward conscious competency, I began to experience the excitement of some improvement. I was ready to take my show on the road and try my golf game out on a real course again. This time I would show the waiting gallery! When it was my turn, I began to methodically go through the lessons I had learned. I fell into my hypnotic golf trance and began to mumble my instructions:

Left arm straight. Eyes on the ball. Keep your head still.

Let the club do the work. Slow back swing.

Turn your hands over.

Point your left shoulder toward the target. Turn like you're turning in a barrel.

It was right about here that I heard someone in the gallery shout, "Oh my goodness, he just took lessons!" A groan escaped from many of those around that golfer. It sounded as if a few of the groans came from my own foursome as I continued. I am not sure if this second round actually moved any faster than my first, but I did show improvement. Unfortunately, because I was so mechanical and slow, it was not the most enjoyable experience I ever had. I, like most new golfers, had settled into Level Three, the Conscious Competent. It was nice becoming a student of the game and learning what I was doing right and wrong. The only problem was that I was driving all those around me crazy. I was determined to stick with it, however, so I kept playing.

Gradually, the more I played, the smoother my swing became, and my game began to speed up. I remembered my golf pro telling me that if I kept at it, I would achieve what he called "muscle memory." I call it Level Four, the Unconscious Competent. At this level, I finally could swing a club fairly effectively and not have to repeat my massive collection of directions. Achieving unconscious competency is a goal most trainees have when they are learning a new skill or process. To achieve this level requires patience by the trainee and encouragement by the presenter.

The Next Level

Much has been written about the four levels of behavior, and all the discussions lead us to believe that the process stops at Level Four, Unconscious Competent. No argument from me that Level Four is our ultimate goal; however, I do disagree that the process stops here. It is unrealistic to assume we simply stop at Level Four and remain there. I would instead refer to these levels of behavior as more of a cycle. What would you guess the next level would be for most of us after Level Four? You are right if you said Level One, Unconscious Incompetent.

If there is a problem with unconscious competency, it is that you are susceptible to complacency. Remember, you are now performing effectively, and you do not even have to think about what you are doing to achieve these results. Think back and recall the first customer you ever worked with. You were probably the model of conscious competency. As a matter of fact, after you recovered from the shock of actually making a sale, you most likely brushed back a tear and in a choked-up voice assured the customer you would be there to make sure all that you promised would happen. Make no mistake about it either, you were there! After a few more of these experiences, you settled nicely into your unconscious competency role of providing good, solid service.

Now let's move forward about 50 customers. Did you give them the same level of service you gave the first person? I doubt it. You actually slipped into Level One, Unconscious Incompetent. After a couple of signals (or complaints), you became Consciously Incompetent, took steps to fix this problem, brushing through Conscious Competent, and resumed your role as an Unconscious Competent. These behaviors are in no way stagnant as the cycle repeats itself over and over again in everything you do.

Summary

Four simple stages that we all go through at our own rate of speed. I've always liked to go over these stages with the audiences I work with because it provides a subtle reminder that no matter at what level audience members might be, the program they are about to go through will be relevant to them . . . and that goes for you, the reader, as well! From new hire to grizzled vet, this model puts everything in perspective.

Chapter 4

The Personality Parade
Training All Different Types of People

S ome people say that training must be a rather boring career. From the looks of it, without ever having been involved in a long-term training project, they appear to be right. Often presenters find themselves teaching the same curriculum, running the same role-play, monitoring the same labs over and over again. How can anyone teach the same materials week after week, in what is often an environment that does not change, without getting bored? It is an interesting question, and one I would probably have trouble answering if it were not for one obvious variable. Although the courses seldom change, *the trainees do*. With those changing groups of trainees come an assortment of personalities, making the job of a presenter anything but boring.

So much can be learned from working with various personality types that it is not unusual for companies to use training positions as stepping-stones to management. The reasoning is quite simple. Anyone who spends a year or two in the classroom, juggling a different assortment of personalities every week or two and finding ways to keep all those in attendance from killing each other, knows a few things about management. As a matter of fact, I would rate the people skills of most tenured presenters to be extremely acute. As with any team that needs to be managed, there is generally a hodgepodge of personalities to try to take care of. A presenter's ultimate dream is to repair whatever personality flaw exists within the trainee and heal that trainee. Reality says that a reasonable goal is to minimize any potential distractions due to personality conflicts and allow both the trainees and the presenter to survive!

There are a couple of flaws in the theory that presenters are ready to step in as managers after a stint in the classroom. If I were to rate a typical presenter on management skills, there is no doubt that when it came to working with personality types, he would get an A+. The problem is that although having the skills to get the most out of any type of individual is critical, so are other generic management skills, such as giving recognition and delegation. Without having taken a management training program for other basic management skills, the individual would get a C–. Combining a management program *with* training works wonderfully in preparing a presenter to be a manager.

Trainees come in different shapes and different sizes with an entire array of personalities. Certain personalities are attracted to various types of training. All presenters will experience a full assortment of personalities. There are two ways to approach this phenomenon. The first way is to react to whatever presents itself to you and take your best instinctive shot at dealing with it. The second, and more preferred, way is to arm yourself now in a more proactive stance to the realities that extreme personalities can create in your training. With a proactive strategy in mind, I now present to you eight basic personality types, the potential problems that might arise when working with them, and solutions. I also hope that you will feel a little less apprehensive about working with these personalities in a practical manner to keep potential difficulties from ever surfacing within your training.

The Loner Trainee

The first type of trainee who may appear in your seminar is a student whom I call the *loner*. As the name indicates, this is a trainee who prefers to be pretty much left alone and considers himself or herself self-reliant. While in class, the trainee typically is attentive and participative, often showing what may appear to be the perfect trainee personality. The only catch is that these trainees often prefer to have as little involvement as possible with the other trainees, can tend to isolate themselves, and may appear somewhat aloof. These trainees are often quite capable as students, which may account for some of their resistance in working with others. My guess would be that if you were able to check back to a report card written as this individual was growing up, you would probably see good grades with a comment that says, "Joey is a fine student; however, he doesn't play well with others."

This type of trainee is not as easy to spot as a lot of the other personality types. Loners usually are very good at coming up with excuses as to why they will be unable to work with other students. They will try to wriggle their way out of any type of group work by saying things like, "If it isn't too much trouble, I would like to work on this exercise alone. I find I am able to concentrate better." Many presenters will not even notice this type of trainee in their seminars because of the trainee's participation. As presenters, our primary focus is on seminar activities and the involvement of the trainees. Within the seminar and in front of the presenter, these trainees appear to be model students. This makes it difficult to look at these trainees with a watchful eye. It is my recommendation that you do. An experienced presenter will tell you that part of the job is to manage the material taught and another major part is to manage the personalities receiving this information. What possible harm can come from a near-model student who does not necessarily interact with the other trainees? Plenty.

One of the biggest problems that can occur within your seminars as a result of a loner is what I refer to as "distancing." Trainees will go only so far out of their way to accept another trainee. After the initial gestures of friendship are rebuffed, the other trainees will back away and distance themselves. Then a strange phenomenon occurs. The class can actually turn against the loner and become hostile. One reason for this is that trainees often are attending a seminar with others in their firm. All of us want to enjoy our training experiences, and a part of that joy involves the closeness that is shared among classes. Many trainees expect that family type of feeling. A complicating factor is that other classes going through the same program may be experiencing that desired feeling. "Our seminar? We're like brothers and sisters!" Now, here is your seminar that, with the exception of one trainee, gets together at night for drinks, lab work, or practice of some sort. A strange type of resentment occurs. It almost seems as if the trainees become jealous that their experiences are not measuring up to the stories they've heard of those other classes, and feel it is the loner's fault. Class members stop trying to include the loner and deliberately distance themselves from this trainee. What's more, slowly, little side comments start being made by the other trainees in the seminar like, "All of us got together last night, well, *almost* all of us got together, to work on this piece." Once these types of comments start, they usually only get worse. Be on the lookout for such behavior and take action.

When dealing with a loner trainee, you can try a couple of tricks. To begin with, make it a basic rule not to go into too much detail when overviewing a course and going over a course calendar. In other words, until you have a handle on the personality types within your training, be intentionally vague regarding the methods you intend to use within your sessions. This allows you some freedom in coping with a loner. The solution I recommend to deal with such trainees does not interfere with what you will be teaching, only with how you intend to teach it. Any curriculum has some poetic license to it. To work with a loner, it will be necessary to exercise some of that license. In other words, lying! Create activities where there are none to force loners into the mainstream of the class.

For example, let's look at an evening activity. My curriculum might say for the trainees to look over a reading for tomorrow. Lo and behold, it comes out of my mouth as a group project requiring two assigned groups to get together in the evening and come up with a couple of questions to use as a review in the morning. I will even go so far as to suggest they take this project to the bar or a suitable relaxing environment. Depending on the setup of your training, you may want these activities to occur in the seminar. Create small-group activities or teams to accomplish tasks that may be written to be done individually. In no way is this solution intended to represent a punishment for the rest of the class. Your job is to make sure that all students get the most they can possibly get out of the seminar you are conducting. As long as you have not already told the trainees about all the evening or seminar activities you have planned, the assignments will not be perceived as anything out of the ordinary.

When working with a loner, you do not want to react too slowly to the situation. Some of the off-the-cuff comments that are made in the seminar can have a terrible effect on the morale of the loner and the rest of the class. Sadly, by the time a presenter actually hears these comments, it may be too late. Most curriculum developers will state exactly what material should be covered. How to accomplish this task is often the presenter's business. Hold back on any early commitments regarding activities and evening work until you have had some time to carefully analyze your participants.

The Quiet Trainee

There are a few constants in this world that we all know and probably feel comfortable with. What goes up must come down. When considering real estate, the three most important factors are location, location, and location. When conducting a training seminar, you are going to have *quiet* trainees. The fact of the matter is that some people in this world are simply quieter than others. Is that a problem in training? Usually not. As a matter of fact, most of the time if these trainees actually do become a problem, it is a result of the presenter's inappropriate handling of them.

The mistake so many presenters make is demanding equal participation from the quiet trainees. Where is it written that all trainees must answer the same number of questions in class? In a few outdated books, that's where! Try to understand that some people are quiet people. They are not slow. They are not troubled. They are certainly not trying to undermine the presenter in any way. They are just quiet people. For some reason, these trainees can unnerve a presenter. Quiet trainees should pose no real threat; however, a few potential problems should be considered.

To begin with, let's look at how the rest of the class may feel about a quiet trainee. Usually the other trainees feel a sense of empathy for this trainee. Students will often band together to help quiet trainees. When a presenter begins to work the quiet trainee hard with questions, there can be animosity toward the presenter from the entire class. At no time do you want to appear to be picking on a quiet trainee.

Another side to the argument regarding the frequency of questions to a quiet trainee is this: If you do not ask questions of the quiet trainee, it becomes awkward for the rest of the class. Some trainees begin to feel as if one student is receiving preferential treatment. "How come he doesn't have to answer questions?" the other trainees begin to think. What's worse, the longer the presenter goes without asking a question of a quiet trainee, the more difficult it actually becomes for this student to participate at all. The trainee's shyness becomes compounded the longer the trainee goes without talking.

I have a couple of recommendations for working with quiet trainees. The first involves looking at the size of your seminar. Some trainees are quiet when there are 10 or 15 students in the seminar. Their confidence is not very high, and they may feel vulnerable. Try introducing a few small-group exercises to the seminar. You would be shocked and amazed at how many quiet trainees come alive when the size of their group shrinks to four or five. It may be a ratio quiet trainees will be more comfortable with. One last point about small groups. Ask that the trainees in the groups take turns with different roles, such as leader and presenter. This will also force your quiet trainee to assume a leadership role within his or her small group and begin to interact with the rest of the class as well. Make sure you have enough small projects so that your quiet trainee gets a turn at the key roles.

My second recommendation, when working with quiet trainees, involves the kinds of questions you ask. Especially early in your training, stay away from questions that can put the quiet trainee on the spot. Questions involving remembering particular facts could wind up being disastrous. Try some easier questions involving his or her opinion. Be extremely supportive (without being artificial) of responses. Even saying things like, "Good answer!" or "Now that's what we are looking for!" can do wonders. The basic point I want to make here is to start slowly and gradually work to build confidence in the quiet trainee.

Instilling confidence within a quiet trainee can be one of the more rewarding aspects of training. Seeing a trainee blossom and come out of his or her shell often is one of the many success stories a presenter clings to. The real world says this is not the norm, however. What you should look for is to create an environment that allows quiet trainees to break out if they so desire and, if not, to at least actively participate at a percentage slightly below the rest of the class.

The Amiable Trainee

Next up in your personality parade of trainees comes the *amiable* trainee. Typically found as new hires, these trainees are about as close to model trainees as you will find. Obedient and ready to carry out the wishes of the presenter, they sit and await your next command. You say jump, and they really will say how high. Whatever you say or do as a presenter must be right. Pinch me, these students sound too good to be true. Okay, here is the pinch.

If I have a concern with amiable trainees, it involves their blind trust. If the presenter were to say, "The sky is green," this trainee would shoot back with "You bet!" I realize this may sound like a dream come true to some of you, but if you take your role as a presenter seriously, this has to disturb you.

The reality of training is that the presenter plays an important role in the professional survival of many trainees. Mastering the skills provided by the presenter may be their lifelines to individual success. Yes, I want the training to be a tremendous experience for my trainees, and I want to be loved by all. I also want these trainees to have long and prosperous careers with the company. It is therefore my responsibility to do all within my power to make sure that the skills I teach can be reproduced by the trainee in the field . . . when I am not there. The fear I have when working with amiable trainees is that I am not always sure they will be able to think on their own. It would be impossible, in most forms of training, to present every possible scenario to trainees. Hopefully, teaching some type of process should help. Nonetheless, a skilled presenter must also teach the trainees to think outside of the box. I do not think a student's agreeing with my every statement accomplishes that goal.

The solution is rather simple; it is not, however, an intuitive one. Most presenters will question amiable trainees to make sure they can think on their own. The problem is, they ask the wrong kinds of questions. If you ask an amiable trainee a question that requires a fact-based response, you will most likely get the answer you are looking for. At no time did I say amiable trainees are slow. As a matter of fact, because they are typically new hires, there is a good chance they will be among your quickest trainees. This can be attributed to either just finishing school and being used to a classroom environment or simply working harder to impress, because they are new. Many presenters think this approach is a way to get an amiable trainee thinking on his or her own. I do not.

A second type of question often asked of amiable trainees is opinion based. The idea here is to solicit the trainee's opinion to a question that has no right or wrong answer. On paper, this appears to be a pretty good solution to getting amiable trainees to think on their own. Unfortunately, the reality is that most amiable trainees will attempt to anticipate the opinion of the presenter and provide that response as their answers. Once again, you are left with trainees who are not fully prepared to think on their own feet.

The correct type of question for an amiable trainee is a case history question. Remember, the concept of a case history question is to present a scenario using information you have just taught. What the case history question does, however, is ask questions that have not been addressed but can be solved using the information taught. It is not unusual to hear an amiable trainee respond by saying, "You haven't taught us that yet." If an amiable trainee says that to you, congratulations. You are doing beautifully. Your job as a presenter is to teach the information necessary to allow the trainee to attempt a logical response. Be supportive of the amiable trainee's answer to encourage future thinking outside of the box.

The good news about amiable trainees is that of all the personality types identified in this chapter, I would probably most prefer to be stuck with these trainees. Other than the potential for the difficulties discussed previously and perhaps a little bit of boredom because they are so obedient, there really is not much to complain about. Keep a watchful eye that they are not too obedient, mix in a couple of case history questions to test the waters, and count your lucky stars. You are going to have an enjoyable couple of days.

The Discouraged Trainee

Let's now turn from the excitement and enthusiasm of an amiable trainee to the negative gloominess of the *discouraged* trainee. You are dealing with a personality type that is often depressed and discouraged and brings these feelings to your seminar. The causes of this behavior can be numerous, but one thing is definitely clear: The discouraged trainee will waste little time making you and the rest of the class aware of his or her feelings.

The causes for this behavior are endless. It could be that these trainees were forced to attend a training seminar they did not want to attend. Some managers who still live in the dark ages use basic training as a punishment. It could be a fear of failure. Some trainees will mask this fear with a rude, insensitive attitude. The trainee could be one who is on the way out of the company due to any number of reasons and for some reason has ended up in your room. Fact number one is this: It is not unusual to have a discouraged trainee in your training room. Fact number two: You had better do something about fact number one in a hurry.

The reason I recommend that you act in a hurry is to combat the basic nature of the discouraged trainee. These trainees love company.

Think back to when you started a new job. You were eager and willing to tackle any challenge that lay ahead of you. You were excited about the new challenges and fearful of the change that you had initiated within your life. For you, and for the rest of us, this moment probably was one of the most emotional times in your life. Then *they* approached you. *They* are the representatives of the "I hate it here and so should you" club. The membership drive started the moment you started your first day. In the blink of an eye, you were informed how miserable it was to work with whomever, for whomever, and the fragile emotional calm you were experiencing was shattered. Perhaps you fought back, but many do not.

Now let's take this experience and relate it to the seminar or workshop you are conducting. Here is a room full of various personalities. Certainly the most vulnerable are your amiable trainees. They want to fit in so badly. Before you know it, what was once an ideal personality is now racked with cynicism and doubt. This gloom can spread across your training room like a cancer.

Fortunately, spotting discouraged trainees is usually easy. No matter what question you ask them, their responses always seem to have a depressed sound to them. This is no accident. What these trainees are really asking, or should I say pleading, is for someone to listen to them. The mistake so many presenters make is not the failure to recognize this personality type or even to deal with it immediately. The mistake made is in *how* they deal with it.

The first error involves listening to the discouraged trainee. The good news is that most presenters will, in fact, hear out this trainee early in their training during the icebreakers. The bad news is they have this conversation in front of the entire class. The discouraged trainee would like nothing better than to air dirty laundry in front of the class at the urgings of a presenter. What a perfect scenario . . . for the trainee. This is where I would like to introduce you to a technique that will be used for a couple of the more aggressive personality types; it is called the "Let's have coffee" technique. Nothing deep, mind you, but you would be surprised at what the conversation will sound like when the discouraged trainee has no audience to perform in front of. A simple "How's it going?" during a break will usually do the trick. What I particularly like about working with this personality type is that if you ask "How's it going?" the discouraged trainee will tell you.

Be prepared to defuse some anger, so a couple of points need to be made here. First, do not apologize or say you are sorry. The reality is, no one is really satisfied with an apology. Usually it does not change the situation anyway. The discouraged trainee has probably heard apologies along the way. In addition to that, the words "I'm sorry" usually cause people to affix blame. The majority of the difficulties that the discouraged trainee tells you about have absolutely nothing to do with anything you have done. Studies have shown that when customer service representatives say "I'm sorry" over the phone, they usually get it from the customer with both barrels. What people really want to hear is an acknowledgment of their problem. A simple "I can understand your frustration" and a restatement of the discouraged trainee's concern typically is more than enough to satisfy this individual. Being a good listener helps, and a nonthreatening reminder of your role as an instructor will more often than not defuse this trainee's anger.

The second common error when working with a discouraged trainee involves the presenter's attempt to make it to the break without calling attention to the problem at hand. One of two things can happen. The presenter can stay away from questioning the discouraged trainee. In that event, the presenter may be sending some unwanted signals to the class that there is a problem the presenter wants no part of. Staying away from the discouraged trainees, in a sense, can alleviate their plight and give them a sort of martyr status. The other possibility is that the presenter can try to soften the questions too much by feeding the discouraged trainee opinion-based questions. By asking a discouraged trainee his or her opinion, you run the risk of allowing the trainee to climb up on a soapbox and vent his or her frustrations in front of the class. Sorry, not for me. I want the best of both worlds: involvement within the seminar but no venting. The solution involves a more careful use of the questions you choose. Make it a rule to stick solely to fact-based questions. Right or wrong, black or white. Frankly, I am not interested in opinions at this time. We will save that for our coffee break.

Discouraged trainees appear to present a major obstacle toward successful training. When they are handled carefully, this simply is not true. Averting any displays in front of the class and taking a genuine interest in their difficulties goes a long way to achieving a workable solution. If you are careful of the questions you use and do not delay in the tactics you choose, the discouraged trainee will not pose any real threat to your training.

The Enlightener Trainee

Most training sessions are not complete without someone in the seminar who seems to know it all. We will call this person the *enlightener*. How many times have you sat through a seminar and watched someone continue to enlighten the class with his or her enormous experience in whatever topic is being discussed? These people can relate to what you are explaining to the class. They have a story that needs to be told. They have an experience that may help you get your point across better. The enlightener brings to the seminar a whole array of potential problems for the presenter.

To begin with, the enlightener poses a major threat to your *timing* of the curriculum. Timing is an issue that will be gone over in more detail later in this book; however, it is critical to a presenter's success. Enlighteners can throw a wrench into the careful timing of a presentation. This, in turn, can cause seminars to run long and force presenters to sacrifice critical material to make up for the lost time. The seminar can appear rushed and hurried.

A second problem that can occur from the well-informed enlightener is damage to your *control* of the seminar and to your *credibility* as a presenter. What often happens when the enlightener gets on a roll is the trainees' attention begins shifting from you to the enlightener. They begin to ask questions of the enlightener and not of you. What's even more frustrating is when the questions are answered by you and the class looks to the enlightener for *his or her* approval.

The final distraction that enlighteners can cause is their uncanny ability to throw off your rhythm. A presenter who is working effectively begins to establish a sort of rhythm. The enlightener's interjections seem to appear in a Murphy's Law manner. Count on the distraction to occur as you are trying to make your most critical point.

Not only can the enlightener's actions create difficulties for the presenter, they can irritate other class members as well. It does not take very long to notice other trainees' eyes beginning to roll as the enlightener brings forth another all-important point. Other trainees can get so frustrated by the enlightener that their participation and morale begin to drop along with their interest in your presentation. Something needs to be done about this right now.

Fortunately, working with enlighteners is fairly easy. To make sense of the solution, first let's look at the typical cause for their behavior. It can be summed up in one, three-letter word: ego. Enlighteners consciously or unconsciously want all those in the room to be aware of how bright they are regarding whatever topic you are discussing. Their behavior is not malicious, nor is it generally intended to create any problems. They often just want to be acknowledged. No harm; that is exactly what you should do with enlighteners. In your acknowledging, though, you had better choose your words carefully.

For example, you would not want to silence your enlightener by saying, "Okay, Frankie, you know a lot about skydiving. I want to hear from someone else now. Do you mind?" As ridiculous as that may sound, it is easy to get to a frustrated point and have your words come out a little hostile. Try it this way, instead. "Well, it looks like Frankie has a lot of experience in this area. I am going to be looking forward to having you share that with us, but I want to hear from the rest of you as well. Come on, don't make Frankie do all your work for you." This type of statement accomplishes two things. It provides your enlightener with an ego stroke, and it brings the rest of your class back into the conversation.

One of the more traditional approaches to working with enlighteners is to simply move up and slightly into their personal space while they are talking. I am not suggesting you pick a fight or anything; just appear very interested, and move in. This approach is especially useful for enlighteners who do not necessarily speak often but have a tendency to ramble. Your movements forward will send an unconscious signal for them to get out whatever they are talking about. If that does not work, be prepared to jump right into their monologues with a statement of your own relating to their points. Then tie it back to your topic and hang on for dear life.

An example of such an exchange would sound like this:

ENLIGHTENER: . . . which can make a difference in how you want to handle this situation. Now, when I was a child . . .

PRESENTER: So, in handling this situation, you would first work with the administrator. You know, you make a good point when you relate how you would want to handle this. In fact, that is what we want to accomplish in this module. People who need people . . .

If I appear to be a little harsh with enlightener trainees, it is because I have seen them innocently drive many a presenter up a wall. I would be terribly remiss if I did not mention that a great deal of the time enlightener trainees are fantastic to have in a seminar. They certainly can assist in helping you break down the Monday morning barriers that you so desperately need to remove. It is amazing how one trainee who is participating in and enjoying your seminar can make others jump in as well. When the class begins to drift away late in the day, it is the enlightener who is ready to speak at any time. Managed properly, the enlightener can be a presenter's best friend.

The Joker Trainee

Similar to the enlightener is a trainee whose personality is rarely kept a secret for long. I am referring to the old class clown who grew up into a corporate environment and who we will now refer to as the *joker*.

The joker is quick-witted and potentially aggressive, so it pays to spend a moment or two getting to know this character.

There are many reasons why an individual behaves as a joker trainee. The first and most basic reason might be that something struck him or her as funny. Just because a trainee makes a couple of humorous remarks does not necessarily mean there is a personality problem in your seminar. It might be just the comic relief your seminar has been looking for.

When the joker trainee's behavior becomes more constant, the reasons may be a little more complicated. Perhaps it is an ego problem or the way this individual deals with stress. Let's again look at possible problems and then at some solutions that will allow us to work with the joker trainee in a peaceful manner.

The first problem that you should beware of is the joker's effect on the timing of your seminar. As with the enlightener trainee, the joker is not shy about chiming in on a discussion. Murphy's Law of training says that these comical additions can come at the most inopportune times. It seems that every time there is a serious point to be made or an emotional statement to be addressed, here comes the joker. Sometimes a presenter builds a presentation to a powerful climax only to see it shattered by an assault from the joker. Potential powerful, magical moments are ruined by an ill-timed joke.

Another concern with the joker involves feelings. Feelings of the trainees or the presenters are often on the line every time a joker opens his or her mouth. When you stop and consider the odds of having just one trainee who may be offended by a joke, you begin to understand the danger of a joker. It could be a harmless joke about New Yorkers, Californians, or any other topic. You never know who may have a connection to the topic. Especially early on, there is no way to tell the sensitivity levels of your trainees. The joker has a dangerous approach to assisting you in finding out in a hurry. What makes matters worse, many curriculum writers actually still write into the curricula suggestions to have a different student start the seminar each day with a joke. These suggestions typically do not stay in the curriculum long once they have been used under fire.

Understanding how to work with a joker requires just a little basic psychology. Why is it that some people require and almost thrive on attention? The answer often is simply to make up for some feelings of uncertainty. Therefore, as with the enlightener trainee, the best approach to working with a joker trainee is to do a little boosting of his or her ego. Actually give the joker an opportunity to perform, but only on your terms. This may come by way of selecting a volunteer or strategically using the joker in a case study. There are only so many of those situations, so I recommend that you let your joker know that he or she is going to be involved well before the actual event. This helps to placate the joker's need to be noticed.

Another approach to working with joker trainees again involves movement from the presenter. As with the enlightener, some movement toward the individual often can help to send out unconscious signals for the trainee to get out his or her story and finish up.

If that does not work, there is still always the coffee break method of asking politely for the individuals to hold back their humorous comments. Be warned: Jokers do not respond well to being singled out and attacked in class. It is not recommended to try to publicly outwit a trainee whose strengths lie in these types of clashes.

Finally, screening a joker's jokes before allowing them to be aired in front of the room may help to avoid any other serious problems.

Remember, these trainees are usually high-spirited, emotional people who have a lot to offer a seminar. Working to channel that enthusiasm in constructive ways can help to harness that energy and put it to work for you. No student personality has a greater potential to warm up a seminar faster and more effectively than the joker.

The Reliant Trainee

One of my favorite and most challenging personality types is the *reliant* trainee. I say this because watching a genuine reliant trainee work his or her magic is like appreciating a unique art form. This trainee is so good at what he or she does, most presenters do not realize they have been had until it is far too late.

When was the last time you felt confident doing a certain task and then the procedures changed? How did you handle not knowing all there was to know about your topic anymore? Many people will find creative approaches to keep from looking foolish and learning new procedures. Reliant trainees are masters of this form of manipulation. Their appearance is one of confidence and coolness regarding everything except what you are teaching. That is where reliants begin to work their real magic. They are usually outwardly confident in many areas but when it comes to other tasks, they will not participate and will rely heavily on others. Thus the name. Often reliant trainees almost have a sense of pride regarding their resistance to learn certain information. They sneak their way out of learning with well-polished phrases, such as, "If you could just do this for me one time, I know I will be able to do it on my own in the future." The only procedures reliant trainees ever really learn are the steps it takes to find someone else to do their work.

You probably have unwittingly assisted many reliant trainees in your time. Maybe it is the friend who "just doesn't do well with that type of customer" or someone who "just wanted you to type that memo this one time." The problem is, there is an office full of people who will offer certain types of assistance on an occasional basis. Take my father, for instance. He could probably build a house from scratch. From top to bottom, there is almost nothing he could not do . . . except work with electricity. For some strange reason, he not only refused to work with electricity, but he took a strange sense of pride in telling you he neither understood nor wanted to learn about electricity. This, of course, then became my specialty out of necessity. After a number of shocks through my lifetime, I later wondered how convenient my father's stubbornness really was.

A common problem that creeps up with many of the personalities discussed, including the reliant trainee, involves time. Unlike many of the other personalities that cause a seminar to slow down, reliant trainees usually have little to say during a seminar. The time problem they cause involves the presenter's time when the seminar is not in session. Before the seminar, during breaks, at lunchtime, and after the seminar, the reliant trainee attacks. It starts with "Could you just take a second to read over this?" and soon becomes "I still can't get it. Could you do one for me?" Before you know it, all your free time is being spent with one trainee. I want to emphasize here that I am in no way opposed to working out of class with a student. I maintain it is a luxury and not a right to have uninterrupted time without students while at a training facility. My argument is that it just is not fair to have one trainee monopolize all your individual time.

This brings me to the second and most important problem a reliant trainee can cause a training department. Falling for a reliant trainee's manipulation fails to correct his or her behavior and can affect the credibility of your training. Remember, often reliant trainees can get away with their behavior for only so long before those around them begin to catch on to their tricks. Training is then suggested by management to try to correct this deficiency. Unfortunately, it is rare to receive any type of biographical information regarding the shortcomings of your trainees. I have never had reliant trainees come to town telling me they have had a history of manipulation and are ready to mend their evil ways! If the trainees return to their office without the skills to correct their performance, it is *your* training that is considered a failure.

Working successfully with a reliant trainee requires the use of a couple of training skills. Start by taking a hard look at your curriculum to get a sense for certain areas that attract reliant trainees. Perhaps it is an area that you have noticed gives trainees trouble or even a more technical process that you sense may cause anxiety. After teaching a curriculum a couple of times, these pieces become fairly obvious. Once you get a sense of where these areas are located, lay out a process for how you will work with people regarding these areas. You may start that particular module with something like this:

PRESENTER: Today we are going to learn a new skill that will be used in introducing yourself to your customer. I will want you to write out your introductions on your own and use them in the role-plays that will be conducted tomorrow. I will not look at them until after you have used what you have once in the role-play. After I hear what you have worked on, I will make written comments and ask that you continue to work on them alone. After three of these role-plays, if you still do not feel comfortable with the process, I will be more than happy to sit down and work with you until you do.

Making a statement like this accomplishes a couple of things. First, it lays down the ground rules regarding how and when help will be given. This allows you to back off and encourage reliant trainees to work on their own. Second, it reassures reliant trainees that they will not be abandoned and in fact will receive help after they have made some attempts on their own. Be prepared to be positive and encouraging to whatever attempts are made by reliant trainees. The better job you can do convincing them they are improving, the better the chances are that they will develop the confidence to use these skills on their own.

Laying out the ground rules in advance is a successful proactive approach. There are also some effective reactive approaches that can be implemented while under fire. A favorite trick used by reliant trainees in front of other trainees is to ask the presenter how he or she would do a certain task. That certain task is, of course, the task they themselves need to do. Using the reverse technique by bouncing the question back to such trainees and stroking whatever answer you receive will assist you in getting them to do their own work. The conversation may sound something like this:

TRAINEE: How would your introduction sound to a typical customer?
PRESENTER: That's a good question. What approach do you think I should take?
TRAINEE: Uh . . . well . . . maybe just a simple third-party reference and a well-thought-out initial benefit statement.

PRESENTER: There you go! Now, that would certainly get the customer's attention and allow us to proceed. Good job.

When working with reliant trainees, it is critical that the presenter first and most important identifies what is going on. Teaching trainees by allowing them to crawl before they walk and walk before they run builds confidence along the way. Perhaps the ultimate irony is that it is not unusual for an enlightener trainee to become a reliant trainee once he or she leaves his or her area of expertise. Call it a bonus if you want to, but you probably will have to work to turn off this trainee initially and then work to turn him or her back on again later. Whenever you get frustrated, however, remember back when you tried to get someone to do your work for you that one time. This may help with the empathy that is required when working with the reliant trainee.

The Sniper

Perhaps the most dangerous trainee of all is the *sniper*. The sniper got this name because many of the comments this trainee makes are not blatantly aggressive. Often the malicious intent is clear, but the sniper trainee can put on an innocent front if challenged. Like a real sniper, this trainee fires shots, his or her cover being the rest of the students in the seminar.

I have many concerns about snipers. The first deals with the effect this trainee can have on the morale of a seminar. It can be disturbing, to say the least, when a trainee comes to a seminar and begins picking a fight with the presenter. For many trainees, this unsettling experience can ruin their training experience. Amiable trainees are particularly susceptible to the negativity a sniper can spread.

Timing is another concern when you are faced with a sniper. By dragging presenters into petty and trivial conversations, snipers can throw a carefully timed curriculum into a tailspin. By the time the presenter has attempted to settle such discussions, he or she may have to sacrifice other more important pieces of material.

Another concern I have about snipers has to do with the presenter's working too hard to placate these trainees. You can spend an entire week attempting to win over a sniper and lose the rest of the trainees in the process.

My final concern with a sniper, as you might have guessed, deals with the presenter's well-being. Whether presenters want to admit it or not, the situation they generally fear the most is dealing with a sniper while they are in front of a class. Without proper preparation, the fight certainly appears to be an unfair one. The sniper, while using the cover of the rest of the class, gets to take shots at the presenter. Maintaining professionalism, the presenter gets to fight back with only one disadvantage. It often appears the presenter is fighting back with his or her professional hands tied behind his or her back. It is the presenter's responsibility to maintain control of the seminar and display professional behavior. A confrontation in front of the class exhibits neither of these responsibilities. That does not sound like a very fair fight to me. As a result, I have seen presenters retreat from the pit and never return. I have seen still other presenters witness a sniper attack in cross-training situations and quit their jobs to avoid the possibility of facing this potentially humiliating situation. I will leave to your imagination the ramifications of bottom-line loss of revenue when a corporation loses a presenter for this reason.

In working out solutions, let's first take a closer look at what makes a sniper tick. To begin with, most snipers, ironically, are created by presenters. No, you did not misread that last statement. It is my strong belief that roughly 80 percent of the contact a presenter receives from a sniper is initiated by the presenter. In truth, because so many presenters want to discuss the more aggressive personalities of trainees, I discuss sniping as a personality trait. The problem is, I have almost never met a trainee who actually woke up in the morning with the intent to maliciously harm a seminar and its presenter. I have, however, seen many of the other personality traits that have been discussed handled poorly, creating a catalyst effect on the trainee. Embarrass an enlightener or a joker or just about any other trainee in front of the class, even inadvertently, and you may create a sniper. Ask the wrong type of question to the wrong trainee, and you may create a sniper. Simply not addressing certain issues up front in your training can create a sniper. How do you know what critical issues you may need to discuss up front? That question will be addressed when we look at how to structure a presentation, shown in the next case study. Suffice it to say, there are a number of reasons why a trainee can assume the role of a sniper. The real question becomes: How are you going to deal with this trainee under fire?

I would like to examine two basic scenarios to prepare you to handle a sniper. The first scenario involves contact with a sniper you already know will be in your room. This is not an uncommon situation. Snipers usually establish reputations for their actions. The second, and more difficult, scenario looks at the same case study, but without the luxury of advance knowledge of a sniper's presence.

How to Handle Snipers Whose Reputation Precedes Them

Let me start by presenting you with what I consider to be a classic case study.

Case Study: The Tale of Rotten Rob Rolles

Rob Rolles is one tough individual. Just ask him. He is intelligent and capable of doing outstanding work. He has been with Widgets 'R Wonderful for over 20 years and unfortunately usually conveys an attitude of boredom. He is generally thought of, by those who work with him, as a fearless employee who tells it like it is. He is also regarded by his supervisor as an employee with an abundance of natural skills. Rob would have been promoted long ago if it wasn't for his tendency to be negative and critical. In his mind, there always seems to be a better way to do things, and Rob enjoys laying it on. His approach often takes the form of needling questions that tend to disrupt the flow of discussions. He does this interrupting with an air of innocence with comments, such as "It won't work!" and "Not this old tired idea again!"

Well, how do you like my sniper? Most people who look at this case study just sigh and say they know this worker all too well. In examining this scenario, the question becomes: What are you going to do about this situation because you know this individual is going to be in your seminar?

When you carefully examine the case study, you find in the third sentence a valuable clue. Usually snipers are not unintelligent people who have nothing to offer. Actually, this intelligence often accounts for snipers getting into trouble. How would you like it if you were the person in your office who knew most of the answers and then found out someone else was coming to town to take over that role? Snipers have large egos and are easily threatened in this type of situation. Unfortunately for snipers, times change and procedures change, and it is often the role of the presenter to come out and deliver that message. So what is the answer? I assure you, I fear no trainee and am in no way a coward. However, in this situation, I recommend one simple, time-tested approach. If you can't beat 'em, let'em join you!

Let's assume you have a one-week training seminar. That really means you are going to be running that seminar for approximately 40 hours. One of the best approaches to working with snipers is to prepare yourself to give up a piece of the show. If possible, try meeting with the individual before the seminar and map out a strategy for his or her assistance. Your discussion may sound something like this:

PRESENTER: Hi, Rob. Thanks for coming. Listen, if it isn't too much trouble, I was wondering if I could count on your assistance in this training. I am well aware of your expertise in _____ [fill in the appropriate topic] and wanted to know if you could give me about 10 minutes on Thursday getting the rest of the class up to speed. I will then go over the new procedures. Can I count on your assistance?

For those of you who are a little squeamish about giving your sniper the floor, notice how you can carefully map out what, where, and for how long your sniper will speak. This should settle any concerns about losing control. If your trainee has no abilities whatsoever to offer the seminar, try "Counting on your help" in passing out handouts and setting up break stations. The magic of this approach is that it often creates a model trainee from someone who once may have appeared to be a potentially volatile trainee. The responsibility of training now falls on both your shoulders, and, given an opportunity, the sniper will rarely fail you.

In reminiscing back to my early training days, I can honestly say that this approach may have provided me with one of my biggest career breaks. The government contract that I was working on called for some important training in Tampa. What we did not know was that there was a sniper lying in wait for one of our top trainers. The two-day training session was so disrupted by the sniper and trainer battles that the training was halted after the first day. Our trainer angrily flew home while the letters began to fly. The government monitor demanded we send someone down to Tampa and "Do the training right!" When the pool of trainers I belonged to was asked for another victim, I volunteered to go under fire. My goal was a simple one: Meet with the sniper beforehand, involve that individual in the training, and try to stroke his ego at the same time. Not only did this solution work, but letters were again generated, this time positively, by, you guessed it, the sniper. I was given my first significant promotion, and, needless to say, I have been a fan of this method of working with snipers ever since.

One irony that seems to be rather consistent with snipers is that they tend to be either really bad or really good. There is not a whole lot in between. When they do behave and write commendatory letters or whatnot, it is almost as if they were saying to those who are listening "See, it isn't me. I have been telling you all along that given a good trainer, I will more than behave!"

What to Do If You're Blindsided by a Sniper

The second and more difficult scenario involves the same type of sniper as mentioned earlier, but this time, you have no warning about his behavior. There you are, happily going through your introduction to the module, when your sniper rears his ugly head with a shot right between your eyes. In the training world, we call this "getting blindsided."

First, let's look at what *not* to do. The first instinct a lot of presenters have is to shoot back. How dare this trainee be so rude! How dare he take such an obvious cheap shot at you! Normally I preach to presenters to trust their instincts in most of the decisions they are faced with, but not this time. The critical point to remember here is that the sniper's behavioral pattern is not a secret to those around him. Other trainees know when a student takes a cheap shot at the presenter. If you felt it, most likely, so did the rest of the class. At this point, even if the other trainees were equally hostile coming into the seminar, they too will be somewhat appalled at the sniper's behavior. Most trainees know it takes guts to stand up in front of a class and will not support inappropriate behavior. That is, unless the presenter fires back. Once a presenter allows himself or herself to get sucked into a confrontation in front of the class, all bets are off. Then the other trainees get subjected to inappropriate behavior from the presenter as well, and the battle lines are drawn. It now becomes a question of which knucklehead they should support.

This leads to my first recommended tactic, which may be something of a disappointment to you: Look the other way. It is from years of experience that I say you will be much better off if you develop a motto that says, "The first one is free." To begin with, you run absolutely no risk of overreacting and alienating the rest of the class. The fact of the matter is that occasionally trainees make rude comments inadvertently. As I used to tell my parents, every now and then I'm going to put a ball through a window accidentally. I'm still a good kid. Often trainees will test a presenter they are unfamiliar with. Granted, I would prefer a different test, such as patting my stomach and head at the same time (I practice that one just in case), but in the real world, some trainees want to see just how well that presenter reacts under fire. On many occasions, these snipers will come up at the first break and apologize for their behavior. In a sense, what they are really saying is that you passed the first test. You did not blink.

Flushing a Sniper Out

Now, let's just say that after turning the other way and muttering to yourself about the first one as being free, your sniper does not go away. One of the most frustrating aspects of dealing with snipers is that they often make their nasty comments hidden securely behind the rest of the class. Sometimes only their slightly sarcastic grins give them away, confirming that you are not paranoid and that the comment you just heard was meant to embarrass you. This next recommendation may sound a little bit risky, but in some situations it may just do the trick. When the sniper is attempting to mask the hostile comments you are absorbing with an air of innocence, you may want to ask your sniper one simple innocent question in return:

Presenter: You know, Rob, that sounded like an aggressive remark. Was it intended that way?

What I particularly like about this technique is that it forces the sniper to put his cards on the table and 'fess up to what is going on. Nine times out of 10, the sniper will back off and choose his words a little more carefully. While staying professional and without being drawn into a confrontation in front of the class, you may very well have passed test number two.

Despite your attempts to handle yourself professionally without overly embarrassing your sniper, there are still those rare individuals who want to have it out in front of the class. You absorbed the first inappropriate remark and attempted to flush out the sniper with the second remark, but the negative comments just keep coming. It is now time to move to the third and final tactic. If you have ever wondered what it might be like to fly without a net, here comes your big chance. The approach I am going to outline for you may seem risky, but it has never failed me or the presenters I teach. The single most effective approach I know of (and have used on numerous occasions) requires relaying the sniper's comment back to the rest of the class. The exchange will most likely sound something like this:

Sniper: Excuse me. I think I speak for all of us here when I say that what you are presenting to us today is really a waste of our time. We have been through this garbage over and over again with no results to show for it. When is the home office going to wise up and leave us alone?

Presenter: So your concern is over the value of the training that is being presented. Fair enough, you make an interesting point. How do the rest of you feel about the value of the training you are in town to receive?

Trainee No. 2: Well, I—for one—am interested in the training and am willing to at least give it a chance.

This strategy is based on the belief that people do not want to see another person publicly humiliated, and even if they concur with the comments that the sniper has made, they will not support him. It is vital to maintain your composure and allow the other trainees to side with you, if for no other reason than to maintain your professionalism. In my years of teaching new presenters, I have ended every class by handing out a business card and asking the students to write me if this strategy ever failed them. To date, I have not received such a response. I am more than happy to make that same offer to you.

Once Trainee No. 2 (whoever that wonderful person may be) comes to your rescue, you are not out of the woods yet. You need no other confirmation; you have a real live sniper in your midst. It is doubtful that he will just go away now. What really needs to happen now is a conversation off-line between the two of you to iron this situation out. The only problem is you may have another 30 minutes until you can take a break and get to the bottom of the situation. There is no sense making this situation any worse than it is, so stay away. If you feel it is absolutely necessary to involve your sniper in the presentation, try to stick to close, probing questions that deal with facts and not feelings. Once you have made it to a break, subtly try to have a private conversation with the sniper. Maintain your composure and try handling the conversation the same way you would work with the discouraged trainee. That is, probe around and see if you can figure out what is disturbing the sniper before you jump down his throat. Assuming this sniper is not going to make your job an easy one and is offering no real reason for his actions, here is a six-step process for confronting the trainee and putting this problem behind you:

1. "I need your help."

Sometimes the most difficult part about confronting an individual is finding the right words to get started. No one wants to be standing there, looking at the ground, hemming and hawing, searching for a way to begin. Beginning your conversation this way sends out a message that you are serious and about to have a frank discussion.

2. "The situation is . . ."

The second step of this process, in my mind, is the most crucial. Starting out by describing the situation really forces both parties to deal with facts, not feelings. This has the potential to be a highly emotional moment. It is easy to disagree with another person's feelings but far more difficult to disagree with facts. State the problem clearly, and discipline yourself to avoid using the word "you." This will also help the individual you are confronting to look at the situation for what it is and will help reduce its emotional aspects.

3. "The difficulties this creates . . ."

Now you can begin to shift gears and let the individual you are confronting see the results or ramifications of his behavior. A couple of reminders: Once again, avoid using the word "you," and stick to facts, not feelings. One other recommendation: Try to avoid using the word "problem." It is a very confrontational word and can emotionally charge your sniper. Try replacing this word with other nouns, such as "difficulties," "concerns," "barriers," or "limitations."

4. "In the future . . ."

At this time, begin outlining the solution or possibly a suggestion to eliminate the behavior you are correcting. Remember, although you are in charge and running the show, you are also in a negotiating position. Allowing the person you are confronting a token piece of the pie is good for all concerned. In other words, try to make your solution a fair and reasonable one for both parties, and then stick to it.

5. "If this situation were to occur again . . ."

I am highly opposed to making threats within a training environment. In this situation, however, you must map out the consequences if the inappropriate behavior continues. This brings me to an important conversation that every presenter must have with his or her immediate supervisor. Before anyone starts training, there must be a clear understanding of the procedures in a worst-case scenario trainee behavioral problem situation. This is no time to be a hero or go out on a limb. Most training departments institute a "send home" policy to aid presenters with trainees who just will not cooperate. This policy empowers the presenter with a tremendous responsibility and obviously should be used only in the most drastic situations. In my years as a professional speaker, I have never sent home a student for bad behavior. The real benefit of such a policy is that it provides presenters with the confidence that they will have management support and that, regardless of the situation, they will win in the end.

6. Gain agreement.

During the conversation that has now been outlined, many trainees will not have a lot to say. As a matter of fact, many will be gazing at the floor or around your office avoiding eye contact altogether. Gaining agreement not only allows you to see if the problem has been solved in the trainee's eyes, but it psychologically makes it more difficult for the trainee to create the problem again. There can be no misunderstandings.

Remember, this technique is recommended when all other options have failed. The realistic outcome of this type of conversation is that the problem will almost certainly go away. That is the good news. The bad news is that your confronted trainee might feel humiliated and may withdraw from the rest of the seminar. I would like to tell you otherwise, but that is the reality of a confrontation of this nature; therefore, use such confrontations wisely.

When dealing with snipers, be prepared for the speech you will have to endure at the end of your training session. It's amazing how frequently you will be subjected to the same, tired words. The speech is usually delivered with other trainees present, and the puppy-dog eyes that go along with the words can make even those with a strong constitution nauseous. At this point in my career, I have the speech memorized. It goes something like this:

Uh, Mr. Jolles, I just wanted to say something if I could. I really liked your training course. I mean, I hope you weren't offended by my words or actions. I certainly didn't mean anything by them. It's kind of how I learn. I really like to make sure I understand everything, so I ask a lot of questions. I know the good instructors like that, and you were just great. Thanks again.

You might need a mouth guard to keep from grinding your teeth during this lame, manipulative presentation, but stay calm. Your sniper is trying to save face. If, in fact, you really do want to alleviate the problem, now is not the time to show your cards. Shake the snake's hand, don't embellish your words, and move on.

In most courses that teach people how to react to feelings of anger, the instructor tells the students to count to 10. Well, when under fire, you do not have the luxury to count off in front of a class, so often turning the other cheek is the next best thing. You have the support of the other trainees, management, and anyone else who has ever had to step into the pit. Maintain your composure and professionalism, treat confrontation as a challenge, and you will do just fine.

Some Closing Thoughts

When you're looking at trainees' personality types, it is important to remember a couple of basic rules. To begin with, you are not a licensed psychologist. Therefore, in no way does any strategy that may be implemented involve curing this trainee of the particular problem. Your basic strategy throughout is survival, yours and the seminar's. Do not be so naive as to think that your solution will undo years of deviant weird behavior. It will not. These trainees have had years of practice. Your goal is not to *fix* any of them, only to *manage* them while they are in your seminar. What your work with these trainees will do is allow you to take a diverse group of individuals who have been thrown together for a period of time and enable them to move from point A to point B as painlessly as possible.

The rule to remember deals with identifying the various personality traits. It is rare for me to lecture on this topic without trainees cornering me after class and asking me what type of personality they or the rest of the class represent. With all due respect, they have somewhat missed the point of this entire topic. In no way am I suggesting that you psychoanalyze every student in your seminar. The key to keep in mind is that you are on the lookout for extremes. I like having someone with a sense of humor in my class. I do not necessarily label that individual a joker. Some people really do know certain pieces of information regarding your topic and want to share it with the class. Fantastic! Your job is to keep an eye out for extremes and attempt to pull these trainees back from their extreme postures.

As far as your reaction to the extremes in personalities being displayed by your trainees, I need to make one final point. I have saved it for last in fear that if I wrote this in the beginning of the chapter, you might not feel a need to read on. If you discipline yourself not to overreact to any of the personality traits that have been discussed and to show just a little patience, often the other trainees will take care of the deviant behavior for you. On many occasions, I have either been told about the message or have overheard trainees telling others to lighten up, quit talking so much, or lay off the instructor. It is when the trainees cannot or will not react that you will have to react for them.

Avoid the Squirrel Mentality of Reaction

Behold the squirrel, one of Mother Nature's true treasures. The squirrel possesses amazing physical traits: speed, agility, power, and strength, to name a few. Yes, sir, the squirrel is truly one amazing creature. Unfortunately, the squirrel is also saddled with one tragic flaw: It cannot make up its mind. Just look in the street if you need a sad reminder. The real tragedy is that as you come speeding around the corner, bearing down on my little friend, he has the ability to easily avoid the inevitable. As he spots you, his keen sense of vision and hearing make many options immediately available to him. He can go left, and he does a few steps. He can go right, and he will a few steps. He can go forward, and he can go back. Unfortunately, at this critical moment of truth, the only thing he cannot do is make up his mind. He does not commit to a decision. Therefore, despite his motions, the squirrel winds up right back in the middle of the road.

You must also avoid the squirrel mentality. You can decide to react, and, if you do, then damn it, be committed and react! You can choose not to react and allow the trainees more time to react for you. Stick with that decision. The worst thing you can do, however, is to make a weak reaction, back off, react again, and appear undecided. You are now looking up at a 2,500-pound car bearing down on you at 50 miles per hour, and you are going to wind up being flattened. Learn from your successes with your trainees and from your failures as well. No two trainees are exactly alike, and neither are their reactions to your solutions. Try not to second-guess yourself; stand by the decisions that you make, and you will live to fight another day.

Summary

There's no doubt about it; if you conduct seminars and workshops on a regular basis, you will become a subject matter expert on different personalities. The key is not just to identify the various personalities that may be a part of your sessions, but to determine if the behavior is extreme enough to address. Usually the rest of the participants will give you the clues you're looking for, and if you make the call, and an intervention is necessary, don't second-guess yourself. It's not a perfect science, but your audience and your instinct will usually show you the way.

Chapter 5

The Pace Race
How to Train Groups with Diverse Needs

One of the most emotional areas that often affects a presenter's performance involves training pace. It is a potentially emotional issue because of the impact that right or wrong decisions can have on a seminar.

When conducting your training, you may feel your product knowledge is sound and your command of the logistics of the curriculum is good. Your next task is determining the knowledge level of your audience. This information will better allow you to adapt to a speed tailored to that knowledge. Now, in a perfect world, you will know the experience of your group ahead of time, and members will all be at roughly the same level. Unfortunately, this is not a perfect world, and training rarely cooperates so reasonably.

The good news is that finding out the pace you may need to communicate is usually not much of a problem. Depending on the size of the seminar, you should run an icebreaker exercise designed to give you the information you need regarding the background and experience level of your audience. Even with larger crowds or in shorter training time frames when the background of your audience is still necessary, there is still hope. All you need to do is poll your audience as to their experiences with your chosen topic. The bad news is that sometimes you may not like what you find out in your poll.

How to Pace a Course for a Large Group with Wildly Diverse Needs
Years ago I was giving a pilot workshop for the National Flood Insurance Program in Los Angeles. This 3.5-hour workshop attracted

an audience of approximately 140 participants. Add to that number another 15 to 20 government monitors from the Federal Emergency Management Agency. Looking back on this experience, I remember with a smile that I had conducted this same pilot one week earlier in Red Bank, New Jersey, and one government monitor showed up. When we moved the show to Los Angeles, the world decided to travel out of National Airport to take a peek. There I was with just a little bit of pressure on me teaching a flood workshop to a crowd of people I knew nothing about. I began to poll the audience to get a sense of what speed I would be working at and received the shock of my young training life. I asked the audience how many of them had written fewer than five flood policies in the past year and about 70 hands went up. I then asked them how many had written five to 10 policies, and no hands went up. Eleven to 15 policies? No hands went up. Twenty-six to 50 policies in the last year? No hands went up. My voice let out an adolescent-type crack as I asked about 51 to 100 policies, and no hands went up. Finally, in a stunned, somewhat apologetic manner, I asked how many of them had written over 100 policies in the year and about 70 hands went up. I am proud to tell you that I did not pass out, but I will tell you I was pretty darn close to doing so.

With a large group like that, there was really only one choice. I told the group that I was probably going to be covering the material at a slightly quicker pace than some of the individuals in the room would prefer. I also told them that I would be more than happy to address questions during the two breaks and stay after the conclusion of the workshop and answer questions for as long as it took. I then told the group that, for some in the audience, the pace might seem a little slow. I told them to bear with me, there were some changes to the program they might not be aware of, and they could use this workshop as an opportunity to brush up on the basics. The off-line questions offer stood for them as well, offering them time to have their more advanced questions answered. Once again, you see the realities of training and a presenter under fire. The result of the seminar? Of the 140 evaluations received, about 70 of them rated the seminar highly but mentioned the pace was a little fast and about 70 of them rated the seminar highly but mentioned the pace was a little slow. I, in turn, felt like a gymnast who had just made a difficult landing without even a little hop. I could have done no better.

Now, you may be saying to yourself, well, wait a minute, how could he be so pleased with such mediocre results? The answer is simple. There is really only one other alternative to the situation outlined, and that is to pick half of an audience and abandon the other half. That solution simply will not work. The result will be that half the audience will love the work you have done and the other half will revolt. With a large group, there are no perfect answers. It becomes a case of selecting the lesser of two evils.

With smaller groups, your success rate with split experience levels actually can improve. You have a greater ability to offer individual attention. The general rule of thumb is to gear your pace about two-thirds below that of your quicker students.

What *Not* to Do when Training Diverse Groups

When you are conducting technical training, the issue of pace once again grows to monstrous proportions. While teaching automation to the government, I have witnessed tremendously emotional situations regarding training pace. Once, while conducting training in a contracted facility, I was one of three trainers teaching the same curriculum to three different classes. Fortunately, I was lucky that week and was working with a group of trainees with fairly similar experience levels.

The trainer next door to me was not as lucky. As the story was relayed to me, when the trainer polled his audience, he found out that of the 16 trainees in the room, 12 had the newest software in their field offices and were actively using the program. Because only about 5 percent of the offices in the country had this software, that level of experience within the room was unusually high. To make matters worse, the other four trainees in the room not only had no experience with the software, but they were from a minority of offices that had not even heard of it. Well, the trainer must have tried using the "eenie, meenie, miney, moe" method of selection because he selected the fast group without compromise. As a result of this decision, the group of four trainees banded together and steadily became more and more abusive to the trainer, culminating with one trainee actually picking up her notebook and slamming it into the wall. The trainer was devastated, ran out of the room in tears, and never taught another class again.

In retrospect, I certainly felt for the trainer, but I felt for the abandoned trainees as well. Especially with technical training, an almost indescribable frustration can surround a lost trainee. Have you ever been lost or stuck while working with a new software program or app? The funny thing about computers is they are not real compassionate with trainees who are close to the right answer. It either is correct, or it is not. If it is not, equipment can be merciless. Nothing is more frustrating than to sit with a locked-up piece of equipment, hearing the trainer calling out commands and seeing your classmates merrily pecking away, while you drift further and further behind. As the trainer, you must empathize with that frustration and do what it takes to catch trainees up.

How to Work with the Slowpoke

Let's now shift our attention to two new trainee roles and look at some methods designed to work with individual trainees who are slipping behind the class or possibly even easing ahead. First, we will look at the potential trouble this may cause, and then we will look at some recommendations to cope with the situation.

The *slowpoke* is a trainee role that most presenters become accustomed to working with. The slowpoke is a trainee who, for whatever reasons, simply cannot keep up with the pace of the rest of the class. This trainee may also suffer from low self-esteem and should be watched closely. The reason I say to watch slowpokes carefully is that they are often embarrassed about their need for assistance and often would like nothing better than to simply go unnoticed.

Sadly, some presenters are more than happy to comply with the slowpokes' wishes to be left floundering alone. Hey, as long as they do not slow the rest of the class down, what could be the harm? Well, your week may in fact seem to run a little smoother when you turn the other way, but we both know that just cannot be done. Good presenters can reach most of the trainees, and great presenters can reach all of the trainees. Your job as a presenter is to attempt to reach all of the trainees with every breath you possess. This attempt to work with the slowpoke must not be to the detriment of the rest of the trainees, so let's look at some ideas that may help.

To begin with, remember that the slowpoke may be somewhat sensitive to the way you offer him or her assistance. There is certainly no need to grandstand and publicize that the class must stop to wait for the slowpoke to catch up. Some of the best ways to work with these trainees require proactive thinking. You might as well face the facts right now that you are going to get slowpokes in your training room, and you are going to have to work with them. One approach I have found helpful is to prepare for this type of trainee by always adding backup exercises for the material I teach. If it is a technical course, try mirroring whatever exercise you have the class doing, but without notes or with different criteria. It is far more difficult working with slowpoke trainees in a technical environment because their inabilities are usually a little more obvious, and you, the presenter, often cannot move ahead without these trainees being on board. By laying out these extra activities, you can buy some time to work your way toward the slowpoke and quietly offer your help.

With nontechnical training, you often can just make yourself available during breaks, lunch, and before and after the seminar. Sounds like fun, huh? The reward of seeing a slowpoke succeed makes it all worthwhile.

How to Work with the Whiz Kid

In their own bizarre way, *whiz kid* trainees can cause enormous difficulties in the delivery of your curriculum. The whiz kid is a trainee who not only knows a lot about your topic but is so confident that he or she constantly insists on moving ahead of the rest of the class.

The whiz kid has the potential to cause two difficulties. To begin with, these trainees have a strange habit of intimidating the rest of the class. As luck usually will have it, the whiz kid will offer some inappropriate, confusing question just as you are attempting to nurse the rest of the class in learning a difficult concept. While the class is precariously teetering between understanding and confusion, your whiz kid will give the fellow trainees a rather unfriendly push, causing an overload and resignation. The problem is, you the presenter are also balancing on a thin line of not wanting to answer the question while assuring the class that the question was not as difficult as it sounded. Sometimes you can accomplish both, as illustrated in the following exchange:

Trainee: Can you give us a better idea of the program's ability to send and/or receive information using the Wi-Fi in an office or home using the 2.4 gigahertz UHF and 5 gigahertz SHF ISM radio bands?

Class: (Nervous murmur and puzzled expressions)

Presenter: I believe Simon's question was in reference to the computer's ability to communicate. Is that right, Simon?

Trainee: Uh . . . well . . . uh . . . yes. I guess so.

Presenter: Well, as I mentioned earlier, I am in town to teach only the information outlined in your course agenda. I would be more than happy, assuming we have the time, to answer off-line any questions that we are not scheduled to discuss in class. Are there any other questions?

Addressing the whiz kid's response this way gets two things accomplished. First, it simplifies the question in an attempt to rebuild the confidence of the rest of the class. Second, it reminds the trainee in a fair and nonaggressive way that questions of that nature are inappropriate in your seminar. This example should also serve as a warning as to the importance of carefully setting up-front expectations in your training. This subject is covered fully in Chapters 6 and 7.

The second problem whiz kids can present in your training involves their own pacing. Whiz kids are notorious for attempting to move ahead of the rest of the class—and for missing out on important information. As you know, I would never advocate lying to any students at any time . . . exactly. In the event you are faced with a whiz kid who just cannot stay put, try this idea. Tell the whiz kid that although he or she may be comfortable with the material you are covering or has been through it before, some changes have been made (this could mean the presenter who is teaching it), and you suggest staying with the rest of the class so he or she can be apprised of these changes. See what a good, well-placed lie can do?

Sometimes you can even pair up your whiz kid and your slowpoke in team exercises. I am all for this technique but strongly recommend you keep a watchful eye out that both trainees are involved in the exercise. Remember, the slowpoke would like nothing more than to have someone do the work for him or her, and the whiz kid would be happy to oblige.

Summary

The pace of your training can have serious positive as well as negative effects on the success of your training. Poll your audiences as to their knowledge levels, and adapt your message to fit their speed. Additionally, keep a watchful eye out for the slowpoke and the whiz kid, and act quickly if needed.

Chapter 6

Anatomy of an 8:00 a.m. Start

Finalizing On-Site Preparations

At last, the preparation is behind you, and it is time for your training to begin. What I would like to do now is take a rather simplistic look at what your morning may look like before you deliver any real curriculum. Sometimes this is the most difficult time for inexperienced presenters who are finally facing the moment of truth and preparing to go under fire for the first time. The strange thing about training is that, regardless of a presenter's tenure, to some degree, all presenters feel that same moment of truth before training is set to begin. The degree of anxiety is often related to a presenter's experience, but it is there just the same. Most anxiety is caused by a fear of the unknown, so let's look at a typical start to training. If you do not usually start your training in the morning, plug in your own times and come along for the ride.

7:00 a.m.: Arrive Early to Ensure Everything Is Ready

It does not matter how many times I have taught a seminar, arriving a full 60 minutes ahead of time is a necessity for me. I will admit, usually all I do is pace off a little bit of nervous energy, but it is time well spent just the same.

Arriving at 7:00 a.m. also gives you some quiet time to run a few necessary checks before the trainees arrive. To begin with, you will be able to check your visual aids. I like my trainees to see the visuals I have prepared only when it is show time. You are much better off checking your focus and equipment well before the trainees enter the room. Especially when using visual aids, you probably are going to need to call somebody if you have a problem more serious than a light bulb.

Believe me, these somebodies have a tendency to take their time in arriving.

With the increase in audiovisual technology, that early start is more important than ever. For instance, if you are using various presentation technology, you are really going to need that extra time. Sometimes it can be as simple as hunting down a power strip, but getting into that room early is critical.

There are all kinds of presentation devices and aids and connectors and connections can be tricky. I go over these points in detail in Chapter 10 on using visual aids. Be aware that adjusting pixels, connecting the laptop, and working with an air mouse can be challenging at times. Starting early gives you additional time to work out the bugs.

At 7:00 a.m., you can also take one last look over the morning's events. At the very least, you can make sure you feel comfortable getting to that first break. When looking over notes, most presenters spend more of their time studying the logistics of the morning than their actual notes. By "logistics," I am referring to the coordination of exercises, activities, and technique. If truth be known, when I'm learning a new course, the logistics usually are more difficult to master than the curriculum itself. Most presenters have some experience in the subject matter they present, so the words themselves do not usually give them much difficulty. Unfortunately, the words do not offer a lot of support in coordinating the actual delivery of the curriculum.

The perceptions of most trainees regarding the competence of the presenter are often based on the *comfort* the presenter shows in delivering the material. That comfort comes from having a firm grip on what comes next. Being able to transition smoothly from one area to another can make a presenter look a lot more comfortable than he or she may actually be. The funny thing is, knowing that you have the logistics part of your presentation under control can give that impression and reduce anxiety. Time well spent indeed.

7:30 a.m.: Arrange Who Sits Where

It may seem like a trivial point, but let's turn our attention at this time to seating arrangements. Who sits where? In the real world of training, it is rare to know much about your audience until they walk into the room.

One thing we do typically know about them, however, is where they come from and their names. In reality, that is all I would choose to know. Sometimes other coworkers or managers will approach me to give me the inside scoop regarding a trainee who will be attending a future seminar. Why not get in the habit right now of giving everyone who walks into your room a fair and equal chance? Frankly, I don't care about what has happened in the past. If trainees are ready and willing to get to work, let the chips fall where they may. You do not need any help in prejudicing their performances in your seminar. Trust your instincts that you will be ready to take action if there is any hint of trouble from a trainee. Innocent until proven guilty.

Now for some controversy. To assign seats or not to assign seats, that is the question. Not to disappoint anyone, I, of course, have a rather strong recommendation. *Assign seats!* Some presenters will tell you that it is hard to predict who will get along with whom, so why not start immediately to create that relaxed atmosphere we so desperately desire and treat trainees like adults. In all honesty, that is the best argument I have ever heard for sitting anywhere, and I made it up. From what I have seen, it is usually stubbornness and laziness that keep presenters from putting name cards on seats.

Once again, the two pieces of information that usually are readily available to me are the students' names and locations of origin. Two strategies here. Use this information to separate the locations and mix the sexes. Separating the locations will help reduce the risk of cliques. Also, it will force your trainees to work harder at meeting the other trainees in the room. Finally, it will help reduce the chances of frequent side conversations that can occur when two good buddies spend a week sitting next to each other in your seminar.

Mixing the sexes will pay off a little more subtly. When you're splitting the seminar into small groups, at least early on, it is far easier to section off the seminar room where the students are sitting than go through a count-off procedure. The real benefit is that you will be assured a good cross section of men and women in each group, which will probably make their discussions a lot more interesting and productive.

As far as name tags are concerned, if you want interaction, please do yourself a favor and do not conduct a seminar without having them in front of the trainees' desks. If you do not receive their names ahead of time, have the trainees fill out tags when they arrive. It is amazing how much more comfortable trainees feel when you call them by name. After a day or two, you cannot help but have memorized them after seeing the names all day long. In an interactive seminar, some trainees will shy away from addressing others if they do not know each other's names. Using name tags on desks will promote not only this type of interaction but more of a family atmosphere within your training room among all the participants.

7:45 a.m.: It's Time for Music to Create a Relaxed Atmosphere

Fifteen minutes before the seminar begins is usually the earliest time your first trainees will arrive. Assuming you want to create a relaxed atmosphere within your training room, you may want to consider playing some music. As with everything else, it is a good idea if you take just a moment to consider the choices that lie before you.

I do not want to create problems where none exist, but you can play correct or incorrect music. Most likely, your favorite kind of music is incorrect. Sorry. The idea behind playing music in your seminar is to try to create a relaxed atmosphere. Therefore, an appropriate music selection consists of music that is basically indistinguishable. If you select rock music, it probably will distract those who do not prefer that type of music. Those who like rock music probably will listen to it too attentively. These disadvantages apply to just about any stylized piece of music. That also means no words.

The rule of thumb is to make a selection that neither attracts nor distracts anyone. What I find to be the best choices are progressive jazz or classical arrangements. I am not particularly attracted to this music, and I do not listen to classical music in my car. I have simply found that such music can blend into the background better than any other music I know. Although I have my own music collection, I offer no endorsements regarding music, but I have become a fan of both Earl Klugh and Stanley Turrentine.

An additional benefit to having a music collection is that you can play it not only in the morning as the trainees arrive but during breaks, after lunch, and while the trainees are working on small-group exercises.

Sometimes, when break-out rooms (additional rooms set aside for smaller group meetings) are not available, the music will assist in keeping your small groups from overhearing each other's work.

7:50 a.m.: Greeting Your Trainees

Most presenters are really not sure what to do with themselves while the trainees are coming into the room. There is an awkward period of time, right as the majority of the trainees are entering the room, that can give presenters a little trouble. If the training that you will be conducting is to be shorter than two hours, or if your audience consists of a large enough number that you do not feel you will be able to spend time with them individually, I would certainly recommend that you plant yourself at the door, put a big smile on your face, and greet your new family. There is not a lot of time, and this could be an excellent opportunity to begin to warm up your audience. Be prepared to make idle conversation. If the discussion turns toward training, be on your best behavior and display a model attitude.

Now let's assume that your seminar is more typical of corporate training in its structure. The seminar lasts for between a day and five days, and you are dealing with anywhere between six and 20 trainees. Here, my approach may be unique. Most presenters will position themselves at the door or in front of the room, making conversation with whatever moves. What's more, many trainees will come into the room with questions for that ready-and-willing presenter to answer before the room gets too full. I happen to feel this is a terrible misuse of time by the presenter for a couple of reasons.

First, what the presenter is unwittingly doing is actually stifling the learning environment. Trainees typically come in a little nervous. The presenter who stations himself or herself in the room cannot help but give off an authoritative presence. What usually happens is that the trainees end up either sitting quietly waiting for the seminar to begin or safely and softly speaking with the people next to them.

The second concern that I have with the accepted practice of waiting in the room for trainees involves the questions that are quietly being directed to the presenter. A question from a trainee usually represents the tip of the iceberg. If one trainee has a question, chances are a couple of others have the same question too. It would be more beneficial to answer that question in front of the entire seminar, not only so all the trainees can benefit from the answer but so you can use the question to show how safe it is to participate in your seminar.

My recommendation is a simple one: Get lost! You will have more than enough time to demonstrate your enormous talents. While the trainees are entering your seminar, mill around outside or possibly even a few doors down the hallway. I like to be in sight to make sure there are not any problems I should be taking care of. In your seminar room, a wonderful event is occurring. Trainees are meeting and greeting each other uninhibited by your presence. The more curious trainees are probably looking around the room trying to anticipate what they will learn and what you will be like as a presenter. Usually the room will be alive with laughter and conversation when you make your grand entrance. In terms of warming up a room, what could be more perfect? My goal in any training situation is to warm up the trainees as quickly as possible, so we can get past our first-date jitters and get some work done.

8:00 a.m.: Let's Get Ready to Rumble!

Assume that the visual aids are ready to go, the curriculum is in place, an overview and objectives are set to kick off the training, and the trainees are in their seats. What are the first brilliant words going to be that escape your lips? I do not want to disappoint you, but reality says, they will probably have a lot to do with housekeeping.

If you are not familiar with the term "housekeeping," it refers to just about everything *except* your curriculum. You will get to your curriculum all in good time, but for now, you had better take care of a few basic pieces of information. These questions are on your trainees' minds so it is wise to remove these distractions by providing answers:

- ♦ Approximately when are the breaks?
- ♦ What power is available for laptops or tablets?
- ♦ When is lunch?
- ♦ What arrangements, if any, are being made for dinner?
- ♦ Where are the restrooms?
- ♦ Are there any evening activities?
- ♦ What sort of recreational activities are available?

+ When does the seminar end each day?
+ When does the seminar end on the last day of training (travel arrangements)?
+ What transportation procedures have been arranged?
+ When is checkout?

Depending on the logistics of your training, questions certainly could be added or deleted. This list gives you an idea of the housekeeping issues that you need to deal with before you attempt to begin your curriculum.

8:10 a.m.: Time to Break the Ice

At this point, I hope I am not frustrating you too much, but you are still not ready to jump into your curriculum. Depending on the length of your training, the next 15 minutes to an hour could be the most important time segment within your training. It is time to begin transforming your room full of trainees into a cohesive team that is eager to learn, and covering housekeeping issues will not accomplish this, nor will jumping into your curriculum. The good news is that it is time to spend an enjoyable couple of minutes learning about your trainees and allowing them to learn about you. It is time for the famous icebreaker.

ICEBREAKERS

You now need to turn your attention to an artful task conducted by just about every presenter under the sun. These next few minutes could set the tone for the duration of the training, good or bad. The problem is that although just about all presenters use icebreakers, they do not really understand what they should be accomplishing and therefore begin to lose faith in the value of such exercises. Let's look at the knock against icebreaker exercises, illustrate some sample icebreakers, and then outline their less obvious and unappreciated benefits.

ICEBREAKER MISCONCEPTIONS

One of the biggest knocks against using icebreaker exercises in training is the time required to run them. Make no mistake, icebreaker exercises can take a while to conduct properly. In a two-week training seminar, I have seen icebreakers last as long as four hours. Often, as the length of training is shortened, so too is the allotted time for icebreakers. Relative to the time you have to deliver your training, the time issue can create a misunderstanding. Certainly, if you have three days to teach your seminar, taking half a day for icebreakers may seem a little excessive. I tend to agree. I do not think it would be excessive to take one to two hours, though.

To understand the value of an icebreaker, it may be helpful to visualize what most presenters feel when they first walk into the room. That is the presence of the wall. The wall is the imaginary border that separates the trainees from the presenter. This barrier also often separates the trainees from each other. Behind the wall, trainees are safe. There is no real interaction or free sharing of ideas or trust, but sadly there is safety. If any type of interaction is desired (and I cannot think of many times when it is not), that wall must be broken down. That is what most presenters use an icebreaker for.

As far as time is concerned, the misunderstanding is that some people believe they can save time by shortening an icebreaker or doing away with it altogether. This simply is not true. No alarm goes off if you jump into your curriculum, and initially your training will shoot way ahead of training by presenters who do use icebreakers to warm up their audiences. The problem this creates, though, is twofold. First, interaction is down, often causing boredom among the trainees and resentment toward the presenter. Second, the presenter must constantly backtrack to learn about issues that should have come out earlier, and he or she must react to situations that could have been avoided by warming up the trainees with an icebreaker.

Time saved by omitting an icebreaker is more fact than fiction. What really happens regarding time can be related to the story of the tortoise and the hare. The icebreaker starts a seminar out slowly and steadily, whereas without an icebreaker, the seminar sprints out to a faster start but ultimately loses the race.

The second and more tragic reason why icebreakers are not used within training is more a developmental misunderstanding than a presenter misunderstanding. Many misguided developers, consultants, and customers argue that icebreakers are perceived as silly and frivolous. I call this a developer misunderstanding mainly because any presenter who has actually been in the pit, under fire, would never support such a statement. Icebreakers form trainees into a supportive, cohesive team.

Bypassing the icebreaker exercise slows down the development of the team significantly. Capable presenters can pull off the icebreaker exercise professionally to guard against any perceptions that the trainees are wasting time.

ICEBREAKER CONSIDERATIONS AND EXAMPLES

Different icebreakers are effective in different situations. Various factors have to be taken into consideration, such as size of the audience. Many icebreakers involve talking to each trainee. When the seminar size begins to creep over 20, this can be a long and tedious process. Large groups don't have to omit icebreakers, however, as illustrated by the following example.

Large-Group Icebreaker First, ask participants to pair up with anyone they wish to in the room, excluding people they already know. Emphasize that participants be bold and seek out someone they would like to get to know better who is not in their immediate vicinity. Their task, once they have found a person to pair up with, is to spend a set amount of time (10 minutes is suggested) learning something significant about each other. You may set up desired questions or intentionally be vague. The idea is for the pairs to meet and begin to feel comfortable with each other. Watch to make sure nobody is left out. If there is an uneven number of students, create a threesome.

Next, ask your pairs of participants to seek out another pair of participants. They may select any pair they want except for pairs with a member that one of them knows. Once they have settled into foursomes, they are given 10 more minutes to introduce themselves and come up with a list of criteria to use in grouping up with another foursome. The only criteria that they should *not* use in making their selections is familiarity. They may select any criteria—from a group with at least one left-handed participant to a group with all participants wearing black shoes.

I usually stop the combining process with groups of eight, but you can certainly keep combining. Once the groups have reached the desired size, you can assign a small task, such as outlining group expectations for or benefits of the topic you are in town to discuss. Your groups' tasks will become clearer to you depending on your topic.

The strength in using this icebreaker exercise is its *flexibility* and *speed*. I have used it with groups as large as 500 and completed it in less than 45 minutes. I guarantee the group will be buzzing after the completion of this exercise and will be a lot more receptive to what some presenters consider to be an impossibility—large-group active participation and interaction.

The time allocated for training will affect your choice of icebreaker technique. If the scheduled training is expected to be shorter than one hour, an icebreaker may be impractical. There are quick techniques to use in these situations, but their effectiveness is questionable. If you must conduct training that is scheduled to last less than an hour, you usually will not have time for a lot of interaction among the trainees. There is still an opportunity to warm up the group with a story, analogy, or questions pertaining to your topic. Moving toward the next step of examining the group's expectations may also do the trick when there is not a lot of time. Expectations are covered in the next phase of the anatomy of an 8:00 a.m. start.

Your choice of icebreaker may depend on the familiarity of the students with each other and with you. Certainly, if the trainees all work together in the same office, they would have little need to familiarize themselves with each other. The same applies if the trainees know you. This familiarity tells you nothing about the many questions that still need to be answered and understood by the presenter. Again, the mistake many make is that they do not understand the other treasured information being collected from an icebreaker.

A final consideration that would affect your choice of icebreakers to use in training involves the level of interaction your curriculum requires. A goal for most seminars is to create an environment that allows the opportunity for anyone who wants to be involved to get involved. If there is a question, feel free to ask it. If you are lost, feel confident to seek help. This type of interaction is a far cry from the type of interaction I am accustomed to, but in some forms of training, it is a reality. For example, some in the training industry believe that there is no necessity in technical training for students to freely exchange ideas. It is hard for me even to write this, because in the technical training I have conducted, I welcomed this form of interaction with open arms. Highly interactive seminars, however, need lengthier icebreakers.

My Favorite Icebreaker (Old Faithful)　　First, pair trainees off. Hopefully, you were able to separate the trainees who came to town already knowing each other, but if this was impossible, try to pair the trainees off with people they did not previously know.

Next, ask the students to take about 15 minutes to interview the trainee they have been paired with. Use a visual aid or a handout to provide a series of questions for their interviews. They may ask additional questions but must use the questions provided as a minimum. Tell the students to listen carefully and take good notes because after the 15 minutes are up, they will use the information collected to introduce their partner to the seminar. Here are some suggested questions:

What is your name?

How long have you been with your current employer? What is your position title?

What other training courses similar to this one have you taken?

What do you hope to get out of this training program?

What are your hobbies and outside interests?

Each of these questions has an essential purpose. Let's look at them one by one, starting with the trainee's name. Most name cards are printed up by taking the trainee's name off some sort of official registration. Looking around your room early on a Monday morning, you may see many Arthurs, Reginalds, Williams, Steffanies, Margarets, Cassandras, Rons, and Rauls. By the time this icebreaker is over, you could just as easily be looking at several Arts, Reggies, Buzzes, Steffs, Maggies, and Caseys. One of the first ways to warm up new trainees is to find out what names they prefer to be called, adjust their name cards, and learn them.

The next two recommended questions refer to length of time with their employer and job title. These questions often can provide early clues to opinion leaders and amiable trainees.

The question about previous experience is one I have really grown to appreciate. If a trainee has experience or taken other courses in corresponding subject matter, there is a good chance you may have an enlightener trainee in your midst. Remember, this is not necessarily a troublesome trainee, and may actually be a diamond in the rough when it comes to warming up the rest of the seminar. If you need a war story or someone you can count on to help break the ice and join in on the conversation, your enlightener is ready and waiting.

Asking trainees what they hope to get out of the training accomplishes two things. First, it provides you with clues for tailoring your message to satisfy particular needs, depending on the subject matter you are working with. The more diverse the subject matter, the more necessary this question becomes. When I teach a Presentation Skills program, this question is critical because of all the different types of training programs that may be represented in my seminars. It helps me a great deal to know where the technical presenters are as opposed to the presenters of more subjective material.

The second benefit of asking a trainee what he or she hopes to get out of a course relates to another potential personality indicator. For example, discouraged trainees tend to use this question to let you know of their unfair situations. The message usually is be tempered by the trainee who is doing the introduction to the rest of the seminar, which allows you to begin the work necessary to turn the discouraged trainee around.

The final question dealing with hobbies also serves two purposes. The first and most obvious reason is that it gives the trainees an opportunity to talk about a topic that is not job related. This in turn provides the greatest opportunity for the trainees to relax and calm down. The faster this happens, the more effective the seminar will become. Some presenters oppose asking this question, thinking it is nothing more than a throwaway question and a waste of time. I do not agree, especially when you consider that these presenters rarely utilize the other less-obvious benefits of the question.

The real benefit of asking about hobbies relates back to the theories discussed in Chapter 2 on working with adults. One of the key principles was to relate the subject matter to adult experiences. As mentioned earlier, adults have an enormous number of experiences to draw on. The presenter can relate these experiences to key subject matter and often can allow adults to make key connections to important material. Learning an individual's hobbies and outside interests often provides you with all the experiences you will need to maximize the use of this technique.

In addition to allowing you to better work with adults, hobbies and outside interests also allow you to work better with quiet trainees, who often need a little extra support to build up their confidence. Relating information to something they know about and feel comfortable talking about may be just the ticket to getting them a few successes they so badly need. What a coincidence, you made an analogy to their hobbies . . . or was it?

The trainee personalities already outlined are not the only ones you can detect with this icebreaker. You will be able to identify the quiet trainee and the joker trainee merely by listening to their introductions. Neither of these personalities does a very good job of hiding who he or she is.

THE PRESENTER'S ROLE IN THE ICEBREAKER PROCESS

Probably one of the biggest mistakes most presenters make during their training stems from the missed opportunities in the opening icebreaker in their seminars. Most presenters are just not active enough. This is your first opportunity not only to warm up the group but to let them learn about you and your style as a presenter.

To begin with, take notes. By taking notes, you can begin to put together some of the valuable information that you should be retrieving now that you are aware no throwaway questions are being asked. It also is one of the best ways to demonstrate to trainees that what they say is important and that you value the information you are learning about them. Truth be known, on many more occasions than I choose to count, I have taken down absolutely useless information for no other reason than that the trainee's eye contact indicated he or she felt the information was important.

I also feel that it is imperative to strike up some sort of conversation with each trainee over time. This technique shows a personal touch and does wonders at warming up a new group of trainees. Some presenters find this difficult because they have to make conversation in front of the seminar with what may be 10 to 20 trainees, one at a time. Guess where a lot of the information you may need will be coming from? The notes you are taking. It is truly amazing what a couple of simple questions to the trainees can do to help make people in a seminar feel more relaxed.

The final task of the icebreaker process is an introduction by the presenter. If you have given the trainees a set list of questions, it is only fair that you use that list to introduce yourself. However, you are better off not pairing off with a trainee; do your introduction yourself. Separating yourself ensures you do not contribute to the creation of a loner trainee and allows you to walk around during the icebreaker and visit with the trainees.

8:30 a.m.: Expectation Time

One of the many reasons I view training as a position under fire has to do with trainees' expectations. Managers can send trainees to attend training for any number of reasons. Once these trainees set foot into the seminar room, these expectations become the presenter's responsibility.

In real-world terms, the presenter inherits whatever misconceptions or problems the trainee may bring to town.

One of the biggest problems that can confront presenters, regardless of their experiences, is a trainee attending a seminar with unrealistic expectations. This can be caused by a number of different factors. Misconceptions by the field is just one example. Most managers have never attended the basic training they send their employees to. They do not take the seminar; they do not audit the seminar. Sadly, it is not uncommon to receive calls from managers who do not understand some of the terms used on the evaluations presenters mail to them. Let's forget, for a moment, the implications that they are in absolutely no position to offer any support or follow-up to the training. They do not even understand what the words mean. Those who have distanced themselves from the training often can inadvertently give trainees the wrong impression of what to expect from the training you are about to conduct.

In addition to a lack of support from the trainee's manager, claims by course promoters can distort expectations. Often those who teach seminars never interact with those who promote seminars. Poetic license takes on a whole new meaning when you read how a seminar is written up to attract attendees. I am not in favor of misrepresenting a course, which often happens in the world of training. Those who attend the seminar are giving their time and money and deserve to get what they have been promised. If you ever want to get a firsthand glimpse at a presenter truly under fire, watch what happens when a trainee shows up expecting information that has been promised but will not be delivered.

For example, once I taught a seminar entitled "Educating the Customer," which combined educational techniques with sales techniques. The main thrust of the course was to teach people that combining good solid training techniques helped ensure a customer who not only understood what he or she was buying but was less likely to be confused by another salesperson into giving up what he or she had purchased. I was asked to design a write-up explaining the intent of the course. The company I was doing this for was to print my write-up, advertise the course, provide the facility, and basically take about 80 percent of the tuition. (Young training consultants sometimes get desperate for contacts!)

It was only after the trainees began to arrive in expensive suits with Mont Blanc pens that I began to suspect there might be a problem. On a hunch, I asked if anyone had a brochure on the seminar, and as luck would have it, one person did. My jaw dropped as I read about "Selling in the '80's, from Cold Call to Close." The write-up was just as foreign as the title. The only piece of information they did not get wrong was my name and the seminar address. Needless to say, my audience was not thrilled with the topic they were about to hear that night. It is the presenter who takes the heat, and it is the presenter who must learn to survive in this situation.

One sure way to survive faulty expectations by trainees is to condition yourself as a salesperson does. In short, check for objections before unveiling your product. Get in the habit of always being suspicious of trainees' expectations, and prepare for some misunderstandings. The mistake so many good presenters make is telling trainees what their course is about and then trying to convince those with different expectations why they still can benefit. Not bad logic, just bad results.

When a salesperson wheels in his or her product or brochure and tells you why you need it, you usually resist. One of the first questions people often ask themselves is: Who is this person, and why does he or she assume I need this product? This situation can give customers the impression that yet another salesperson is trying to sell something they do not need. One of the best techniques in selling is still simply listening and asking questions. The customer will tell you all you need to know and like you better if you just listen and ask questions. Customers perceive salespeople as more trustworthy and empathetic when they follow those two basic rules. Trainees perceive their presenters as more credible and interesting when the presenter adheres to these rules as well.

How to Set Expectations

The most successful approach that I can recommend is to, from this day forth, hide all course maps, put away schedules, and listen to your trainees. Basically, keep your product out of sight until you find out what your trainees are looking for. This approach can benefit a presenter in three ways. To begin with, the exercise itself can act as an icebreaker. If the program you are teaching is very short and there is not a lot of time for an icebreaker, just use the act of gathering expectations as a warm-up. Even if there is sufficient time, finish your icebreaker portion of the program by collecting expectations.

The second benefit of collecting expectations is the up-front information from your trainees regarding what they are looking for from your seminar. As mentioned earlier, you are in a much better position to convince trainees of the benefits of your material before you tell them what you are going to cover in the seminar. If the trainees' expectations match your material, terrific, no problem. If the trainees' expectations are unrealistic or do not match your curriculum, you can probe further and discuss it without looking defensive. In short, you are still holding your cards.

Another benefit to collecting trainees' expectations before you go over your own expectations involves the value of the responses. When some trainees, particularly new hires, hear what you intend to teach, they often will parrot back what you have already gone over. It is impossible to get a feel for what they were really expecting. With an honest list of expectations, a presenter gets a good indication of what information may need to be covered more carefully or may need to be added. Without changing the curriculum, the presenter actually can tailor the message somewhat to fit the trainees.

Collecting expectations before addressing them is a necessity. I would even go so far as to recommend that if you post nothing else during the duration of your training, post the expectations. This sends a message to the trainees that you are serious about your desires to see their expectations fulfilled. Tacking these expectations to the wall allows you to keep a watchful eye out for what needs to be covered. If you choose to place the trainee's name by his or her respective expectation, you can even include the individual who requested it in your discussion. This increases participation and again sells the message that the trainees' expectations are important to you.

However, as important as the expectations are to you and your trainees, I have one more suggestion concerning what you will do with these expectations. The conventional approach to training recommends that you address them at the end of your training session, whether it's a day later or a week later.

Well, I have a bit of a different viewpoint on this subject. I suggest you *do not* go over these expectations with the students. Don't get me wrong. I study these lists throughout the training. I just find it artificial to go back and check with the trainees item by item: "Well, Johnny, your expectations from Monday said that you wanted to learn more about objection handling tactics. Did you?"

At 4:50 p.m. on a Friday, after a hard week's work, I doubt that Johnny is going to make waves and tell you that he did not learn what he wanted to about objection handling. Besides, if Johnny does open his mouth, those who are dying to get out and catch a flight are going to kill him.

With that said, you need to let the group know that their expectations are important to you. Tell them how you will work diligently to address these points but that when you don't check this list at the end of the session, it won't be due to an oversight.

Finally, there's nothing wrong with referring to the list from time to time during the program as various topics connect to it. It is a more natural approach to working with this material and will allow you to get honest answers from your trainees. There's also nothing wrong with an occasional expectation that doesn't match up with what you have planned in your agenda. Getting this disconnect identified early gives you multiple options to clarify or take the point off-line and cleared up.

Once you have collected these expectations, you can go over the course map and present an overview of what you have planned for the training. At this point in training, you walk a tightrope between not telling too much and telling enough to generate interest within the seminar.

Summary

There's a lot that goes on before that 8:00 a.m. start, and the better prepared you are before your program starts, the more relaxed you'll be once your program starts. You'll need to be sense of calm because the most important few minutes of your entire delivery is just about ready to start. Take a deep breath and stay enthusiastic because the best is yet to come. It is now time to learn the secret of successful training.

Part II

Delivery: The Art of Making Great Presentations

Chapter 7

The Secret of Success
Selling Your Presentation

Although I have been running seminars and workshops on my own for over 25 years, this isn't the first time I have operated a private consulting company. When I was in my mid-20s, I put out a shingle and gave consulting a try. I had no difficulty attracting clients, worked when I wanted to, and somewhat lived the American dream. I was a sole proprietor. What in the world would possess any successful entrepreneur to ditch it all and go to work for a massive corporation? Most people work the other way around. First, you work for the massive corporation, then you work for yourself. But I was looking for something more to teach people when it came to actual training technique. I wanted something tangible, something process driven that could be taught to anyone incorporating any topic.

There were only about three different companies I would have left my business for, and Xerox was one of them. One reason for my fascination and respect for Xerox was its *commitment to training*. A corporation that builds a training facility that sleeps 980 students on 2,300 acres obviously takes training seriously. (Although I'm sure the company still takes its training seriously, sadly, the facility was sold, and the land it sits on has been developed.) My second and equally important criterion for selecting Xerox was its reputation for being *process driven*. By "process driven," I am referring to working with concepts that teach predictable and repeatable steps.

As a consultant, I could demonstrate effective training techniques to you at the drop of a hat. I could analyze your own speaking style and curriculum and make delivery recommendations. I could even make creative suggestions regarding some approaches to getting people interested in your presentation. The problem with me and most consultants is we offer no real process. Before learning the process I will be teaching you in this chapter, I would tell trainees about appealing to adult learners and to address the concerns outlined. The problem was I never really told them *how*. This is where a process is critical. Forget statements such as "The first thing you want to accomplish is clearing the air with your audience." I want to know how! When you learn from a process, you basically learn, "Do this, this, this, and then this, and you will have cleared the air with your audience."

It has been said that "You only have one chance to make a first impression." In this chapter, I want to offer the most critical piece of information I can give to any presenter. I want to *systematically*, within a process that is *repeatable* and *predictable*, show you the most effective approach for addressing basic adult learning needs, selling your information better, and establishing credibility as a presenter. I do not want this to be subjective in any way. What I offer you is a process that you can see, measure, and use no matter what the circumstance, no matter what the topic.

One of the largest presentations I ever conducted was at a hostage negotiation seminar put on by the Baltimore County Police. Police officers came from all over the country to hear about how Xerox negotiates with its customers. The thinking was that the hostage negotiators could pick up some tips from the top sales training organization in the world. What does a copier salesperson from Silver Spring, Maryland, know about hostage negotiation? The truth is, in my selling I had a few people who were unhappy with my products, but I never had one customer take any of my machines hostage. Okay, I might have been a little out of my league, but I know about selling, and I believe negotiation is negotiation. The trick was, I had to figure out a way of getting that point over to my police friends quickly or my message, no matter how good, would fall on deaf ears. In a sense, this situation is a microcosm of what all presenters face at the beginning of their presentations.

I plugged in the process I am about to show you, and within 10 minutes I had the audience excited about my material; they gave the presentation the highest rating in the 12-year history of this annual seminar. With the former guest speakers including Ted Koppel and Ronald Reagan, and an audience that I had been told was skeptical as to my very presence, I was more than satisfied. I was elated, and I had my process to thank.

The nature of seminar delivery and the realities of going under fire demand a process. Learning the process I am about to teach you will benefit you personally by making you feel a lot more confident about whatever training assignments you have. Corporate training burns many people out quickly. If I had no way of knowing what I was doing that was contributing to my success or failure, I would not last long either. This process will answer those questions, making you feel much better about the seminars you conduct.

A second benefit you can derive from following a process within your seminars is the change you will notice in how you perform your job. Following the process will assist your trainees in learning more effectively, thus making for smoother seminars and better trainee evaluations. This is not merely an indicator of satisfied customers; it is also an indicator of a good presenter doing great work in one of the most public positions within the company.

Your company also benefits from the process you are about to learn. No profession I know touches as many internal and external customers as training. When a presenter performs effectively, it is the company that is looked on favorably and that ultimately benefits.

In this chapter, I want to teach you how to build your presentation. I want to provide you with a process that will, step by step, lay out what it takes to deliver a phenomenal presentation. I want you to feel that it is a process that you can use regardless of the topic or nature of your presentation, and I want you to use it within the seminars you conduct.

To accomplish this, I walk you through the critical overview process. We then look at some approaches for constructing the body of your presentation and a process for concluding your presentation. The plan is to start and finish strongly.

We do this by breaking down the steps of the process. This will give you a solid foundation on which to build your own presentations. I also provide you with a sample of the process outlining the various steps. This sample is designed to act as a model you can go back to and use for quick brush-ups when necessary. Finally, I provide you with two worksheets that will help you in constructing your own presentations. I suggest you make copies of these worksheets for future presentations.

When this chapter is complete, I hope that those of you who use the process outlined within this chapter in its entirety will fill out the reply card in the back of this book and mail it to me, or email me with your feedback: training@jolles.com. This will let me know how the process is working for you. It is my firm belief that at least 95 percent of you will respond favorably, enjoying the immediate success this process can offer.

The information for most of this chapter comes from a source I have come to know well. That source is Xerox. When I first went to the Xerox training center, I was asked to rewrite the Train-the-Trainer program being delivered to Xerox personnel. There were 10 modules, and I conducted major rewrites of nine. The only module that remains untouched to this day is the module that lays out the process you will now be learning. It was written in 1972, is a timeless piece that needs no adjustment, and to this day remains one of the most significant lessons I have ever learned in training.

Perhaps one of the most telling events that I can recall involving this subject occurred with a close friend of mine. They say that opposites attract in relationships, and, in my opinion, this certainly holds true for friendships as well. I have a friend named Claude who illustrates this point well. At first glance, we do not appear to have much in common. To begin with, Claude is about 10 years older than I am. He is somewhat quiet, while I am, uh, well to put it nicely, not. Even our occupations are dramatically different. Claude is a computer science major from the late 1960s and has worked with computers for more than 20 years. I, in contrast, am more of a people person. For years, Claude and I have conducted a mutual teasing of each other's careers.

The one thing Claude and I do have in common is a quiet, common belief in friendship and loyalty. Claude, quite simply, is a friend for life. Well, one day this friend for life showed up at my doorstep somewhat pale. It turns out that my friend Claude had been interviewing with another company and had successfully completed three phases of interviewing. Only one more phase to go, but this is where his lack of color came in. You see, Claude informed me that night that he would be giving a 20-minute presentation in the morning that would determine whether or not he got the job. Talk about the power of a presentation!

There was no career teasing in his eyes that night, only fear. I asked him what he had prepared, and like a good computer whiz (sorry, Claude), he produced a 20-page document. Remember, this was supposed to be for a 20-minute presentation. I will not belabor the point. To make a long story short, we threw out the mess he walked in with, took 30 minutes to reconstruct the presentation using the process you are about to learn, and the next day Claude delivered the presentation of his life. He not only got the job, but he has become a fan of the process, and he is not what I call a man blessed with natural training abilities.

So get comfortable, get ready, and let me show you some ideas on how to bring your presentations to life. I hope that not only do I hear from you after using the method in your seminars, but that you find the same success I have found in working with a process that makes presentations a breeze.

Introducing the UPPOPPR Process

Let me ask you a few questions. Are you curious about what I have to show you? Have I gotten your attention? Are you interested in what you are about to learn? I believe you are. I believe you answered yes to all three questions because I have already performed the UPPOPPR (pronounced YOU-POP-ER) process on you in the introduction of this chapter. Maybe some of you were already excited and ready to learn. Maybe, just maybe, some of you were not. This is what a presenter faces every time he or she approaches a new group of trainees or even a new topic. Trainees have many questions that they may or may not ask. You read in Chapter 2 about working with adult learners and the fundamental needs these adults have. You have also heard me say over and over again that a presenter is guilty until proven innocent. Well, we are now going to take care of those adult learning needs, clear the air of any misunderstandings, and start more powerfully than you could ever imagine. We are going to do all this with the help of the acronym UPPOPPR, and all within the first 10 minutes of each major module within your presentation. Here is what UPPOPPR stands for:

Utility
Product/Goal
Process
Objective
Process Justification
Proof of Ability
Review

UPPOPPR

Utility: Conveying the Benefit of the Training Program

The "U" stands for the *utility* of the subject you are prepared to teach your trainees. The utility attempts to provide benefits to your trainees that show them *why* it is *necessary* to learn the subject you are about to teach. There is no accident as to the order of this acronym. If a trainee sees no *benefits* to learning what you are about to teach, you have no audience. So many trainers and speakers go into their topics without ever really knowing whether their audiences see any importance in what they are about to learn. You read in Chapter 4 about all the different types of personalities that may appear in your training room and recommendations for handling them. One of the best ways to avoid personality problems is to not allow the situation to occur in the first place. Establishing some utility for what you are about to teach goes a long way toward making trainees *want* to learn.

In Chapter 2, you read that adults must have a need to learn. Establishing utilities does just that. Once again, you have to approach every training situation understanding the basic fact that your audience is selfish. We are all selfish to a degree. Trainees unconsciously apply a universal thought to every training topic the presenter brings up: "What's in it for me?" Every trainee who will ever walk into your training room will listen to you with that thought on his or her mind. Some will verbalize it; some will stew about it; others will remain silent. All will think about it.

The single biggest problem that presenters face is the participant who does not want to be in your program. If you felt there was nothing you could get out of a class, would you want to be there? Again, it is critical for a presenter to appeal to people's sense of greed by letting the audience know what is in it for them; but let's talk about how. One approach is to get expectations of the participants up front; this information tells you exactly what the trainees want to learn. If you commit to addressing these needs and take those lists seriously, you at least have a head start. Unfortunately, you cannot list expectations for larger audiences, but an overhead question that samples the audience's interest or a pre-polling might help.

Now let's get back to the UPPOPPR and the approach within the process itself. As you begin your presentation, you must address the utility of what you have to say. You can do this one of two ways. The first, and more traditional, way is to show consequences. As children, most of us were brought up by learning to do certain things based on consequences. "Finish your peas or no dessert" was one of the earliest lessons I can recall. Funny thing is, I never learned to like peas. As we grew, so did the consequences. Bad grades, bad jobs, bad lives. Unfortunately, the only real lesson learned from most subjects motivated by consequences is rebellion. This is not to say that utilities supported by consequences are all bad; it is simply a reminder that you should carefully examine your topic and choose to motivate adults by consequences only when there are no other options.

Examining another option brings me to the second approach to establishing utility. That approach is by showing value. If at all possible, I like to show value, or how the material will help the trainee. This tends to be a more positive, motivating technique and appeals to most adults more favorably. Whether you establish utility through consequences or value, you need to address three questions:

1. "How will it affect me personally?"
2. "How will it affect me on the job?"
3. "How will it affect the organization I work for?"

In examining each of these questions, you can now look at how I addressed these issues in the beginning of this chapter. (As I mentioned, I have modeled the entire process in overviewing this topic.) Let's start with the utility addressing the value of this topic to you personally.

Here's an example of what you might say to your audience:

The nature of seminar delivery and the realities of going under fire demand a process. Learning the process I am about to teach you will benefit you personally by making you feel a lot more confident about whatever training assignments you have. Corporate training burns many people out quickly. If I had no way of knowing what I was doing that was contributing to my success or failure, I would not last long either. This process will answer those questions, making you feel much better about the training you conduct.

Simply stated, by learning this information, each member of the audience will benefit personally. That is what is meant by *a personal utility*.

The second question that needs to be addressed is how the topic will affect the trainee on the job. Here's an example of what you might say:

> *A second benefit you can derive from following a process within your seminars is the change you will notice in how you perform your job. Following the process will assist your trainees in learning more effectively, thus making for smoother seminars and better trainee evaluations. This is not merely an indicator of satisfied customers; it is also an indicator of a good presenter doing great work in one of the most public positions within the company.*

Most trainees will become more interested in your topic when they see how it may benefit them on the job.

Finally, you need to answer the question of how your topic will benefit the trainee's company or organization. It is the last small piece that will ensure an effective utility. Here's an example of how to convince them:

> *Your company also benefits from the process you are about to learn. No profession I know touches as many internal and external customers as training. When a presenter performs effectively, it is the company that is looked on favorably and that ultimately benefits.*

If the members of your audience are demotivated and disgruntled with the company they work for, I would not necessarily recommend this third part of the utility. I will say that establishing organizational utilities gives a certain polish to a very critical part of your presentation.

When establishing a utility, there are a couple of different styles that can be used. Often presenters deliver their utilities in a lecture-type format. Sometimes these utilities are initiated by questions to the trainees. The third approach, and my personal favorite, is to begin to establish utilities by telling a story that involves your topic. If you noticed in the beginning of this chapter, that is exactly how I started the utility for this topic. I gave you not just one story; I gave you two. Here they are again:

> *Although I have been running seminars and workshops on my own for over 25 years, this isn't the first time I have operated a private consulting company. When I was in my mid-20s, I put out a shingle and gave consulting a try. I had no difficulty attracting clients, worked when I wanted to, and somewhat lived the American dream. I was a sole proprietor. What in the world would possess any successful entrepreneur to ditch it all and go to work for a massive corporation . . .*

> *One of the largest presentations I ever conducted was at a hostage negotiation seminar put on by the Baltimore County Police. Police officers came from all over the country to hear about how Xerox negotiates with its customers. The thinking was that the hostage negotiators could pick up some tips from the top sales training organization in the world . . .*

The bottom line to establishing a utility is summed up with this humble Jolles motto: "Don't tell 'em, sell 'em!"

By this, I mean a lot can be learned from selling an idea to an audience the same way a salesperson sells an idea to a customer. Effective salespeople don't approach clients with a product and tell them why they need it. Just the opposite is true. Top salespeople get customers to want their product and then show them the product. Creating utilities for a presenter does just that. The idea behind establishing utility for your topic is that it puts you in a position to create interest and get your trainees to want your topic before you show them your product. Utilities are not only the most *difficult* aspect of the UPPOPPR; they are the most *critical* as well. If you now have an audience that cannot wait to hear what it is you have to talk to them about, you are in a most enviable position.

U**P**POPPR

PRODUCT: SETTING A GOAL FOR THE TRAINING PROGRAM

The first "P" of the UPPOPPR acronym stands for *product* (or *goal*). As I mentioned in Chapter 2, adults want to know what the big picture is. Understanding this may clear up any questions or doubts the trainees may have. It is a lot easier for adults to learn when they can see what the goal of the seminar is. Typically, the product is the shortest part of the UPPOPPR and can often be stated in one or two sentences. In some situations, after being tantalized with some crafty utilities, this is the first time the trainees are actually told what it is they are about to learn. Here's an example:

> *In this chapter, I want to teach you how to build your presentation. I want to provide you with a process that will, step by step, lay out what it takes to deliver a phenomenal presentation. I want you to feel that it is a process that you can use regardless of the topic or nature of your presentation, and I want you to use it within the seminars you conduct.*

Allowing your trainees to see the big picture about what you are preparing to teach them helps adults learn and allows them to see the goals of your program. Keep it short and to the point. More detail regarding the subject you are introducing is right around the corner.

UP**P**OPPR

PROCESS: DESCRIBING THE APPROACH TO TRAINING

The second "P" of the UPPOPPR acronym stands for *process*. With the product that preceded it, the intention was to provide the trainees with the big picture or goal of your seminar. Now, quite naturally, it is time to give the trainees a better idea of how you expect to *achieve* this goal.

The process portion of the UPPOPPR can be broken into two parts. What you need to cover in this part of your overview is not only *more detail* on what you are going to be talking about but *how* you intend to talk about it as well. When describing "what" you are about to talk about, there is no need to get into too much detail. A light touch on the major points of your presentation will do. For example:

> *To accomplish this, I will walk you through the critical overview process. We then look at some approaches for constructing the body of your presentation and a process for concluding your presentation. The plan is to start and finish strongly.*

Most training modules comprise three to five major points. In this section of the UPPOPPR, you must discipline yourself from giving up too much information. The intent is to overview the material, not to teach it.

The second part of the process portion of the UPPOPPR begins to deal with the method, or how you are going to teach the material. Most presenters unconsciously address the content, or "what" they are about to speak about, but rarely do they address "how." This is a mistake. Once again, and not to sound like a broken record, you are guilty until proven innocent. This means, if trainees came to town a year ago and were bored to tears during a seminar, they will assume your seminar will be boring as well. As a matter of fact, the realities of being a presenter are that whatever negative experience trainees have suffered in the past are expected in the future. Nobody said training was fair. It is my hope that this book will inspire you to think outside of the box and be more creative. Why keep this a secret? Tell the trainees how they will be learning this information. By addressing this key point of the process, you also begin to address a host of adult learning characteristics.

Here is an example of a presenter communicating *how* the material will be taught:

> *We do this by breaking down the steps of the process. This will give you a solid foundation on which to build your own presentations. I also provide you with a sample of the process outlining the various steps. This sample is designed to act as a model you can go back to and use for quick brush-ups when necessary. Finally, I provide you with two worksheets that will help you in constructing your own presentations. I suggest you make copies of these worksheets for future presentations.*

Remember, you must address the major adult learning characteristics:

♦ Adults learn more effectively when they are motivated.
♦ Adults learn more effectively when they are kept interested.
♦ Adults learn more effectively when they are involved in activity.

Here, those adult learning characteristics begin to take form. Have you ever sat in a seminar, frantically taking notes, only to find out that there was a handout at the end of the seminar with all the notes in it? This is your opportunity as a presenter not only to reduce any fears the trainees may have but to influence the way *you* want them to learn.

Do you want questions throughout? *Tell* the trainees how you want them to participate. Are you walking into a hostile situation? Tell the trainees to hold all questions until the end. The key is to make the rules here when you tell them *how* the module will be taught.

For challenging modules that are difficult to learn, this is your opportunity to keep the trainees from getting frustrated too early. The process in this module is a classic example. I know the UPPOPPR is challenging. One of the goals within the UPPOPPR process I laid out for you was to give you confidence in your ability to master the technique by letting you know up front that I would be providing you with a sample and a worksheet. If you are not careful to lay out *how* you are going to teach something, you may lose a significant number of trainees who become too frustrated and give up.

UPP**O**PPR

OBJECTIVE: WRITE SPECIFIC TRAINING GOALS

The fourth step in the UPPOPPR approach to training is to focus on training *objectives*. Numerous books and courses have been devoted solely to the art of writing objectives. This is a topic that has been made much more difficult than it needs to be. The problem and confusion stem from the fact that developers attempt to include far too much in their objectives. This may be a result of trying to package too much of their overview in the objective. One thing is for certain: Most trainees, and presenters for that matter, are completely confused by the term "objective." Let me make a few suggestions to keep you from acquiring any of the bad habits associated with objective writing.

One bad habit to avoid is becoming intimidated by the subject of objectives, causing you to not want to get involved with writing them. I would love to be able to tell you to look the other way when it comes to objective writing, but that just is not possible. Objectives are just too valuable to presenters; and although many presenters are not asked to create them, you often will have no choice. You see, if you are in the pit and trainees are unclear as to what is expected of them once the training is complete, it is you who will be receiving the sniper fire, not the program developer. An important adult learning characteristic previously discussed is that adults want to know what is required of them before the seminar begins.

Instead of avoiding objectives, look at the tremendous value a well-written objective can offer you. To begin with, an objective allows both presenter and participants to evaluate how well they are doing. If an objective has been established and some trainees could not meet the objective, they begin to see where they are in relation to where they should be. You also have the ability to see how well you are doing as a presenter. If 50 percent of the seminar participants could not meet the established objective, you are the one who needs to do some reevaluation. It is not time to panic or become upset. It is simply time to take that 15-minute review you had planned in the morning and make it 30 minutes instead.

The first terrific benefit of training with objectives is that you will be providing a gauge for you and the trainees as to how well you are doing. An exciting indicator as to the success of your objectives often can be found in simply watching the participant guides. When the trainees are meeting your objectives, they usually leave their participant guides on their desks at the end of the day. When they are unable to meet the established objective, the participant guides mysteriously vanish for the night.

Another strength behind writing objectives lies in your ability to influence what you want the trainees to learn. Whenever we present information, there is always a mixture of "nice to know" and "need to know." A good objective deals with the "need-to-know" areas. If I tell you that you will be using a particular portion of the material at the end of the module, you probably will listen harder when that point is covered. Carefully crafted objectives will even assist you in your selection of visual aids. Adults learn through their sense of sight, but adults will not learn as effectively if everything is visual. Therefore, you can plan your key visual aids around your objectives. This, in turn, will help your trainees to retain and achieve more. So, what is the secret to writing a good objective? Each objective should include four simple steps:

1. Action
2. Requirement
3. Degree
4. Benchmark

1. **Include action in the objective.** This step, "action," is probably the most misunderstood step. Typical objectives read: "At the end of this module, you will have a greater appreciation for . . ." or "When this module is complete, you will be able to . . ." I want to be somewhat delicate here, so let me just say I think these objectives are a bunch of bunk! How do trainees know if they are able to do something unless they do it? Most objectives look more like recipes than real-live objectives.

   Therefore, the first step that I recommend is an actual "action" or activity: "At the end of this module, you *will* demonstrate [role-play, participate, show, etc.] . . ." The classic example of action that most of us were raised on is testing. In fact, it is an accurate objective action. The only problem is that it lacks creativity. It may sound corny, but I have a dream that trainees will look forward to an objective rather than fear it. One way to accomplish this is to get more action in the objective. Try to have your trainees actually do what it is you are teaching. If you are training people how to answer a phone, do not give them a written test on the skills taught. Have them actually do it.

2. **State the requirements of the training program.** Stating the requirements of your objective up front is another way to reduce the fear behind objectives. What are the rules? For some reason, these are kept as closely guarded secrets in many schools. Isn't the intent behind education to teach rather than terrify? You study your notes and are tested from your book. You study your book and are tested from your notes. Sorry, folks, I just do not accept this form of education. When I'm conducting a training session, one of my goals is to have my trainees be able to accomplish more, using what they have learned, than they have achieved from any other seminar. Pop quizzes and other such mysteries on a corporate level do not help people learn; they intimidate.

   I would rather *motivate* you to learn than frighten you to learn. As a student, when I heard we were going to be tested, I wanted to know the "requirements." I was the obnoxious voice in the back asking if it was an open book or a take-home test. I had no idea that I was asking such a reasonable question!

It certainly would have changed my approach to learning. If students know that they will be tested from their notes, it makes sense that they will take good notes. What is so wrong about teaching the objective? Not word for word, but it should be a focus. Explain the "requirements," for example:

♦ Tell trainees they will be asked to volunteer.
♦ Tell them there is a time requirement.
♦ Tell them they will be selected at random.
♦ Tell them they will all participate, or some will participate.

Whatever your requirements are, clear up any misunderstandings and let trainees know what those requirements will be.

3. **Explain the degree of accomplishment expected.** How well should the trainee be expected to accomplish the action you have created? Once again, you were conditioned during testing. You were told that you would need to get a certain number of questions right to pass. You do not have to ask trainees to perform perfectly the activity you are planning. Perhaps you will give them three opportunities or maybe assist them once. The intent here is to provide the trainees a yardstick as to how well they are doing versus how well they should be doing.

4. **Benchmark the performance of trainees.** You must give the trainees a standard for the activity they are performing. If you were teaching players how to hit a baseball, you could tell them that they will each hit three baseballs at the conclusion of your presentation. (That is your action and requirement.) They are to hit at least one baseball down the right field line. (There is your degree.) The problem is, if you do not provide the trainees with a benchmark, they can try to accomplish this any way they want to. Because you are teaching a seminar on hitting, I assume you want them to use the techniques provided in your lecture. Therefore, that fact becomes your benchmark. It could be an author, a visual aid, or even yourself, but there must be a benchmark for the trainees to measure their results against.

EXAMPLE
So, do these four steps look difficult? As with anything else, they take a little practice. Now let's look at the objective established for this module

and see if you can distinguish among the four parts that have been outlined:

> *When this chapter is complete, I hope that those of you who use the process outlined within this chapter in its entirety will fill out the reply card in the back of this book and mail it to me, or email me with your feedback: training@jolles.com. This will let me know how the process is working for you. It is my firm belief that at least 95 percent of you will respond favorably, enjoying the immediate success this process can offer.*

- ♦ Action: . . . fill out the reply card . . . and mail it to me, or email me . . . This will let me know how the process is working for you.
- ♦ Requirement: When this chapter is complete . . . those of you who use the process . . .
- ♦ Degree: . . . 95 percent of you will respond favorably . . .
- ♦ Benchmark: . . . outlined within this chapter in its entirety . . .

A successful delivery often boils down to one key question: Did you meet your objective? The irony is that your success does not, in fact, depend on whether you actually meet your objective. Success lies in whether you can answer the question. With the four steps you have just seen, trainees will know, without question, what is expected of them. What's more, with a little creativity on your part, they will be eagerly awaiting their opportunity to show you just how much they have learned.

UPPO**P**PR

PROCESS JUSTIFICATION: IDENTIFYING THE SOURCE OF INFORMATION PRESENTED

A logical question that is often asked during a presentation involves where the information that you are using came from. It is no coincidence that *process justification* follows your objective. Chances are you have just given the trainees a benchmark within their objective. It is now time to finish that thought for the trainees. Where did the information that you are using come from, and why did you choose that particular source? Sometimes this source may be you. Sometimes it could be an author you chose to select. Here's an example:

The information for most of this chapter comes from a source I have come to know well. That source is Xerox. When I first went to the Xerox training center, I was asked to rewrite the Train-the-Trainer program being delivered to Xerox personnel. There were 10 modules, and I conducted major rewrites of nine. The only module that remains untouched to this day is the module that lays out the process you will now be learning. It was written in 1972, is a timeless piece that needs no adjustment, and to this day remains one of the most significant lessons I have ever learned in training.

The importance of including the process justification often depends on your material and your audience. Guilty until proven innocent. Why take chances? Trainees have a right to know where the information you are using came from and why it was selected. It is a good idea to head off any potential conflicts and offer this information to your trainees.

UPPOP**P**R

PROOF OF ABILITY: DEMONSTRATING THE SUCCESS OF THE TRAINING APPROACH

As you are preparing to deliver your curriculum to your trainees, there is only one other point that needs to be covered. Is there a *proof* source? Has what you are about to teach ever really helped someone in the past? Does it really work? At this time, you have systematically attempted to get people to see what is in it for them and told them the goals for your seminar. You have explained what you will be doing and how you will be doing it. Additionally, you have told them what is expected of them, where the information came from, and why you selected that information. The only question that may be left unanswered by the trainees is "Will it work for me?"

The intent behind stating a proof of ability is to provide the trainees with some sort of proof source designed to build confidence in their minds. This proof source could be how what you are teaching helped you personally. It could, just as easily, be how what you are teaching helped someone else. For example, I cited this experience earlier in this chapter:

Perhaps one of the most telling events that I can recall involving this subject occurred with a close friend of mine. They say that opposites attract in relationships and, in my opinion, this certainly holds true for friendships as well. I have a friend named Claude who illustrates this point well. At first glance, we do not appear to have much in common . . .

. . . He not only got the job, but he has become a fan of the process, and he is not what I call a man blessed with natural training abilities.

When putting together a proof of ability, you can use a story or an analogy. The idea is to provide one last push to fire up your trainees and instill confidence in the fact that they *can* accomplish whatever it is you are teaching.

UPPOPP**R**

Review: Emphasizing the Critical Information

I know what you are probably asking yourself "What can we *review*? We haven't entered the body of our presentation yet." When you start using the UPPOPPR overview, you will find that this entire process can last anywhere between five to 15 minutes, depending on your timing and the length of the module. It is a good idea to lightly, very lightly, touch on three critical areas. Those areas are the process, objective, and utility. The idea is not to rehash exact "what" and "how"; the intent is to net out the critical pieces of these three areas. For example, I do it this way:

So, get comfortable, get ready, and let me show you some ideas on how to bring your presentations to life. I hope that not only do I hear from you after using the method within your seminars, but that you will find the same success I have found in working with a process that makes presentations a breeze.

Try to avoid transitions into your review, such as "In conclusion . . ." or "To summarize . . ." Gently remind the trainees of the need-to-knows of the process, objective, and utility, and jump on it. You are now ready to rumble!

Mastering the UPPOPPR

Well, what do you think? Mastering the UPPOPPR is challenging. The rewards, however, will make it all worthwhile. One of the most important lessons that can be learned from working with this process comes from the art of *selling*. Think back on the teachers or presenters who really made a difference in your life. Did they just dispense information, or did they touch you in some way? Salespeople do not just tell; they sell! That should be your motto as well, regardless of the curriculum.

Some presenters will look at the UPPOPPR and assume it is too time consuming to use. In reality, using the UPPOPPR can be equated to the case of the tortoise and the hare. Rather than jumping into your topic and constantly going back to address issues that should have already been explained, you slow your entry into the body of your presentation a bit by using this process. In return, you will methodically move into your presentation without having to stop to clear the air answering questions that should have been addressed already.

With regard to actually writing a UPPOPPR, try using the UPPOPPR worksheets (see Figure 7.1) to guide you in addressing the critical points. As with anything else that is worthwhile, the rest is up to you. Practice, practice, practice, and use the reply card to let me know how it is working for you.

THE BODY

The actual body of the presentation is the easy part. Typically, the body of the presentation is that lifeless creature sent down from the home office developer's desk. If you are writing your own curriculum stylistically, you can choose one of three methods.

One method of writing your curriculum is the "manuscript" method, which means writing out every word of the presentation you are to deliver. It works well for TV anchorpeople who are reading off teleprompters, but it can be a nightmare for a presenter. Nothing will be more embarrassing for you, as a presenter, than to fumble about, looking for your place in your script. It is often a good idea to manuscript a UPPOPPR, but only to make sure you are confident that it is complete before you begin to synopsize it.

Another approach to writing the body of your presentation is to use a sentence outline. This technique provides the presenter with bullet-ized information in broken-sentence form. A sentence outline may be helpful for capturing transitions and a well-rehearsed UPPOPPR.

Finally, there is a word outline. As the term suggests, this is an approach that forces you to capture key areas of your presentation in a single word. This method is recommended for presenters who know

UPPOPPR Worksheet
Page 1

Utility

Story, analogy, lecture _____

_____

_____

_____

_____

_____

_____

What's in it for them: _____

1. Personal_____

2. Job   _____

3. Corp.   _____

_____

_____

_____

_____

_____

Product/Goal

The big picture _____

_____

_____

_____

_____

_____

FIGURE 7.1 UPPOPPR worksheet

UPPOPPR Worksheet
Page 2

Process

Content: "what" _____

_____

_____

_____

Method: "how" _____

_____

_____

Objective _____

Action _____

_____

_____

Requirement _____

_____

_____

_____

Degree _____

_____

_____

_____

Benchmark _____

_____

_____

_____

_____

_____

FIGURE 7.1   UPPOPPR worksheet (*Continued*)

UPPOPPR Worksheet
Page 3

_____

_____

_____

_____

_____

_____

Process Justification

Where info came from _____

_____

_____

Why this source _____

_____

Proof of Ability

Build confidence_____

_____

_____

_____

Review

Touch on process, objective, utility_____

_____

_____

_____

FIGURE 7.1   UPPOPPR worksheet

their material extremely well. The idea is to use the outline only as a guide to make sure you do not skip over an important point.

Often presenters mix and match techniques depending on their familiarity with their topic and curriculum. It often is a question of style.

THE FINAL REVIEW

I happen to believe that there is a common link between presenters who consistently dazzle their audiences. Although each has his or her own unique style, one similarity can be found time after time. They start their presentations strongly and they finish their presentations strongly. If you adhere to the structure of the UPPOPPR, I can assure you that your presentations will start strongly. If you remember to incorporate these next three steps, you will finish strongly as well.

The first step in finishing your presentation is to review the major points from the body of your curriculum. To find these major points, you probably will have to look no further than the Process portion of the UPPOPPR. It is difficult to say just how much time you will need to spend reviewing the material. Factors such as nonverbal cues, participation, difficulty of the material, and time allocation will help you decide. The goal, however, is not to review everything but just the most important points. Once again, depending on timing, you can do this using questioning techniques or just a presenter's summary. One technique that I use when I review with questions is to make this deal with the trainees. I tell them, I promise not to ask them any questions directly if they promise not to look at their notes. This way no one is put on the spot not knowing an answer, and I am able to determine what information has actually stuck.

The second step is really more of a reminder. During the UPPOPPR, you carefully created an objective for the seminar. It is time now to test your objective and evaluate performance.

The third and final step should be logical as well. You started your presentation generating interest and answering the question "What's in it for me?" It is only appropriate to now tie the presentation back to that utility. Now, I am not suggesting that you rehash all the benefits. Doing so could start to sound a bit redundant. I think it is effective to end on a positive, reassuring note, and that means briefly explaining the basic utility once again. That is the intent, and that will allow you to finish strongly with confidence.

Introducing the UPPOP Process

For those who are not conducting training but are presenting shorter programs like keynotes, the UPPOPPR can be a little too much, given the shorter time frames and the limited amount of content actually delivered. No worries. You can trim the process down to a UPPOP (pronounced YOU-POP) and move a little faster into the body of the presentation without losing too much.

When executing a UPPOP, you'll just need to shorten what you're doing as follows:

U—Utility. No matter how rushed you may feel you are, I would never shortchange a utility. From the creative beginning to the presentation you choose, to the three utilities for the audience, don't change a thing in the most important part of your presentation.

P—Product. It's only one sentence, and it gives your audience a sense of the big picture. No change here either.

P—Process. Here's an area we can trim a bit, but only because the presentation itself will be trimmed as well. Unlike a full training program that's replete with agenda items, a keynote presentation is much shorter, and so is this list of items found here.

O—Objective. With larger audiences and shorter speaking times, the objective found in shorter presentations is shorter as well. A simple explanation of what it is you expect out of the audience at the conclusion of the presentation should do the trick.

P—Process Justification. Every audience needs to hear where the information came from and why you are the person delivering it, so no shortcuts here.

The proof of ability is usually unnecessary for shorter presentations, but that would depend on how shaky or unsure the audience may be regarding the topic you are there to deliver. The review is also unnecessary because the presentation is shorter and doesn't have as many moving parts. Figure 7.2 is a worksheet that will guide you in addressing the critical points of this streamlined version.

**UPPOP Worksheet
Page 1**

Utility

Story, analogy, lecture _____

_____

_____

_____

_____

_____

_____

What's in it for them: _____

1. Personal _____

2. Job _____

3. Corp. _____

_____

_____

_____

_____

_____

Product/Goal

The big picture _____

_____

_____

_____

_____

_____

_____

FIGURE 7.2   UPPOP worksheet

UPPOP Worksheet
Page 2

Process

Content: "what" _____

_____

_____

_____

Method: "how" _____

_____

_____

Objective _____

Action _____

_____

_____

Requirement _____

_____

_____

_____

Degree _____

_____

_____

_____

Benchmark _____

_____

_____

_____

_____

_____

FIGURE 7.2   UPPOP worksheet (*Continued*)

UPPOP Worksheet
Page 3

_____

_____

_____

_____

_____

_____

Process Justification

Where info came from _____

_____

Why this source _____

_____

_____

Notes: _____

_____

_____

_____

_____

_____

_____

_____

_____

FIGURE 7.2   UPPOP worksheet

Summary

There just isn't a more important moment than the first few minutes of your delivery, and whether you use a full UPPOPPR or a shortened UPPOP, your command of this process will change the way you approach a presentation forever. Start strongly, finish strongly, and the body will take care of itself. I'd suggest you use those worksheets and give yourself some time to not just create a strong opening, but practice it. I can assure you, you'll be glad you did!

Chapter 8

Thirty Tips on Maintaining Interest

One of the hottest issues in training involves the topic of this chapter. How do you maintain interest? Whether your program is 10 minutes, 10 hours, or 10 days, the reality most presenters face is that a great deal of their success or failure will most likely be judged by how well they keep their trainees interested. Through my years in the pit, I have tried many creative, and sometimes bizarre, ideas to maintain interest throughout my presentations. Over the years, I have developed a fascination with this topic.

Do not forget the intended message behind this topic—maintaining interest. It is my hope that two key points have already stuck from your readings thus far. First, no presenter is immediately interesting when he or she appears in front of a seminar for the first time. Oh yes, I must admit that I have walked into new classes that have neither seen nor heard of me and have been greeted by thunderous applause. Unfortunately, that is about the exact moment the alarm clock goes off and it is time to start a new day. The art of creating interest is employed gradually and, at least early on, subtly. The second point from the preceding chapters is that the UPPOPPR overview is designed to initiate interest, not sustain it. My hopes are that once a group is properly prepared for a topic using the overview, the ideas in this chapter will keep the momentum going in your favor.

I think it is only fair to warn you that maintaining interest is a never-ending brainstorm. What is right for some may be totally inappropriate for others. It is therefore my intent to shower you with as many ideas as possible with the hope that a handful will find their way into your presentations.

1. USE YOUR VOICE EFFECTIVELY

One of the biggest fears most people have when they are asked to speak publicly involves their voices. The worry often involves how our voices sound. There is an easy way not to worry about that problem, because there is nothing you can do about it. Most people do not like their own voice when they hear it played back. It sounds different from the way we hear it when we are speaking, and that tends to bother people. What you should focus on is avoiding any hints of monotone.

An example of this involves a story I once heard about Mark Twain. It was written that Mark Twain had a terrible habit of cursing, which bothered his wife a great deal. She would try to correct him, but it was no use. As the story goes, once, while shaving, Mark Twain cut himself and let out a long string of curse words. His wife, who was in the other room listening, was so upset at his language, she wrote down every word he said. When he finished shaving, she marched into the bathroom and read back every word—to which Mark Twain patiently replied, "That's very good, honey. You've got the words; you just don't know the tune." Now you need to think about the tune. *How* you say it is as important as *what* you say.

2. TELL ANECDOTES

Anecdotes or stories that relate to your topic are another way to keep adults interested in your presentation. As with most of the ideas presented in this chapter, too much of anything becomes a waste. Used selectively within your presentation, these stories not only create interest, they often help to relax you as well. A prime example of an anecdote is the story you just read about Mark Twain. Certainly while you're telling a story that relates to your topic, there is no need to be stuck behind a lectern at the mercy of your notes. Often when presenters launch into an anecdotal story that involves their subjects, you will observe a noticeable change for the better in their facial expressions and body language.

The biggest trick to using anecdotes within your presentation is to remember to actually tell the story. A recommendation here is to put a word or title in the margin of your notes to remind you to tell the story. When you are under fire, things happen very quickly. There is nothing more frustrating than finishing your training only to realize that you forgot to tell a couple of key anecdotal stories. With reminders clearly visible in your notes, the only reason you will not tell a story is because you made a conscious decision to skip over it.

3. Keep Moving while You Talk

In my mind, movement is one of the easiest and surest ways to keep trainees interested in a presentation. Perhaps you can tell an anecdotal story that relates to your subject and move around as you tell it. There is something truly wonderful about a presenter who moves around as he or she speaks. It communicates comfort with the subject matter, credibility, and, most important of all, interest.

In corporate training, a horseshoe-style seating arrangement benefits a presenter for two reasons. First, it helps the trainees by allowing them to see each other, learn each other's names, and get comfortable around each other. Second, it creates an open area (which I have been referring to as the "pit") that presenters can move around in to generate interest.

4. Vary the Pace of Your Presentation

The rate at which you speak, or your pace, can also add to the interest you are creating within your seminars. Some presenters speak quickly and others speak slowly. Each is successful in his or her own way.

So, which is correct, fast or slow? The answer is both and neither. The key is not necessarily to adapt a speaking style that is fast or slow. The key is to adapt to your own style and vary the pace. We can hear at about 325 words a minute and generally speak at about 170 words per minute. Our minds can receive as quickly or as slowly as someone wants to speak. To maintain interest, all we need to do is vary the pace. If you naturally speak quickly, force yourself to slow down at times. If your pace is naturally slower, give yourself an occasional kick in the pants and speed up. The actual words per minute is not the trick; the *variance* of the pace is.

5. Distribute Handouts

Most presenters do not like to hand out materials because they are afraid they will lose the attention of the trainees. I happen to agree with that philosophy, but I would like to offer a benefit to waiting to hand out certain materials. If timed properly, handouts can actually help create a little interest within your training room. The obvious plus in holding handouts until you are ready is that you can focus the trainees' attention at the proper time.

What most presenters fail to realize, however, is that there is another plus as well. You can incorporate movement and pass out the handouts to each trainee yourself. Next time you take a seminar, notice that when the presenter passes out any handouts, he or she most likely drops a pile on one trainee's desk and asks that the stack be passed around. Instead, you can make this a wonderful opportunity to get in each trainee's face a little bit. You can incorporate some movement and get a little more benefit out of an easy, interest-sustaining idea.

6. Incorporate Trainees' Names into Your Discussion

Name involvement is a technique that is subtle but effective. To incorporate name involvement, all you have to do is use some of your trainees' names in a rhetorical sense. This approach is especially useful when you are delivering a lecture or slower curriculum. An example of the approach would sound like this:

Presenter: Now John may not agree with what I have just shown you and Tom might. The key is that both have formed opinions that are valid and strong.

The intent behind name involvement is not to *embarrass* but to *refocus*. No one should be put on the spot. Use trainees' names only within your conversation. Gone are the days when presenters pounce on a poor, defenseless trainee with questions they know their trainee cannot answer. This dangerous technique is still used to shock trainees back to reality. In the real world of working with adults, not only will this approach cause anger and defensiveness from the trainee, but it can also act as a catalyst for a sniper attack down the road.

7. Use Visual Aids

Visual aids are a natural for kicking life into even the dullest curriculum. Visual aids can be used to appeal to any of the five senses. A well-timed presentation aid can break up a difficult module. Be selective, watch your timing, and remember the motto from before: "If you emphasize everything, you emphasize nothing." Also look over Chapter 10 on visual aids.

8. ASK QUESTIONS

One of the best ways to keep generating interest throughout your training is to keep a steady flow of creative questions going between you and your trainees. A very common mistake from presenters is the positioning of questions. Often the questions from the presenter come in bunches. Twenty minutes will go by, and then the presenter will begin to ask questions, as if trying to fill a quota. The idea is to maintain the interest level of the trainees throughout the presentation.

Try mixing up the types of questions that you ask the trainees to fit the curriculum. For instance, you might want to begin a module with opinion-based questions, develop the topic with case study and comparison questions, and review at the end with fact-based questions. The key is to keep a somewhat steady flow of questions throughout and to vary your questioning techniques.

9. CONDUCT SMALL-GROUP ACTIVITIES

One of my favorite techniques to maintain trainees' interest and improve learning retention is to use group activities. When delivering a seminar, it's easy to fall in love with your own voice. Letting participants find their way to your conclusions through small-group activities is a can't-miss approach to maintaining interest. It also helps participants learn more effectively.

One of the biggest shocks I received before I rewrote Xerox's Train-the-Trainer program was in the area of participation. Here was a course designed to teach new trainers how to teach. During the four days of lecture before the individual presentations, there was plenty of talk about the need for small-group activities. The problem was, we did not practice what we preached. There were *no* such activities. We also averaged about three deliveries a year.

When I rewrote the curriculum, I updated and added some information in almost all the modules, but these changes were not drastic. The major change took place on the delivery side, where now not a morning or afternoon goes by without some sort of group activity reinforcing the curriculum being taught. These activities total 14 in four days. As a footnote, when I left Xerox, that Train-the-Trainer was averaging about 18 deliveries a year with a healthy six- to nine-month waiting list of trainees from all over the country trying to get in. Amazing what small-group activities can do for a course!

10. Utilize Role-Plays

A more specific type of small-group activity that can create interest within your seminars is role-plays. A role-play allows participants to use your materials in a real-world environment. It also provides another unique benefit: It ensures relevance.

Frequently, when working with repeatable processes, one of the challenges presenters have is tying their process to specific client needs. Clients don't want to apply your process to widgets; they want to apply it to their specific situations. When appropriate, role-plays allow you to marry your process to the clients' specific situations. Clients are thrilled because you have demonstrated knowledge of their business and have made your material relevant to their needs. You're thrilled because you also incorporated a wonderful interest sustaining idea.

11. Personalize Your Presentation

A simple and fun idea, personalization can add some real sizzle to your presentation. Personalization techniques involve taking whatever your topic happens to be and creatively individualizing some of the key areas. Doing this can involve unique signs or slogans involving you or your participants.

12. Create a Case Study

It goes without saying I'm a fan of role-plays and always will be. I recognize that they tend to make people uncomfortable, but how else do we take what has been learned and apply it in a real-world setting? The answer is case studies, that's how.

Case studies allow participants to work with what has been taught and sift through it. Isn't that how the material will be used in the real world when the training has been completed?

Case studies also permit a kind of freedom that audiences crave. Processes are great, but when people forget that those processes are merely guides, they can lose confidence in the value of the ideas that are being taught. With case studies, participants are encouraged to make their own decisions based on scenarios they are familiar with. That creates confidence not just in what has been taught but in how it is to be used.

13. CREATE A SIMULATION

One of the most intense forms of small-group activities that can be utilized within a seminar environment is a simulation. A simulation is an activity that combines multiple actions to bring about what often can be an unpredictable solution. In my mind, a well-written simulation may be the most powerful activity that can be inserted into a seminar. It may also be the most difficult.

Let me provide you with an example of one of the greatest simulations I've ever seen or conducted. When Xerox was attempting to create a culture of quality and problem solving to compete with the ever-growing competition that was eroding its market share, it began to teach a "Leadership Through Quality" program. This theory-driven program didn't get a whole lot of attention. The flaw in the program was that what was being taught could not be seen. The program that was designed to "save the corporation" was in critical condition.

Then one significant change was made to the program—a simulation was added. Once the theories of problem solving and quality improvement were taught, the groups of 20 participants were put into three groups to physically build a product called a "Geezenstack." This created an environment that allowed participants to see, touch, and feel the processes they had been hearing about for two days. The simulation itself took another day and a half, allowing participants to measure what they were doing. The participants went through the steps to problem solve the approach they were taking and to improve the quality of the results they were getting.

The results were magical. Getting participants to take the program was no longer an issue, as word of the simulation spread fast. Participants understood and retained the processes that were taught. Ultimately, this little simulation and the Geezenstacks that were so much a part of it may have saved one of the largest corporations in America.

One last point about simulations and case studies. The idea is to allow participants to pick through what they have learned throughout the session and apply it based on the information received. This means you are not evaluating performance based on a perfect use of the materials provided, but rather how participants manage these pieces and make decisions. This will mimic real-world scenarios and allow participants to gain confidence in what you are teaching them.

I frequently create simulations and case studies that intentionally do not require some of the key steps I have taught. It takes a bit of courage to sacrifice the use of your favorite tactic or skill, but by showing participants that even the strongest tactics aren't necessary all the time, you remind them that what you are teaching is not a straitjacket but a set of skills that is available as needed. In a sense, you lose the battle to win the war.

Simulations don't have to last a day and a half. They can be pared down to much shorter periods of time, but beware. The idea is to allow participants to use what has been taught and to discover real-world lessons. It would be a shame to rush participants through such a wonderful seminar opportunity.

14. Show a Sense of Humor

Humor is a valuable tool to some presenters that can come in handy during some of the drier sections of the curriculum. It certainly makes the list of interest devices, but in no way is it a necessity. I have seen some extremely good presenters who did not incorporate a sense of humor within their style. Sadly, there are still those who believe the only way to succeed as a trainer or public speaker is to incorporate a sense of humor. Please do not get me wrong. I think a sense of humor is helpful to a presenter, as long as it is natural.

One of the most frustrating aspects of being a consultant involves this very topic. Often I was asked to work with fairly prominent individuals in various organizations to assist them in their public speaking duties. A first request from many was for me to write a joke to start their presentation off. Most of the time I begged them not to use a joke, but it was no use. The jokes were told, the polite laughter followed, and the message was sent out loud and clear to the audience: "This person is not funny."

There is one other recommendation I would like to make when incorporating humor within your training. *Do not overdo it.* Presenters who are too humorous can run the risk of losing control of the seminar. In any seminar, the goal is to create a relaxed and open learning environment. It is not a carnival. I, too, have been down this road. In my eagerness to get my trainees to loosen up, I used to loosen them up too much. This would create a lack of control and discipline. Unfortunately, once you lose control it's a lot more difficult to regain it. Once a presenter encourages trainees to relax and have fun, it is difficult to change the rules all of a sudden. Presenters can be perceived as phony and inflexible. This is one of those situations when presenters must walk a very narrow tightrope.

15. Use Nonverbal Communication

If I may quote a lesson learned early in most of our lives, "It is not what you say, but how you say it." This holds true with this next interest device, nonverbal communication. This form of communication can include facial expressions, hand movements, body movements, or any type of gestures. Much has been written on the subject of nonverbal communication, and some is fascinating. Personally, I think you can overdo it a bit. For a presenter, the key to incorporating nonverbal communication is to try to pay attention to just a few things. First, if you are using a lectern, make sure that you do not hold onto it. Doing so is a noticeable indicator of anxiety. It also blocks a major portion of your nonverbal communication. If you free your hands up, the rest will come naturally. In a sense, nonverbal communication is a little bit like breathing. It is difficult to do only if you think about it.

Once you free yourself up to let your nonverbal communication take over, there is only one other tip I would recommend. Try to keep your gestures as open as possible. It is somewhat contradictory to be asking trainees for questions and strolling around the pit while your arms are crossed tightly in front of you. Loosen up! Generate some excitement through your nonverbal communication, and keep those gestures open to invite participation.

16. Mix Up Your Techniques

One simple and effective approach to maintaining interest can be accomplished by mixing up your techniques. Some presenters are comfortable acting as facilitators while others prefer more of a lecture style. Still others prefer a take-charge authority role. Each method can be effective at different times for different presenters with different curricula. The key to creating interest, regardless of which approach you prefer, is to change techniques throughout your training.

It is important here to emphasize that I am in no way suggesting any deviation from the written curriculum. I am recommending that you use the available delivery techniques creatively to keep the trainees' interest.

17. Use a Team-Training Approach

Another solid technique that can be used to spice up your training may be to use a team-training approach. "Team training" refers to more than one presenter in the seminar. Sometimes presenters develop what I call "vocal rapture," which is a deep affection for their own voices. This affliction can cause presenters to lecture too much. It can also cause them to be a little shortsighted in looking beyond the resources that may be available. Most trainers never even consider giving up the floor to another trainer.

No matter how talented a presenter is in delivering material, a second speaker, strategically placed, can only add to the interest the first presenter has created. In reality, I am talking about the potential of 39 hours and 45 minutes for the presenter and 15 minutes for another speaker. That is not exactly a huge risk or loss of control on the presenter's part. With this in mind, let's look at three possible areas where you might be able to find the help you are looking for.

The first, and most common, is another presenter. Perhaps you are in the process of cross-training a new presenter. This might be an excellent opportunity to allow this individual to get his or her feet wet by teaching a module, conducting a feedback session, or even role-playing a character for the seminar participants. Maybe another presenter is floating without a seminar that week. Typically, presenters are off for a reason, say to clear their minds or take care of other business. We are, however, talking about a limited period of time to give your seminar a shot in the arm. With a promise of reciprocation, you may find a more-than-willing partner. Given that many training departments still consider the teaming of presenters a luxury, let's look at two more areas that usually are available to everyone and may be right under your nose.

Peer training is one approach that is a natural, utilizing the team-training concept. Often members of your seminar have some experiences that may be pertinent to your topic. What a wonderful opportunity to tap into these experiences and create a little interest within your seminar at the same time. You can even use some of your more talkative trainees or sniper trainees to assist you. Now you have not only stroked their egos, which helps you to get a lot of these types of trainees under control, but you have generated some additional interest as well. The only other important recommendation here is to make sure you lay out the parameters of how these trainees are contributing. The most important rule of all is to be very up front and clear regarding time. Emphasize that you are going to give them 10 or 15 minutes, and stick to it. Doing this should help to reduce any worries you may have about losing control of the seminar.

A final recommendation for team training involves the use of a possible guest speaker. Now, I know what you are saying "Guest speakers do not grow on trees. I'll never find one!" Well, that is where you might be wrong. I am not necessarily talking about finding the type of speaker you would find at a high school graduation. I am referring to the less obvious, the often overlooked. Let me provide you with an example of just such a case.

Years ago, I was conducting a five-day class in Nebraska. The topic was automation training, and I was forewarned that the employees there were famous for their lack of energy and interest. As I was setting up for the class, I was racking my brain as to how I could make the class more interesting. Then I noticed a custodian cleaning up the day's office debris. It hit me like a flash. I asked him if he could come in later in the week and talk for 15 minutes or so about how the automation of the office I was teaching in had changed his job. I did not have to ask this man twice. He was very excited about being a speaker. For three days, I tantalized the class with the promise of a guest speaker who specialized in the effects of office automation. When the day finally did arrive, this man delivered a presentation that would have made many presenters envious. The trainees loved it, the custodian loved it, and the class was a success. What more could I have asked for?

18. THINK OUTSIDE OF THE BOX REGARDING THOSE GIVEAWAYS

The seminar world is littered with forgotten giveaways. Golf balls, pens, key chains, mugs, T-shirts, and the tired list goes on. I can assure you, I'm not against giveaways; I'm against *boring* giveaways. Think about it for a moment: You are about to give something that is supposed to make a statement. Is a pen with your name on it really the best you can do?

I'm a guy who prides myself in thinking outside of the box, and the greatest giveaway I've ever had is something that you would call a "bobblehead" but I call a "Robblehead." I had 100 of these guys made a few years ago, and although they were not inexpensive, the giving of a Robblehead is a moment few forget. Maybe it's the Robblehead's uncanny likeness to me . . . or maybe it's the *2001: A Space Odyssey* music that plays while the Robblehead emerges out of flames on the screen in front of the audience when it's time for him to make his entrance.

In the end, the cost of this giveaway is not that much more than a book giveaway, and although I take pride in my books, my Robbleheads are never forgotten. There are a number of stock body positions that are available, but choosing one that holds business cards has gone a long way to keeping those Robble's in front of my clients. Coincidently, my website is tucked neatly on the base to not be forgotten as well. Not that I'm all that competitive, but I always smile when the professional speaker before me whips the audience into a frenzy by giving away a white T-shirt with his or her company's logo on it, and I know what's up my sleeve and ready to emerge. (By the way, notice what's also on that Robblehead's base.)

19. ENCOURAGE COMPETITION AMONG TRAINEES

Everybody has his or her own favorites when it comes to trying to create and maintain interest. Competition happens to be one of mine. It is astounding what a little friendly competition can do to an otherwise dull curriculum. I have seen presenters use all sorts of prizes and awards to create a competitive situation. Unfortunately, those who focus on the prize too much are missing the whole point behind the strategic use of competition. It is not the actual prize that so many of us crave but rather the thrill of winning. Ironically, when the prize is too expensive or overdone, trainees lose their focus on learning and become blinded by winning the prize.

In my career as a professional speaker, I have seen others give away items ranging from 50-dollar bills to company merchandise. I have also witnessed trainees who were at each other's throats trying to win these valuable prizes. There is no sense of teamwork, and even a sense of professional jealousy often arises. If the winner's answer is at all subjective, there can be resentment by other trainees not only toward the winner but toward the presenter as well. Some trainees can become somewhat hyper while others will simply shut down. In this situation, the emphasis is too much on the prize and not enough on the event.

The prizes that I would recommend should be far more symbolic. Let me give you a couple of examples. When I taught for the National Flood Insurance Program, one of the worst courses to teach was a seminar that required trainees to rate premiums for insurance policies. Not only was the course a bit boring, but the trainees themselves were not the most lively bunch. Getting them to rate 20 individual policy examples was like pulling teeth. Without making any changes to the curriculum, I started to pair up trainees (also utilizing idea 9 for maintaining interest) and have them compete for "valuable prizes." The prizes turned out to be certificates that read "Oh Boy, Can I Rate a Policy" and the all-important Baby Ruth candy bars that accompanied those certificates. Funny thing was, the trainees learned the material, had fun, and no one got too worked up over the prizes.

Now, to be perfectly honest with you, I should confess that I have, in fact, given money out in some of my seminars. The only difference is that I will give somewhere between a nickel and a quarter. Once again, it is more the thrill of winning than the actual prize.

One last point about competition. You do not have to look too hard for areas in your curriculum to introduce this technique. A trick I like to use in some seminars is to work competition into answers to questions. For example, if I am bringing a study into the seminar to show a statistical breakdown of some sort, I merely ask a couple of volunteers to take their best shots at guessing what the results are. Of course, I do not get much of a response until I tell them a prize is on the line. Then my only worry is to limit the number of volunteers I will accept. Great participation and interest is immediately created the moment I introduce competition.

As far as prizes are concerned, keep them simple. To this day, one of my most successful prizes happens to sound a little arrogant, but it works like a charm. For winning a contest, or even answering a tough question correctly, I give out an $8^1/2'' \times 14''$ poster. Of what? you ask. Me! As a matter of fact, I have about three or four posters of me in the most obnoxious, arrogant poses you'd ever want to see. Depending on the course and the timing of the award, I usually put some sort of caption across the top. Of course, no Rob Jolles poster is complete without an autograph slashing across the middle. A couple of reminders if you are interested in this particular idea. Wait a while before distributing these prizes until the trainees get to know you and understand you are poking fun at yourself. Also, I don't recommend this idea in potentially hostile environments. Talk about adding grease to the fire!

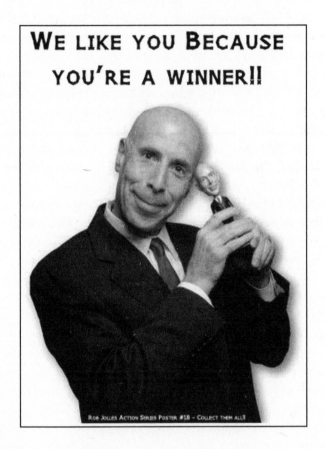

We like you Because you're a winner!!

Rob Jolles Action Series Poster #18 - Collect them all!

20. Try an Offbeat Approach

Now, doing something offbeat is not necessarily an area that I would dabble in . . . exactly. If I did, however, I would probably recommend a number of ideas that I have used.

One of my favorite unique finds actually came to me as a result of a trip to the supermarket. At the time, I was battling a boredom problem at work. My trainees were writing papers every night, and every morning I would read them and return them with my comments. I began to get creative and put symbols like checks and smiley faces on the homework, but that still just did not seem to be motivating the trainees one way or another. Then I stumbled on an amazing find. It happened to me harmlessly enough. I slipped away from my wife at the grocery store, promising to pick up a couple of items. One item I usually volunteer for is the cereal. I do this because for some strange reason, I still like to see what is being offered on the back of those cereal boxes. As a kid growing up, I used to send away for many of the strange little items and then anxiously wait for their arrival in my mailbox. I have never gotten over this thrill. Well, on this fateful day at the supermarket, my perseverance paid off. As I began turning cereal boxes around, I became transfixed by the Cheerios box. For a whopping $1 (and a couple of proofs of purchase), the company was offering to take a photo you sent them and make a rubber stamp out of it. With four boxes of Cheerios in tow, I ran home and put my plan into operation. No more smiley faces; now I could be using *my* face! I immediately shot two pictures, one of me happy and one of me not so happy. Cheerios was kind enough to make good on *this* kid's request and provide me with a stamp of each. The great thing about these stamps is that my trainees become seriously concerned when they see the Unhappy Rob and vow to do what is necessary to get the Happy Rob next time.

21. DEVIATE FROM YOUR TOPIC

This idea is probably one of the most misunderstood in the list. Simply put, topic deviation is nothing more than allowing trainees to stray off the topic you are covering and letting them go for a few moments. This particular phenomenon happens in most seminars. The reason I say it is misunderstood stems from the average presenter's reaction. What most presenters do is immediately assume an authoritative role and wrestle the conversation away from the trainees and back to the topic at hand. What a waste!

The idea is to try to create a training environment that is *conducive* to discussion. With that expectation comes the probability that the discussions will not always be exactly what you want them to be. So what? You should be flattered that trainees feel comfortable enough to discuss issues openly in your training room. Often the presenter should slip back out of the pit and let nature take its course. When you do so, watch for nonverbals from the trainees. They typically will signal you when the discussion has gone on long enough. On the average, these conversations will last between two or three minutes. Once some trainees begin to look at you instead of those who are speaking, it is time to enter with a closed probe and bring the seminar back on target. Your reentry may sound something like this:

Trainee No. 1: (after a few minutes) . . . that is how we do it in our area.

Trainee No. 2: Well, in our district, we have been known to tell people.

Presenter: (breaking in) So it sounds like there have been a variety of approaches used in the field. Well, if you look at some of the tactics that we have been discussing, you will see a variety there as well. To begin with . . .

Sometimes, when breaking in or waiting to break in, you may hear a trainee slyly comment about you losing control of the seminar. Do not get defensive or feel obligated to explain your conscious decision. What they don't know won't hurt them.

22. Use Music

As I mentioned in Chapter 6, music can be used in training not only to create a mood but to create interest as well. Playing simple, middle-of-the-road music when trainees are entering the seminar helps to set a certain tone for the rest of the training. The idea behind this recommendation is not to stop here. Look carefully at some of the small-group exercises or activities, and see if you can mix in some quiet music while trainees are working. Many of my musical selections are based entirely on the type of exercise the trainees are working on.

For example, in a Quality class that I teach, the trainees participate in a culminating simulation. The entire class works together, using all the skills they have learned, to complete one final task as a team. During that simulation, I play the theme from *Rocky* and other similar motivational songs. The bottom line is that music often can make a good small-group exercise or activity just a little better.

23. Take Breaks

So far we have looked at a number of creative approaches for maintaining interest within your training. Now let's look at an interest-sustaining device that tends to be taken for granted. Breaks are often a presenter's best friend. Similar to topic deviation, this technique is also often misunderstood. Let's take a look at some of the misunderstandings and then at some suggested solutions surrounding the idea behind breaks.

The first misunderstanding regarding the idea of a break is that it should be carefully tied to a particular spot in the curriculum. Often a presenter opens an instructor guide only to be greeted by the developer's references to where to take breaks. The intent behind these references is legitimate and typically corresponds to shifts in curriculum. The mistake presenters often make is to misinterpret these *suggestions* as *requirements*. The developer may want you to break on page 25 and the book may say to break on page 25, but if the trainees are drifting away on page 20, you had better think again.

A second misunderstanding that preys on many presenters concerns the preset timing of seminar breaks. In some seminars, preset breaks are scheduled at the same time every day. For example, you may be conducting a seminar that starts at 8:00 a.m. with a planned break at 9:30. That is all well and good, but once again, What if the trainees are falling asleep at 9:00?

The solution regarding breaks? Watch your trainees. *Read their nonverbals.* You usually will not have to look too hard to pick up on when trainees need a break. If you are pressured by management, developers, or even your client into breaks that are far apart, work in short five-minute breaks. Insist that trainees stick to the five minutes and start back up on time. This conditions the trainees to learn you mean business. What usually happens is that those who need to run to the restroom do so, and the others will just stretch and mill around. Ironically, that five minutes probably will allow you to teach more in a day rather than less because the trainees will be better able to focus on your topic.

One other technique you can use with breaks is what I call "foreshadowing." Sometimes trainees come back from a break and, within 20 minutes, begin nonverbally signaling for another. You may want to say something like, "We'll be taking a break in a couple of minutes, so hang in there." It does not sound like much, but you would be shocked at how many trainees snap back just from hearing the work "break." Okay, it's a cheap trick. All's fair when you're working that pit!

24. Pony Up, and Pay for the Video

As you will see from reading this book, I'm a big fan of incorporating video into seminars and workshops. Nowadays there seems to be a video that will support just about any topic. These videos are usually very well done and can provide a terrific change to the lengthier deliveries.

The hitch is the initial cost. This is because companies know that once they sell a video to an organization, that organization can show it as often and to as many audiences as it wishes. For that reason, don't be surprised to pay studios that represent these films from $500 to $1,000.

But don't let costs deter you from using this fantastic, interest-sustaining idea. Remember, one seminar will more than pay for this video, which you may find yourself using for years to come.

25. Make It a Game Show

A seminar isn't a seminar without some kind of review in the end. This next idea takes a little time and a lot of preparation, but it sure can help ending your seminar with a bang. One of the most popular game shows to try to re-create is *Jeopardy!*

This is a favorite activity of mine because it allows you to create review questions from the material you've taught. You can work this idea from a low-budget approach or put a lot of money into this idea. Once you've created the 40 questions you will need, you're ready to go.

The low-budget approach requires fake money (I use Monopoly money), a flip chart, and three call bells. Once the participants are seated, give each person a simple call bell found at any office supply store. Prepare your flip chart with four columns of just numbers (i.e., $100, $200, $300, etc.). On a second page, do the same thing but double the numbers. Keep your questions in front of you on the lectern. As each question is answered correctly, put the money in front of the appropriate individual. Things move quickly, so I suggest that you not get involved in taking money away from those who answer questions incorrectly. Set yourself up for a final *Jeopardy!* question, and you're ready to go!

The high-budget approach requires the same questions, but the rest can get more interesting. There are companies that sell *Jeopardy!* game boards, *Jeopardy!* software programs, scoreboards, and even systems that allow participants to buzz in. One company I like to use for this type of merchandise is the Trainer's Warehouse (www .Trainerswarehouse.com). Check out the site, and you'll get plenty of ideas and a price range that should meet your needs.

The more participants you can get involved with this activity, the better, and it will work with large audiences. Obviously, this game is not recommended for shorter, keynote presentations, but for longer presentations, it is very enjoyable.

26. Time Those Activities

This next idea is not earth-shattering, but it does create interest. It also helps you manage many of the other ideas that you have been reading about. For many of the activities that require participation, you will need to time the events. Doing this allows participants to manage their time better and keeps you and your seminar running on time. You can shout out the times to your participants. Or you can use a tool that makes this easier—and a little more interesting.

For a few years I've been using a software program that provides a simple clock that counts down on my computer. Because I use Keynote for just about every presentation I deliver, I can project this countdown on the screen in front of my participants. I assume there are a few of these programs available, but I recommend simply going to www .trainerswarehouse.com. At that site you'll find numerous items that will help you time your activities. It's a nice touch, easy to use, and adds a little spark to what you are doing.

27. Work on Those Name Cards

We've all seen them, those folded tent cards waiting for participants when they enter a training room. Sometimes we put the participant's name on the card, and sometimes we let participants do it for themselves. However, it's not what's on the front of the card I'm suggesting you look at; it's what's on the back.

There's some valuable blank space that's just dying to be used right there under the participants' noses. I'm quite sure you'll be holding your audiences in a nonstop, interest-sustaining spell, but the mind of every audience member drifts a bit. If they do, imagine the participants seeing things like this on the card facing them:

- *Always* feel free to ask questions.
- Challenge the information being presented.
- Bring something powerful to the conversation.
- Engage your neighbor.
- Stay focused.

You can tailor what you want printed to fit your meeting, but giving participants something to look at will certainly help in keeping them interested.

28. FEED THEM RIGHT

What you feed your audiences will go a long way toward helping them to maintain their interest in what you say. A few years ago I was asked by a major car rental company to do an evaluation of its training program. It was a fantastic program from start to almost finish. The one unusual part of the training was the snacks. A few times a day, in came candy bars, potato chips, popcorn, soft drinks, and more. Soon after each snack fest and the sugar highs dissipated, heads started to drop. Not wanting to be a killjoy, I convinced that company (and many others) to put out healthy, more nutritious snacks.

29. INCENT THE BACK OF THE ROOM

How many times have you walked into a seminar and watched those back tables fill up? Why not? If you sit back there, you won't really have to engage with the speaker. But I like to kick the interest up and frequently show up with a bunch of pens. When I'm done speaking, I thank those who sat in the front row and give every one of them a pen. I then look at the back of the room and say, "Maybe next time you'll come up here and join us!"

30. Show Enthusiasm!

Last, but by no means least, is enthusiasm. I haven't listed the interest-maintaining devices in any particular order because each is appropriate in its own way, depending on the audience and style of the presenter. I would like to break from that rule at this time, however, and present you with my number one interest device: *enthusiasm*.

When presenters ask about maintaining interest (and it is the most-often-asked question during a Presentation Skills program), I tell them to sit through the course for a week and that I guarantee, if they keep their eyes open, they will get plenty of ideas. It all starts with enthusiasm. Think of it this way. You've misplaced an overhead? Trainees will forgive you. You stumbled over an extension cord? It could happen to anybody. You're fairly new to the curriculum and are forced to read more than you would like to? That's okay. Drop a stack of handouts on the floor? Pick them up; it could happen to anybody. You see, the bottom line is that when delivering seminars, workshops, or corporate training, audiences will forgive just about anything. Anything . . . but a lack of enthusiasm. It is no coincidence that if you look over the performance of most presenters, you will find that usually, each time they teach a new course, there is a strong trainee reaction. By that, I mean the trainees usually bond closely with the presenter and each other. You see, the first time a presenter teaches a new seminar, regardless of tenure, there is a feeling of *eagerness* and *challenge*. This often translates to added enthusiasm and thus satisfied trainees. As the presenter becomes more accustomed to the new curriculum, that enthusiasm dwindles.

Perhaps the single most challenging aspect of corporate training revolves around maintaining enthusiasm. This maintenance takes a tremendous amount of self-discipline. The fact of the matter is that some days it is extremely difficult to find the enthusiasm necessary to do the job you know you are capable of doing. I suggest you keep a couple of reminders in your head. Lesson number one comes from an article I read about a fighter named Marvin Hagler. Hagler had an interesting attitude toward his physical training. On days he felt up to conditioning himself for an upcoming fight, he worked very hard. On days he did not feel up to doing the things he knew were necessary to prepare, he worked twice as hard. Pound for pound, Marvin Hagler was considered one of the greatest fighters of all time. His reign as middleweight champion stretched from 1980 to 1987. Few fighters won more bouts. Few worked harder. That attitude of working so hard on those days you don't feel like working quite as hard needs to take place within your training.

With respect to maintaining enthusiasm for your training, lesson number two comes from the attitude adopted by an actor. If an actor had to recite the same lines to the same audience each night, it would not take long for boredom to set in. Fortunately, the audiences change nightly. Likewise, although presenters may feel as if they have told a story or an analogy one too many times, the trainees are hearing it for the very first time.

As for me, I demand a great deal of enthusiasm from myself. I will continue to be enthusiastic teaching my seminars, workshops, and training classes. When I can no longer muster up that enthusiasm, do not feel sorry for me. There will not be enough time. I have vowed that when I can no longer put the enthusiasm necessary to conduct corporate training on the level that I feel is appropriate, I will learn to do something else very well and move on. Presenters must take responsibility for maintaining their own enthusiasm. It is just too important to do without.

What to Do about Sleepy Trainees

Up to now, I have presented a list of ideas designed to help trainees stay awake and interested in your training. No matter how skilled you are as a presenter and how many interest-maintaining ideas you implement, some trainees are still going to get sleepy in your seminars. How are you going to react? The first point you should consider is why it is happening. Try to remember that the average time an adult learner can go without a break is somewhere between 45 and 55 minutes. Class segments in school are usually 45 minutes, with lectures in college averaging about 50 minutes. For whatever reason, most corporate training curricula sched-ule a break every 90 to 120 minutes. This is not good and tends to put a lot of pressure on the presenter.

A second reason that trainees may be falling asleep is the plain and simple fact that they may be tired. Too often presenters' egos get hurt from working hard in the pit only to look up and see the whites of a trainee's eyes. It can be demoralizing as well as debilitating. What you need to remember is that some people may absolutely love what it is you are talking about and how you are presenting it. Unfortunately, they are tired. This could be due to time change adjustments, sleeping problems due to stress or unfamiliar surroundings, or any number of other reasons. Think back on your own experiences as a trainee. Were you ever fascinated with the topic and with the presenter but had trouble staying awake?

The real issue becomes how you are going to react. Hopefully, from your own experiences, you will be empathetic to those who are having trouble staying awake. It is not an insult, and it is not a signal to speed up. It is reality. You are not dealing with children. Gone are the days when a sleepy student was pelted with a piece of chalk or an eraser. This form of humiliation will most likely result in aggressive behavior from the trainee, and rightfully so. My hope is that sleepy trainees will inspire you to work even harder.

Now let's turn our attention to how to strategically work harder with trainees who are dozing off on you. To begin with, one classic technique is to move toward the sleepy trainee. It is important to note that I am not suggesting you call on him or her with the intent to embarrass. I am merely recommending you move near the sleepy trainee and perhaps increase your volume just a little bit as you continue your conversation with the audience.

Movement is effective in some situations with sleepy trainees; unfortunately, in other instances, it is not enough. When trainees are very sleepy, they will tend to snap to it as we brush by only to succumb to sleep again once we move away. When I was teaching flood insurance, this was a chronic problem for most of the trainers on staff.

A solution that I came up with then and still use to this day was the Thriller Chiller. The intent behind this idea was to assist those who were overly tired. If my moving toward these trainees was not enough to keep them awake, I would move to phase two. I would return to the lectern where I kept the Thriller Chiller—a pitcher loaded with ice water—pour some out into one of the paper cups I kept with it, and return to the pit. This time, however, I would not only brush by the offending trainee's seat, but I would subtly drop off the cup of water. The trick was never to break from the conversation I was having and to call absolutely no attention to what I was doing. The effort was and always is appreciated.

Summary

No presenter starts a seminar by making it instantly interesting. The good presenters aim to build interest throughout and generate excitement as they go. Alone, few of the ideas you have just read through will provide you with the level of interest most presenters desire, but in combinations, four, five, or six of the ideas in a module begin to add up and create interest. Before you know it, your trainees will be referring to you as the Thriller III.

Chapter 9

The Art of Effective Questioning

Getting Trainees Involved

What is it that makes one seminar jump while the one across the hall bumps? What is it that transforms ordinary curriculum into dynamic text? Finally, what is it that separates the great presenter from the good presenter? The answer lies in the presenter's ability to get the trainees participating and involved.

The best way of accomplishing this can be stated in one word: *questioning*. The title of this chapter suggests that becoming skilled in this area is the equivalent to mastering an art form. That is because effective questioning can bring even the most difficult text to life the same way an artist brings a blank canvas to life. As mentioned earlier, I am a firm believer that most conflict arising between presenters and trainees is initiated by the presenters. Additionally, I feel that one of the contributors to this problem involves questioning.

Types of Questions

When you're first examining the art of questioning, it is important to understand that, as a presenter, you can ask your trainees many kinds of questions. Each kind can be effective, depending on various criteria. So many presenters make the mistake of seldom using more than one kind of question within their training sessions. As you will see, there is a whole world of questions out there that will not only get people involved in the material being taught but will help to promote the kind of stimulating training environment that so many presenters search for.

FACT-BASED QUESTIONS

Let's start with the kind of question that is most often used in training today. A fact-based question is a question that has a right-and-wrong answer. A fact-based question is the kind of question that most people associate with a learning environment. As a matter of fact, because, once again, the only teaching models most of us have are school-teachers, most presenters will use fact-based questions within their training. This becomes perhaps the single biggest mistake presenters make when attempting to use questioning within their presentations. Guess which kind of question is the most dangerous to ask in a training environment? Murphy's Law strikes again! There are pros and cons to using this kind of question within your training, and I will be more than happy to examine both, but right now I want to emphasize that, when used improperly, fact-based questions can often do more bad than good . . . and they are often used improperly. Here are a couple of examples of fact-based questions:

PRESENTER: Which of the techniques are most commonly used?

or

PRESENTER: What are the proper steps, in sequence, to logging on to your computer?

One of the key goals any presenter must work toward is to create a stimulating training environment that is both participative and alive. You are attempting to conduct your training using adult learning principles to create such an environment. As a matter of fact, about 90 percent of this book is dedicated to allowing you, the presenter, to use proven techniques to assist you in putting on the most informative and fun training programs imaginable. Fact-based questions can undo a lot that has already been done. Why? Because fact-based questions put trainees on the spot in front of the rest of the class. One thing you do not want to create within your training is a threatening environment. When trainees feel threatened, they tend either to stop participating or to become aggressive toward the presenter. Remember the last time you did not know an answer in front of the rest of the class? Your reaction to being put on the spot and possibly embarrassed will vary depending on your personality. It is hard to predict exactly what this reaction might be, but chances are it will not be positive.

Up to now, it may appear as if I am not much of a fan of fact-based questions. The fact of the matter is, there are times within training and for certain types of courses where fact-based questions are necessary. Technical courses, for instance, require trainees to learn definite right-or-wrong responses. Many of these programs are computer based, and the funny thing about computers is that a computer is not interested in your opinion. The answers provided are either right, or they're wrong. In addition, fact-based questions are often quite effective during review sessions at the end of modules. My only concerns about fact-based questions are that they are often overused and can intimidate. Also remember that if you are going to use fact-based questions effectively, you should study up on some of the techniques recommended later in this chapter.

OPINION-BASED QUESTIONS

The second most frequent kind of question asked within training is opinion based. As the term suggests, this type of question does not have a right-or-wrong response. It is a safer kind of question to ask a group of trainees whom you do not know because of the decreased chances of putting anyone on the spot. Sometimes this type of question can be a little frustrating for presenters, because you must remember the basic principle that states "Everyone is entitled to his or her own opinion." Clearly stated, you are not allowed to tell someone his or her opinion is wrong, Some examples would be:

PRESENTER: What is your opinion of this technique?

or

PRESENTER: How do you feel about this type of training?

The only disadvantage to using opinion-based questions within your training is that often trainees' responses will lack substance. By this, I mean you are often simply asking trainees how they feel. They are not necessarily using any of the information that you have given them to formulate a response. I often think of opinion-based questions as a way to take a temperature reading within the seminar. This type of question will allow you a small peek at what the trainees are thinking, but probing for too much more defeats the whole purpose of this kind of question. You can gather additional information by using a couple of other kinds of questions that are discussed below.

The advantages of opinion-based questions are simple. First, and foremost, they help reduce anxiety within the training room. Once a presenter demonstrates the fact that no opinions will be openly challenged, trainees begin to participate. The old saying "Walk before you run" certainly pertains to this situation. I am in no way suggesting that you ask nothing but opinion-based questions throughout your training. I am saying, however, that early on in training, opinion-based questions, used strategically like icebreaker exercises, are terrific for preparing a seminar for active participation.

Another advantage to opinion-based questions centers around the personalities in your training room. The faster you can figure out the types of trainees you are working with, the better you will be able to appeal to their learning styles. Opinion-based questions allow trainees to express themselves freely. That gives you the opportunity to determine attitudes, interests, and personality types in your training room.

COMPARISON-BASED QUESTIONS

Now that you have reviewed the two most common kinds of questions, let's look at some types of questions that are not used as often. As the name might indicate, a comparison question asks trainees to examine similarities and differences of the topic in question. Comparison-based questions are similar to opinion-based questions but require more of a response from trainees. Typically, the response is somewhat opinion-based, but it is often lengthier and more substantial. A couple of examples of this type of question are as follows:

PRESENTER: Based on what you have learned so far, how would you compare the educational approaches used in your school days with some of the approaches recommended in this course?

or

PRESENTER: Given the current method of accessing information for the customer and the automated method that has been demonstrated for you today, how would you compare the two?

This kind of question is more challenging to trainees and rarely can be answered in a word or two. Once you have asked a comparison-based question, you can often count on some sort of discussion within the seminar. The only danger in asking comparison-based questions once again involves your timing. I do not recommend asking a question of this complexity until the trainees have settled in and gotten to know you. Once this has been accomplished, this kind of question begins to create a nice bridge between feel-good, opinion-based questions, and work-harder, case history–based questions.

CASE HISTORY–BASED QUESTIONS

Perhaps my favorite of all questions that can be asked within a training environment is the case history–based question. The disappointing reality is that it is also the most seldom used of the kinds of questions recommended. A case history–based question requires trainees to think on their own by providing a scenario without a conclusion. Trainees are then asked to provide a solution based on the information that has been taught so far. Let me give you a couple of examples:

PRESENTER: Let's say you were set to give your first training seminar. Everything appeared in order until you noticed that on the schedule, the time committed to your training had been increased from one hour to two hours. Given the points we have covered so far, what strategy would you use to lengthen your training without wasting trainees' time with unimportant filler?

or

PRESENTER: Aren't interactive skills wonderful? Suppose the next phone call you received came from an irate customer whose first words to you were to suggest you not use any damn interactive skills or other such foolishness and solve his or her problem . . . now! What approach would you take with this type of customer, and why?

As you can see, case history–based questions require a lot more work from trainees. Picking up where the comparison-based question leaves off, now trainees must use not only the skills that you have taught but some of their own intuition as well. This is a tremendous kind of question to use when trainees are riding along taking in what is said without question.

The only real danger in using case history–based questions is the risk that a trainee may have no idea of an answer. At this point, you have come full circle from a one-dimensional, fact-based question that requires regurgitating memorized information to a trainee who is thinking and breathing on his or her own two feet. As far as suggestions for working out some of the negatives to asking questions, these factors can be addressed in the "Techniques for Asking Questions" section later in the chapter.

Preparing and Coaching Trainees to Answer Questions

In deciding what kinds of questions you may want to use within your training, you may want to consider a few suggestions. First, as far as your *timing* is concerned, try to spend some time learning the various personalities within your room. Until you do, try holding back on asking the fact-based questions. For example, Monday morning is not a good time to begin firing these high-pressure questions at your trainees. Give the class some time, and learn which types of trainees you have in your room. Then you can more carefully introduce the kinds of questions that are most appropriate for the personality types you are training.

The second preparation you must make when preparing to use fact-based questions within your training involves *coaching*. Take a proactive position right now, and anticipate that some trainees are not going to know the correct answer. Do not wait for this to happen in front of the entire class. Take my word for it, it will. What are you as the presenter going to do?

Remember, when a trainee is stuck or having difficulty with your question, it is not only the trainee who is uncomfortable. The other trainees in the seminar feel uncomfortable as well. Once I took a course (a Presentation Skills program of all courses), where a trainee was asked a question he did not know the answer to. The presenter waited and waited and waited. The other trainees, sensing the embarrassment of the trainee who could not answer the question, began raising their hands in an effort to help out. The presenter insisted they put their hands down and allow the trainee in question to respond. After at least two agonizing minutes, the presenter finally moved on. This one situation created an air of anxiety and tension that never left the seminar. It was apparent that all that was accomplished by putting this trainee on the spot was limiting the flow of further questions or responses. As with most seminars, trainees began nervously to second-guess themselves and shut themselves out from active participation.

Forcing responses out of students may work in television dramas, but it does not work when training adults. It would be unfair to say that trainees will no longer participate in front of the class; they probably will. But you may not like the form of participation you receive. Unfortunately, the reaction will probably come in the form of an attack somewhere down the road.

When a presenter embarrasses a trainee in front of a class, the trainee often retaliates much later. Trainees do not want to appear argumentative or negative so they often wait for the right opportunity. When they see it, the presenter gets it right between the eyes. Maybe it is a controversial point. Maybe it is an unpopular stance that you the presenter must take. Maybe you simply misplace a handout. Rest assured, this sniper you have created, or perhaps another trainee who sympathizes with the individual who was attacked, is waiting to "pounce." Often we as presenters are left wondering "Gee, what got into him?" It could very well be that our own insensitivity and rudeness created this situation.

I cannot emphasize enough how important your sensitivity to your trainees is. With questions, you have a rare opportunity to prove to the class what you have been preaching all along: This is a safe environment where your input is taken seriously and highly regarded.

Knowing that despite the disadvantages, you will still need to ask fact-based questions, prepare yourself to coach all responses that are necessary. Try to keep rewording and subtly feeding more of the answer you are looking for. Your conversation may sound something like this:

PRESENTER: What kind of question do you use more often in your technical training-type courses . . . Danny?

TRAINEE: Uh . . . um . . .

PRESENTER: Remember, it was the type of question that had a right-and-wrong response.

TRAINEE: Oh, well that would be . . . uh . . .

PRESENTER: Based on . . .

TRAINEE: Facts! Fact-based questions.

PRESENTER: Excellent!

In addition to this technique, it is by no means inappropriate to move the question to another volunteer. This approach may be helpful, depending on the personality of the trainee being questioned and the cohesiveness of the class.

Sometimes trainees will not hesitate at all. As a matter of fact, they will proudly and confidently give you the wrong answer with a big smile. Here too, the subtle approach can spare a trainee from unnecessary embarrassment. Try to find something, anything that may be close to your answer, and then simply fix the rest of the response. Here is an example:

PRESENTER: What kind of question do you use more often in your technical training-type courses . . . Jessie?
TRAINEE: Definitely the opinion-based questions.
PRESENTER: What is your reasoning behind this answer?
TRAINEE: Simple. Everyone has an opinion, and in this type of training, finding out their opinions would be very helpful.
PRESENTER: You make a good point. We certainly cannot go wrong finding out an individual's opinion in any type of training we conduct. You may also want to consider fact-based questions to ensure that trainees have learned the correct processes. Good answer.

Another example of the compassion I am referring to can be borrowed from an old sales technique. When a customer has misunderstood a point the salesperson has made and is objecting to it, rather than risk egos being hurt, the salesperson may simply use a process called "feel, felt, found." The idea is to gently nudge the person from the misunderstanding without making him or her feel foolish. The "feel" portion of your answer does just that. The "felt" portion of your answer adds empathy, and the "found" portion gently provides your trainee with the correct information. Putting it all together would sound something like this:

PRESENTER: What kind of question do you use more often in your technical training-type courses . . . Jessie?
TRAINEE: Definitely the opinion-based questions.
PRESENTER: You know, that's kind of interesting you say that. A lot of people *feel* the same way you do. If they are going to ask questions,

they want to start slowly with those opinion-based questions and work their way up. I *felt* the same way myself when I first started to conduct technical training courses. Strangely, what we *found* was that for technical training, often the best approach centers around fact-based questions to ensure that trainees have learned the correct processes.

With either of these two examples, do not worry that you may not be clearly communicating the exact, textbook response in this particular case. As I mentioned earlier, adults learn by repetition, and this answer is a prime candidate to not only be repeated but cleaned up as well. In some cases, it is also a classic example of perhaps not quite winning the battle but eventually winning the war.

Techniques for Asking Questions

So far we have looked at different kinds of questions that you can use within your training sessions and ideas involving participation and coaching. Now I would like to turn your attention to various techniques for delivering or using these questions. It would seem logical to learn more about who is in your training room and try to figure out the best kinds of questions to ask of your seminar, but the question that still needs to be answered is "How?" The truth of the matter is that although you should give a lot of consideration to the kinds of questions used within your training, you should give just as much, if not more, attention to how to ask them.

GUIDED TECHNIQUE

One of the most common techniques used by presenters in asking questions is a guided question. Guided questions are aimed directly at trainees, giving you complete control over who is going to answer the question. A key strength to using guided questions lies in the control it gives the presenter when working with seminar participants. Many individuals simply will not participate unless a question is guided directly at them. In addition to this, there are other trainees who will attempt to answer *every* question unless the question is guided away from them. Guided questions allow you to choose who will answer the question.

Unfortunately, guided questions are not without risk. This approach can be viewed as somewhat threatening if overused and can also inhibit the potential for spontaneous participation. The good news is that the biggest problem with this questioning approach can be easily avoided with a little discipline on your part. You see, what almost all presenters do when they ask a guided question is start off by addressing the trainee who will be asked the question. Sounds somewhat logical. The question may sound something like this:

PRESENTER: *Danny*, given the skills you have just learned and the text provided, what would you do if there was no system administrator to help you through the process just taught and an irate customer called wanting immediate action?

Here you have a rather classic case history question using a guided technique. Looks harmless enough, doesn't it? The problem is that the moment the trainee's name was introduced in this question, the trainee tuned in . . . and the rest of the trainees tuned out. In this example, the typical trainee most likely hears "Danny, given the skills," and left sometime soon after to dream about the next scheduled break. Seems like kind of a waste for such a well-thought-out question. A much more effective approach would be as follows:

PRESENTER: Given the skills you have just learned and the text provided, what would you do if there was no system administrator to help you through the process just taught and an irate customer called wanting immediate action [pause], *Danny?*

Formulating the question and then pausing will allow all the trainees to mentally work toward an answer. Then guide the question to the student you select. Also, the pause lets you look at the group and choose someone who shows a sign of recognition. This may very well help you to avoid the embarrassment of choosing someone who is without a clue. Looks easy? The next seminar you attend, watch how often this technique is used. I will give you fair warning; you will seldom see it. The only thing easy about this technique is how easy it is to forget. Using this approach will allow you to involve all your trainees in the questions you ask. With some practice, it becomes a snap.

OVERHEAD TECHNIQUE

Just as common as the guided technique in delivering questions is the overhead technique. You are basically allowing anyone in the seminar to take a shot at answering them. One key advantage to using this approach is called "Day One." Day One represents the beginning of any training that you may conduct. The trainees are typically a little tense, and it is your job to begin to create the type of environment that is conducive to learning. Icebreaker activities help, and so does the demonstration of a nonthreatening environment. Overhead questions also allow you to begin to learn about the various personality types within your seminar. Overheads allow those who want to talk a chance to talk and those who need a little more time a little more time. You will begin to get an insight into the nature of your trainees by observing how they react to the overhead, allowing you to carefully strategize the kinds of questions you intend to use. As you begin to demonstrate the safety of participation, the room begins to thaw.

The actual delivery approach for overhead questions can be done a couple of ways. Sometimes if you just ask the question and extend your arms out, trainees will assume the question is aimed at anyone who wishes to respond. Of course, you may wish to not be quite so cute and may try asking a question similar to the following example:

PRESENTER: Can anyone tell me at least two of the four behavioral styles that were discussed earlier?

or

PRESENTER: What are at least two of the four behavioral styles that were discussed earlier today [pause], anyone?

The second approach is recommended once the class has had a chance to warm up. It allows all the trainees to begin to work out a solution, not knowing if you will guide the questions toward them and ask them to answer it. The only real disadvantage to the overhead approach to questioning arises around total participation. Some trainees just will not volunteer an answer unless a question is guided directly toward them. Just remember to be patient. Often trainees who do not appear to be involved may just need a little more time. There is no law that says everyone must participate on day one by 9:00 a.m. If you give these trainees some time, you may find that they too will participate and get involved with questions delivered overhead to the class.

Relay Technique

Another technique that you can use when working with questions is the relay technique. This approach involves the presenter asking a question of the class and then simply moving that same question around the room getting input from other trainees. This technique is particularly effective when combined with case history– or opinion-based questions. Here is an example:

Presenter: Let's say for a moment that you are approaching a training situation where you know there are going to be some unhappy trainees. What are some of your thoughts regarding your initial participation [pause], Jessie?

Jessie: Well, I think I would probably make an attempt to figure out, before the training is to begin, what their particular grievances are.

Presenter: Good idea. How would you approach this situation [pause], Artie?

With the relay technique, you can ask the same question of each trainee. You benefit by getting to know the trainees and by keeping them involved. Trainees benefit by being exposed to a variety of opinions and solutions to a given question.

Reverse Technique

The final technique that you can use when questioning trainees is called a "reverse." The reverse technique actually is initiated by the trainees. Often many presenters are totally unaware of the opportunity at hand. This is what happens. A trainee asks the presenter a question, and before you can say "Bob's your uncle," the presenter has answered it. Newer presenters often gobble up questions, because of their desire to achieve some credibility. What a wasted opportunity! Here is a chance to really get one of your trainees thinking about an issue relating to your curriculum, and it is gone. Add to that the fact that there are many shrewd trainees out there who will pick up on your weakness and try to get you to do their jobs for them. A reverse approach solves all of these problems by putting the question right back into the trainee's lap. Here is an example of how it may sound:

TRAINEE: Uh, excuse me. What do you think is the best approach for us to use in our role-plays tomorrow morning?

PRESENTER: That is a good question. What approach do you most strongly favor?

TRAINEE: Well . . . I . . . uh, thought maybe the strategic tactical approach.

PRESENTER: What benefits do you think could be gained by that tactic?

TRAINEE: I could use both processes taught and still be in a position to think on my feet if I was not receiving the kind of information anticipated.

PRESENTER: Excellent! I could not agree more. Allowing yourself the flexibility to react in the role-play should in fact be a major factor in the approach you select. Good job.

This response could have just as easily been relayed to even more attendees in the seminar to hear their responses. The key is that presenters should not waste chances like these to get trainees more involved in the curriculum. You will also notice something else that is important when you're using this technique. In the example, you will notice that the presenter adds support to the response where necessary and in a way puts the finishing touches on the trainee's answer. Some presenters will argue that they do not want to appear as if they do not know the correct answer. They probably get that feeling from watching some other poor presenter nervously try to get at a response from the class to a question they obviously do not know the answer to. Once a response has been given, the presenter nervously nods and moves on to another topic. I will not lie to you and tell you that I have been 100 percent sure of the answer to every question I have relayed or reversed back to the trainees. I will tell you that I will use the resources available to me in the room, which is often other trainees, and offer my opinion in support of their responses.

Reversing questions is a wonderful approach to helping trainees to think on their own. Many trainees have strong opinions about questions they pose to the presenter, and it is simply safer and easier to have the presenter answer the questions for them. Certainly not for every question, but in many situations utilizing this technique provides a gold mine of an opportunity for you to gain participation within the seminar and help trainees to think for themselves.

Do's and Don'ts of Questioning

Whether it is asking questions of or receiving questions from your trainees, there are some definite dos and don'ts. Let me finish our discussion about the art of questioning by presenting you with an outline of each, starting with the dos.

Have a Positive Attitude toward Questioners

For starters, do maintain a positive attitude when addressing questions generated by your trainees. Too many presenters make the mistake of appearing defensive when handling questions from the class. Unfortunately, questions often are viewed as something bad when just the opposite is true. To begin with, questions from the trainees show interest in the material taught as well as an environment conducive to a discussion. This type of atmosphere should be cherished by the presenter, not feared. Truth be known, in my years of delivery under fire, I have seen just about everything. With these experiences behind me, I can honestly say there is not much that will rattle me . . . except the absence of questions. Nothing is worse than talking and talking and talking and then being faced with dead silence when searching for questions from the class. That makes even Rob a little uncomfortable. Remember also that usually when one trainee has a question regarding something that is being covered in the seminar, other trainees have the same question. Often the question posed to the presenter is more the tip of the iceberg than the exception to the rule. With this in mind, you should be flattered to get questions and carefully explain those areas of information that are unclear for the benefit of the kind soul who asked the question as well as for the rest of the class.

Know Your Material

Do try to know your material as well as you can. The reality of corporate training is that there is always going to be a first time, a new seminar, or an unrealistic time schedule. Do the best you can within reason, and try to anticipate the more difficult areas by looking over your notes. This will give you added confidence and credibility.

An example of this comes from my insurance days. When I sold insurance for the New York Life Insurance Company, I was considered a pretty good group health insurance agent. I must admit, I do not think I knew that much more than my competition, but I was conscious of one subtle difference. When I was learning about health insurance, I became totally confused (along with the rest of the public) with an area of the policy called "preexisting conditions." This part of the policy dealt with what would and would not be covered in the event the insured switched policies and had already received treatment for an illness. Within this provision, there were rules dealing with 30, 60, and 90 days that dramatically affected coverages and liabilities. Now do not worry, I have no intention to try to explain this to you any further, but it was a critical issue for the insured. I studied and studied this provision, anticipating questions in that area, and I was not disappointed. I was one of the few agents who had a clear understanding of this area, and I was able to explain it to others. This ability translated to increased credibility and, in that profession, increased income.

UNDERSTAND THE QUESTION

Make sure you understand the question being asked of you. With the typical presenter's mind moving at a highly accelerated pace, it is quite easy to misinterpret the question being asked. Occasionally I am guilty of this error in judgment. You see, when a presenter is attempting to control the training room, many issues are swirling around in his or her mind: what is being said, what key points need to be made, what is coming up, personalities and timing, to mention just a few. Therefore, it is extremely easy to hear a question and mentally jump to a point that you have been wanting to make. To complicate matters a little more, it is not uncommon for trainees to ask rather vague questions. Under fire, in the pit, it is the presenter's responsibility, not the trainee's, to make sense of what has been asked. It is rather embarrassing to answer a question, see a confused expression on the trainee's face, ask if that answered the question, and hear: "No, not really." Oops! Here is an example of how easy it is for a situation like this to occur:

TRAINEE: What is a good way to apply this technique?
PRESENTER: That is a good question, I'm glad you asked. This technique can be applied on just about any customer as long as you are working with the decision maker. That is a topic I want to discuss now. Does that answer your question?
TRAINEE: Uh, no, not really. All I wanted to know was how you get started in learning the technique itself.

A recommended technique to avoid this embarrassment is called "restating." Restating simply involves repeating the question asked by the questioner to confirm your understanding of what was asked. Once the trainee agrees to the restated question, you have the green light to go with an answer. An example of restating would look like this:

TRAINEE: What is a good way to apply this technique?
PRESENTER: Okay, the question has been asked "What is a good way to apply the technique that has been taught?" I assume you are referring to customer applications, is that correct?
TRAINEE: No, just some ideas to help us learn the concept.

Another benefit to restating the question is to ensure that all the trainees were able to hear what was asked. For trainees, it can be frustrating to be sitting in a training room, hear someone on the other side of the room mumble a question that they cannot make out, and hear the presenter say, "Boy, I'm glad you asked that one! Tuesdays and Thursdays without fail." Many trainees will not ask what was said; they will simply sit back and stew. A few minutes, an hour, a day later, the presenter gets sniped by the trainee who could not hear and wonders, "What's that guy's problem?"

Making sure you understand the question may appear obvious, but it is well worth your time. In a small seminar, with a trainee who speaks clearly and loudly and words his or her question so that there can be no confusion, do not worry about the formality of restating and clarification. Make that decision the exception to the rule, however, and remember, in a large training environment or where the acoustics are bad, you have no choice but to restate and clarify. Consider this technique an insurance policy to handling questions effectively.

ASK QUESTIONS IF NONE HAS BEEN ASKED

It always amazes me to sit around a table of trainers at lunchtime after the first day of training and hear some of the stories: "I've got the dullest group of slugs you have ever seen," or "Boy, you could hear a pin drop in my classroom this week." Not wanting to disturb the slightly large ego of most trainers, I usually quietly ask these trainers if they are asking questions of their trainees, to which I get the standard answer, in stereo: "Of course!" Earlier in this chapter, you read about the different kinds of questions that you can ask and the techniques for asking them. What I failed to mention is that sometimes trainees are not ready for even the simplest opinion question. Oh, they will certainly answer it, but there still may be an air of apprehension hanging over the room. Your job as a presenter is to get rid of the uneasiness trainees feel and promote interaction. In this case, you do need to ask questions of the trainees if none has been asked. The difference now is that, as with other issues relating to training, you may have to crawl before you walk and walk before you run.

Let me give you an example. You have a group of trainees who, as fate would have it, are all rather quiet. There are a couple of trainees who would normally talk, but not until a couple of others were speaking first. There you have it, a standoff. Many presenters will ask a few simple overhead opinion questions, get no takers, direct a question at someone, and try a couple of more times. Eventually, the presenters will resign themselves to the fact that there will not be much interaction, so here comes the lecture, full steam ahead. Why not back up one step and ask questions that really do not require answers? Here are examples of some questions designed to warm up trainees slowly:

Presenter: This concept was difficult for me the first time I saw it, how about you?
Trainees: (Grumbling, mumbling, and nodding collectively)

Not exactly a word, but I'll take it! That is what I call "crawling." Now let me show you what walking might look like:

Presenter: Of the three items you see before you, which do you think will be most helpful in assisting you in your everyday duties?
Trainee: (Eyes averted, looking down or away) Number two.

Now you have them walking, by giving you real words. A few more questions like these, and you should have them dancing with sentences in no time. Then it is more appropriate to ask the more involved opinion questions.

Bad combinations of trainees? There really is no such thing. The presenter may need to work harder, however, to bring some trainees out of their shells. The results you witness within your training rooms will certainly be rewarding.

Handling questions from your trainees properly provides many rewards: Increased credibility, opportunities to involve other trainees, and the creation of a training climate conducive to the sharing of ideas are just a few. There are some pitfalls that must be avoided, however. Let's now turn our attention to some of the negative approaches to handling questions.

Don't Discount or Discourage Questions

Perhaps the single most destructive act a presenter can inflict on a seminar is to discount questions that are asked. Discouraging trainees from asking questions is not something most presenters actually plan, but nevertheless they are often guilty of it.

One of the most blatant examples I can provide occurred when I was a student attending a technical writing class at a local university. There was little to no interaction in a class of 20 that met once a week. Now, there are those who would say that there is not a lot of need for interaction in a technical writing class, but I would strongly disagree. The class was three hours long, with most of the students remaining conscious for about the first two hours. I guess you could say that it was the responsibility of the student to stay awake or risk a failing grade, but as you know, I come from the school of thought that believes you motivate students in other ways. I would also have loved to have heard what the other students were working on and the obstacles they were facing, but without any interaction, the class remained full of strangers.

On one magic night, about eight weeks into the class, a strange thing happened. At first, I did not know exactly what it was, and then I recognized it. A student was raising his hand. We looked back and forth from the teacher to the student, nervously waiting for the teacher to turn around. Finally, in midsentence, the teacher turned around and, with an indignant leer, stopped talking and stared at the student for what seemed like an eternity. Mercifully, the teacher then asked the student what his question was. As the student anxiously began to ask his question, the teacher's face began to register a kind of disgust. (I quickly decided I liked the leer better.) Once the student finished his question, the teacher started her response with "I can't believe you asked that question. We just went over that a couple of minutes ago. Were you listening or just daydreaming again? The answer is . . ."

To this day, I still do not know the answer that was given. I was too mortified with the teacher's response to care. I do remember that when the teacher finished answering the question, she then asked if there were any other questions. There were no more questions that night, nor were there any more for the remaining eight weeks of the course.

The ramifications of discounting student questions are very real. You run the risk of creating a potential sniper trainee, alienating a class, and destroying your chances for group interaction. I am one who does not like to dwell on the negatives, so let me relate a story that deals more with the positive aspects of not discouraging questions.

When I was a training consultant, I once assisted in a listening seminar that an acquaintance was giving. I did not know much about the seminar, but for a waiver of the $100 admittance fee, I agreed to help with registration at the door. I also knew that my friend had a good reputation as a presenter. The one characteristic I had been told to look for was his ability to relax his audiences and get them to participate. As I helped to seat the last of the 175 participants, a sly smile appeared on my face. "So in less than seven hours, this guy is going to get this mass participating? Fat chance," I thought. Sure enough, as he began his presentation, he mentioned his desire for the audience to feel comfortable, ask questions, and participate. Sure! Twelve people, maybe; 175, forget it. Then, after a rather quiet first half hour, it happened. It started innocently enough with one hand being raised in a sea of humanity. The presenter quickly finished what he was saying, smiled warmly, and asked the trainee for his question. What happened next is something I will never forget.

Trainee: When you mention sound and different noises, is it kind of like a butterfly and a train?

The rest of the audience found this question strange, and a confused murmur filled the room. My sharp professional speaker's eye caught a subtle leg buckle of the presenter as he reached to pull on his chin in thought. In a split second, the presenter's smile reappeared, as he remarked:

Presenter: Well, when you consider that a butterfly makes a quiet sound, much like our own communication, and the train makes a loud sound, much like many of the day-to-day distractions we are all faced with, then, in fact, they are very much related. I guess it becomes a matter of which will be more likely to win. I am rooting for the butterfly, and maybe some of the ideas we discuss today may help us all to deal with the trains in our lives. Excellent question, thank you!

The trainee who asked the question smugly nodded to the answer that was given to his question and rather arrogantly sat back down in his seat. I looked around the room. Many of the trainees were peering off in a confused kind of daze, but this soon changed. The glazed expressions were replaced with almost universal understanding. The message the presenter sent was clear. No question would be rejected. At that moment in the seminar, you could see the trainees thinking, "If he got away with that one, then I have a question."

A transformation had occurred. The seminar continued with active participation from a crowd most presenters would consider impossible to warm up. To this day, I have given serious consideration in my larger seminars to actually planting a trainee to ask one or two questions that are off the wall. Fortunately, when the numbers are that large, chances are a plant will not be necessary. You should have the real McCoy. You see, the last time you taught a course and someone strange appeared out of nowhere, you may have been lucky. You just did not know it!

The skill demonstrated in the following example is a technique every presenter should practice. Many times you will be in a position where you are not receiving the question or response you are looking for. It is critical to make the questioner feel that his or her participation was worthwhile. It therefore becomes necessary for you to find value in whatever the trainee is offering. Sometimes, as in the example just illustrated, doing so can be quite a challenge. The rewards make it all worthwhile. Trainees know when you show empathy to them or their fellow trainees. Sometimes it almost becomes a question of whether the glass is half full or half empty.

A good illustration of this type of exchange recently came up in a program I was conducting. The question I asked related to a customer service issue the trainees were discussing. They had just watched a tape showing a rental car clerk being somewhat rude to a customer. I asked the class if they felt the problem they had just witnessed was a people problem or a process problem. The response that I was looking for was a process problem. The point I wanted to bring out was that 85 percent of the problems of this nature are process problems and 15 percent are due to people. Here was our exchange:

PRESENTER: From the video you just watched, do you think this problem was a people problem or a process problem?

TRAINEE: A people problem, for sure!

PRESENTER: I see. Well, you are in good company because a lot of people feel the same way you do. Fifteen percent of the time you are right. What's really surprising is that 85 percent of the time it is a process problem.

To me, it is most challenging to turn a response around when it is so emphatically stated incorrectly. Try not to put yourself in that type of position and avoid catch questions altogether. Let me illustrate this point with another example from that same quality class. I used to ask students to finish this statement: "If it ain't broke . . ." The response that I was looking for was really "fix it better," but that is not what I received. Often I would get trainees who would not only finish the statement with the immortal "don't fix it," they would go on to sing the praises of this statement's wisdom. Why put yourself in that position? I still ask that question in the quality class I teach, only I changed it a bit. I now say "Finish this statement, but let me warn you now to be careful. 'If it ain't broke . . .'" With this fair warning to the class, I have not had a problem since. The trainees do not feel tricked, and the question becomes a fair one.

Finally, you may receive questions from trainees that are so far off the wall, that you cannot even relate them to anything that you have talked about. In that instance, the best statement I can recommend is to look at the questioner, pause purposefully, and say, "That is an excellent question, one I haven't even considered before. Let me work on it a bit and get back to you." It has not failed me yet, but make sure trainees have not read this book before using it.

DON'T RUSH TO FILL IN THOSE MOMENTS OF SILENCE

They say that time flies when you're having fun. Well, that can be true when conducting training as well. This feeling of speed can make a presenter susceptible to another problem that needs to be avoided. Do not become uncomfortable with moments of silence.

To begin with, these moments (due to all the fun you are having) are really shorter than you think. It is quite common to hear a presenter ask a class, "Are there any questions?" and about one one-hundredth of a second later say, "Good, let's move on." To the presenter, it seems as if he or she has taken a long pause, but to the trainees, that pause went by in a flash.

Often, when a presenter asks a class if there are any questions, initially the trainees will not offer any. The reason for this is simple. When the presenter is conducting training properly, most trainees are left thinking about what was just said. It takes a few seconds for them to digest the information and then pose a possible question. When a presenter moves on quickly without slowing to see what questions the trainees may have, the presenter is wasting a wonderful opportunity for interaction. By the way, this slowing down and listening for questions is easier said than done. I usually force myself to count (using my fingers behind the lectern) to eight.

If you need one more piece of evidence to slow you down, consider this little experiment I run in my Presentation Skills programs. I tell trainees of my recommendation to slow down. I then tell them that over the course of the week they are in town to take Presentation Skills, I will model what I am teaching and wait for questions. I tell them that I will ring a bell every time I receive a question after at least five seconds of waiting, reminding them that these are questions and discussions they would never normally hear. I bet them that the bell will ring at least 10 times within the week. That is one bet I have not lost yet.

Don't Worry about Questions without Answers

One of the biggest fears many newer presenters experience is of not knowing the answer to a question asked in a seminar. Although this fear may be somewhat illogical, it needs to be addressed just the same. I say it is somewhat illogical because when you consider the idea that one individual should know everything there is to know about a topic, it does seem rather ridiculous. We do not necessarily expect this from someone who is training us, but we do expect it of ourselves. Hogwash! Repeat after me:

I do not have to know everything about my topic. What I do know will be much more than what the vast majority of my students know.

When you are teaching a course, especially for the first couple of times, you may want to take a proactive approach to this issue. Rather than waiting to be stumped in a topic that is fairly new to you, try clearing the air while still in your overview with a statement similar to this one:

PRESENTER: . . . and as for the material that we will be covering, I am certain that I will be able to answer the vast majority of your questions. Of course, no one knows all the answers, including me, but I do know where I can get the answers. Therefore, what I do not know I will write down on this pad (or flip chart), and I will get you the answers by _____.

Before you start your training, make sure there is a contingency plan in place that will allow you to get answers to questions you cannot answer. This may mean someone you can call, a place you can go for the answers, or even another presenter who may have more experience with the subject matter in question. Whatever the solution, make sure you communicate this process to your trainees. This may mean answers by a certain time in the week. It could also mean a memo to all attendees clarifying issues that could not be addressed in the seminar.

By discussing this point at the beginning of training, before there are any problems, you will feel a tremendous weight lifted from your shoulders. You are not expected to know everything. Get rid of some potential anxiety and get that issue out in the open early. If a trainee is asking for your opinion, then make sure you emphasize it is just that, your opinion. If someone asks a question that requires a factual response, then answer the question just that way, factually. The critical point here is to *never*, under any circumstance, *make up an answer* to a question you are unsure of. This is the quickest way to destroy credibility that I know of.

Now, I believe I have made my point regarding this issue, but be forewarned. It is easier to violate the trainees' trust than you may think. Recently, a colleague told me about his experience teaching a course that he had taught many times before. A participant asked a question in an area that the presenter had not been questioned about before. What's more, he did not really know the answer. Before he could stop himself, he heard a voice take a guess at the answer. The voice did not indicate that this was a guess or an opinion; the voice stated the answer as a fact. The voice was his own! He told me it happened so fast that he almost threw a hand over his mouth, but it was too late and, besides, survival instincts began to take over. The major problem he was now faced with was attempting to sell this answer to the class while he thought of a way out of this mess.

Unfortunately, the saying "O, what a tangled web we weave when first we practise to deceive," was far too real. My friend believes that some of the trainees sensed his discomfort and his less-than-usual conviction when speaking on an issue, because every time he attempted to move on, he got another question from a trainee and another puzzled expression to go along with his new response. Apparently, he was in too deep to reverse his answer, so he did what any red-blooded presenter would do: He conveniently shut down further questions due to time, promised to revisit the issue later, and moved on with a nauseous feeling in the pit of his stomach. He told me that he did, in fact, revisit the issue the next day after getting the correct answer, and he told the students that they could consider the new response as a viable alternative. (He never exactly told the whole truth.)

His story gave me a new respect for not making up answers. As a presenter, your guesses will be interpreted as fact unless you state otherwise. It takes self-discipline to continuously tell the trainees what you do know and what you do not know.

When you really stop and think about it, are you not even a little skeptical spending 5 or 10 days with one presenter who knows *every* answer? I can understand that a presenter might know *most* of the answers, but *every* answer? I personally would begin to wonder. As strange as this may sound, there is one time I will not tell the truth within the training I conduct. On some occasions, I actually tell trainees I am unsure of a response to a question I know the answer to. I then go through the motions of confirming the answer through the designated channels and follow the process that the trainees and I established from the outset. This not only inspires *more* trust from the trainees in the answers they will be receiving but solidifies a lot of the responses already given. Remember, this is an acceptable lie in the name of good, honest training.

THANK TRAINEES FOR THEIR QUESTIONS

One last minor point I would like to make regarding handling questions from your trainees is a friendly reminder. Do not forget to thank the trainees for their questions. As emphasized throughout this chapter, receiving questions from participants benefits a seminar in many wonderful ways:

- ◆ It demonstrates interest from the trainees.
- ◆ It allows you, the presenter, some insight into the clarity of your message.
- ◆ It assists in keeping people interested in your topic.

To receive this type of participation is flattering, and you should continue to encourage it. One of the best ways I know to accomplish this is to get in the habit of thanking the trainees for their questions before major breaks, such as lunch and the end of the day. This little thank-you should help you to pick up where you left off in terms of predicted levels of participation.

Summary

It is hard to state in quantifiable terms exactly what makes a good presenter and what makes a great presenter. If I was forced to choose a couple of skills, however, questioning would certainly be one of them. Challenge yourself to ask more thought-provoking questions and use the techniques discussed to better manage the personalities within your seminars. I firmly believe that if you can master the key areas outlined in this chapter, you too will find the art of questioning a pivotal tool for your own personal success.

Chapter 10

Using Visual Aids

Years ago, when I decided to hang up my insurance sales shoes and become a trainer, I attended my very first Train-the-Trainer course. As I nervously entered the room, I began searching for my name tag. The trainees' list read more like a who's who from various Fortune 500 companies. With little to no training experience behind me, I was a walking sponge. The room was fairly quiet, with trainees fidgeting nervously with the training materials when the trainer entered the room. The room immediately fell silent. I was struck by the fact that the trainer made little to no eye contact as he headed for the overhead projector. Without a smile, without an acknowledgment, he flicked on the projector. A newspaper article that had been copied onto a transparency appeared. The headline read: "Expectations for Trainers in the Workplace to Decrease 75% by 1994." There was a moment of uneasy silence, which was soon broken by nervous laughter and finally conversation from all in the class. It seemed as if everyone was discussing the article and the ridiculousness of it when the trainer again moved into the pit, turned the overhead off, and began to speak. "Now that I have your attention," he said, "I want to start talking about the wonders of training." The four-day class was not yet 30 seconds old, and I already knew I was going to like the course and the trainer who was teaching it. That is an example of the potential of a well-thought-out visual aid.

Do your presentations *jump*? Up to now, we have spent a great deal of time talking about the *words* you are going to use in your training presentations. Now we will talk about how you can enhance those words with visual aids. Ask trainers about the importance of a well-prepared visual aid and they will sing its praises. Remember, 75 percent of what you learn comes from your sense of sight. The more visual aids you use, the more your trainees can retain.

So why are visual aids so often poorly used or not used at all? One reason is fear. There are risks you must take when using a visual aid. Fortunately, the rewards far outweigh the risks. The second reason comes more from our previous learning experiences. All of us, at some time in our lives, have witnessed a presenter who has had problems with the visual aids he or she intended to use. We swear to ourselves that it is not worth it.

Visual aids are just too vital to your training to avoid. You must use them to strengthen not only your trainees' retention but your own presentation as well. We'll take a look at presentation software and other high-tech options available in the next chapter. However, due to budget constraints and other factors, more traditional visual aids might be the only devices that are available to you. If you are going to use them, you need to use them correctly. With that in mind, the intent of this chapter is to explore the strengths, weaknesses, and ultimately the proper use of some of the most commonly used visual aids.

Flip Charts

The flip chart is a visual aid that just keeps hanging on. There's nothing flashy or splashy about this device, but it is the visual aid of choice for many presenters. When you see its strengths, you will know why. Let's first look at the weaknesses of the flip chart.

The first and most obvious weakness is the flip chart's message size. Depending on the shape and setup of your room, chances are that once your group goes over 50 participants, the flip chart will no longer be effective. For large groups, the flip chart is of little use.

Another major weakness of the flip chart is its inability to travel comfortably. I am not referring to working with blank flip charts. These can be rented onsite, or added to the cost of the training room you may be renting. I am instead speaking of prepared flip chart materials. Typically, flip chart work is prepared on heavier paper, allowing for the wear and tear of everyday use. This paper usually cannot be rolled and must be transported flat. If you frequently conduct training on the road, this visual aid is probably not for you.

The flip chart's final weakness can be traced to the markers being used. The problem that many presenters run into when using flip charts is messages bleeding through. Depending on the markers and paper that you use, you may see portions of your writing coming through to the next page, creating a ghostlike image. This can be somewhat distracting, not to mention wasteful because of all the unused paper.

With all the weaknesses of the flip chart out in the open, let me tell you why this visual aid is such a popular tool in corporate training. For starters, it can be used very spontaneously. When a presenter is struggling, the flip chart is often just the ticket to help answer a difficult question or clear up a confusing concept.

The affordability of a flip chart also helps make it an attractive choice of visual aid. Markers, pads, and stands are inexpensive to purchase. Even the cost of rental of such items when you're working on the road is negligible.

Perhaps the biggest strength in working with a flip chart is its positive perception by the trainees. For some unexplainable reason, flip charts carry with them an adult connotation when it comes to training. Why knock it?

Now that you have been shown both the weaknesses and strengths, let's focus on how you are going to use the flip chart properly. First, let's clear up the weakness of messages bleeding through. This can be accomplished two ways. If you insist on using heavier markers, you can staple the bottom corner of two flip chart pages together. This will allow you to turn the page without fumbling for two pieces of paper. Another suggestion (if you want to avoid waste) is to change markers. I particularly like the water-soluble markers called Vis-à-Vis. The advertised benefit of these markers is that they can be washed off a transparency. I like them because they do not bleed through a flip chart pad, and they are a little smoother to write with.

In terms of the words you are going to write, try to structure your writing using an outline format. In other words, you do not need to write down every single word. You may choose to use bullets and abbreviated English. A second suggestion is to watch the actual number of words you choose. I try not to use more than 12 words. The 12 words is a rule of thumb, not a law. When I am writing the expectations of a class or something that is more for my use than that of the class, I write more.

Finally, to use a flip chart properly, you need to consider your positioning. To begin with, you should have the flip chart in a location that allows all trainees to see it clearly. You should be positioned to the side of the flip chart, making sure you do not obscure the trainees' view. As with an actor on a stage, you should not be so far back as to upstage your visual aid, nor do you want to be in front of it. Ideally, the trainees should be able to see both you and the flip chart together and not be forced to choose. Position yourself on the side of the flip chart according to your dominant hand. In other words, if you are left-handed, try to stay on the left side of the flip chart. If you are right-handed, work on the right side of the flip chart. The idea is to try to keep your dominant arm from reaching across the flip chart and turning you away from the trainees.

As always, room assignment may put you in a position of working with what is there, but it is my hope that you will have enough control to set up your room in a way that best meets your needs. Considering the audience support by adult trainees, the flip chart may be the way to go for you.

Video

Video offers you the opportunity to introduce a lot of creativity to your training. Easy to embed right into your presentation software, motivational videos or even videos that are not directly related to your topic allow for a great deal of flexibility within your training. I attended a management training course once that used video brilliantly. The class was not really coming together, and there was little interaction or discussion. Then the presenter showed a segment from a movie called *Twelve Angry Men*. This old classic movie deals with the deliberations of a jury and the emotions that are brought out. The presenter related it to certain responsibilities that all of us had as managers, and the discussion was on.

A second benefit to using video within your training once again involves perception. Video allows you not only to see dramatizations of situations relating to your subject but to create them as well. You can accomplish this using a video camera, tablet, or smartphone, one of the most beneficial tools available in training. Despite what people might think and despite the appearance of an extra five pounds, the camera does not lie.

Regarding the proper use of video, you must get in the habit of testing the links before you use it. You must also check whatever equipment you are using early. When video does not work, it is not the kind of visual aid that you can repair quickly. Five minutes before your seminar begins is not the time to check your clips. Leave yourself enough time to take a stab at fixing the problem and then get a specialist in to help you.

When selecting a video, look for clips that are not too long: "Emphasize everything, emphasize nothing." Too many strong messages get diluted by clips that are just too long. Remember, video is a visual *aid*. Actual length can depend on several factors, such as the length of the seminar or topic relevance. Clips in the two- to four-minute range are good for most purposes.

Objects for Demonstrations

Sometimes you might find yourself bringing in different objects to show your trainees. This scene could resemble an adult show-and-tell. It seems harmless enough, but done improperly, some problems can arise. Objects tend to be a huge distraction if not handled correctly. Try to get out of the habit of allowing trainees to pass around your object during the seminar. Not only does it distract the individual who is looking at the object, it also distracts the next couple of trainees who are eagerly awaiting their turns.

Positioning is also an important consideration when you're working with objects. If you are going to show an object to your trainees, show it to all of them, not just a few fortunate souls. Avoid working one side of the room and showing any type of favoritism.

If you want to show an object to your trainees, start at one side and physically walk the object around to each person. If you are showing a particular piece or movable part, continue to repeat the action and verbiage for each couple of trainees. When you have made your rounds, inform the trainees that you will place the object in a certain area for them to come up and look at during the next break (a necessity for larger groups). This will allow you to keep the trainees involved and let them get a better look at the object if they so desire.

Pointers

I remember when I first decided that I was going to be a trainer. The dreams I had! The thrills, the challenge, the discipline, and, oh yes, the pointer. What trainer uniform could be complete without the pointer, loaded and ready for action? This, of course, was before I met with the reality of a pointer. Yes, if you are working a large room with a screen across the room, you will probably need a laser pointer. Otherwise, if I may say so in my delicate, opinionated way, forget it! Pointers are more trouble than they are worth. If you want to play a practical joke on a friend who is a trainer, give him or her a pointer right before he or she is set to present. It is nearly impossible for a presenter not to fidget with the pointer as he or she is speaking. Additionally, the pointer often becomes an unintentional weapon as the presenter wields it about the room, distracting those trainees who prefer their ears, eyes, and noses to remain unharmed. In short, pointers and pointer pens are good for the kids and are loads of laughs at parties, but this professional speaker would not wish one on my worst enemy.

Dos and Don'ts

Often, it's not the equipment that fails us, but our lack of understanding regarding how to work with the equipment being provided. Here are some simple dos and don'ts to be aware of.

WATCH YOUR SHOULDERS

Unless you are working in a large room, with monitors on the floor in front of you, often the only way to see your slides is to turn and face them. However, this turn can be a bit tricky. Too often when we make that turn, we turn our entire body and head. Try being aware of this and simply turn from the shoulders. No matter how hard you try, if you're trying to sneak a peek at your slide for your own reference, do it quickly, and try to make it look like you are drawing the audience's attention to that particular point on the slide.

WATCH YOUR BODY POSITION

When you are working in front of a small room, it's rather easy to remember to stay to the side of your screen. A blinding screen light will remind you if you forget. But in larger rooms, with big stages and elevated projectors, it's easy to walk right in front of the screen and not only avoid the bright light in your eyes, avoid blocking any information your audience is trying to see. That's because the screen is usually well above your head, and frequently projected from the rear. It's still often necessary to pick up a word, or gesture from the screen. To do this smoothly and to keep as much of your body as you can facing your audience, make sure you are standing to the side of the screen. This will let you work comfortably and keep your head facing the audience.

WATCH THOSE SPEAKERS

Watching a great presentation is like watching a great movie. The audience can be riveted by the message and get lost in the action. Imagine if you were watching a movie and someone all of a sudden hit an air horn. That would certainly get your attention. Well, being miked up and walking in front of a speaker can just about do the same thing. It's a feedback issue, and your local AV tech can *sometimes* help keep you out of trouble. My suggestion is to pace out the room during your mike check. Check all parts of the room for feedback, particularly near the speakers. Rather than cross your fingers and hope the AV tech has the problem solved or that you'll remember where your line is, put a piece of tape down to show you the line you cannot cross, and enjoy yourself.

DO NOT FORGET TO PRACTICE WITH THAT REMOTE

Most professional speakers carry their own remotes, but beware. When you are presenting in a larger room, with AV onsite, you often will not be allowed to use your own remote or your own laptop. AV personnel are not big fans of changing laptops over, so you'll be stuck with their remote. Advancing the slides is usually not a problem, but moving backward can be. Practice using the remote, understanding what buttons do what, and figure out what the unique range of the remote you are using might be.

DO NOT PREPARE TOO MANY SLIDES

The mistake of providing too much information plagues most speakers, and unfortunately this problem often spills over to the slides they produce. Too many slides are often used as a crutch, and create a lack of spontaneity for the speaker and a sense of boredom for the audience.

And if the problem of having too many slides isn't bad enough, usually those who suffer from this problem put too much onto the slides. Too many slides with too much information on them can bring even the best presentations down.

Do Not Forget to Show Up Early

Most professional speakers know to show up early, and most speaker's bureaus include a clause about showing up early in their contracts. The rule of thumb seems to be 60 minutes early. If you're delivering a small workshop and you're 100 percent in control of your AV, an hour should be enough. However, if you're speaking in a larger room and do not have control of the equipment being used, I'd suggest you get there early—*really* early! The best time to show up is when AV shows up, and that's usually around 6:00 a.m. This will give you time to work out the kinks because at 6:00 a.m., the room will not be crowded. Set up your equipment, test it, get comfortable with it, and go get a cup of coffee. You'll have plenty of time to relax.

Some Final Thoughts

In this chapter I have discussed the pros and cons of working with some of the more common visual aids. I have also provided some ideas on how to use them properly. I would like to leave you with two other reminders. The first deals with the amount of time you expose your trainees to your visual aids. I have a little motto concerning this very point: "Use it, then lose it." This means that when you are done showing your visual aid, get rid of it. You have control over where you want your trainees to focus. Try not to clutter up your message with visual aids that relate to earlier material. This is not to say that I do not favor strategically posting certain aids around the room. I am really referring to visual aids whose messages were delivered but not moved away or covered.

My final suggestion for working with any visual aid is to rehearse. Practice with the visual aid so its use offers you confidence, not concern. If you are going to mask or shield, rehearse. Visual aids will make a statement. Used improperly, the statement is negative toward the presenter. Used effectively, the statement is positive. Rehearse, follow the techniques outlined, and your experience with a critical training tool will be a rewarding one.

Summary

Over the years, no chapter has changed as much this particular chapter. Overhead projectors were replaced by 35mm slides, VHS players were replaced by imbedded video on large hard drives, and my Apple music library, and a small Bose speaker have replaced my trusted CD player. What has not changed is the effect visual aids have on an audience, from helping them learn, to helping sustain interest. The devices might change, but the need to incorporate these devices has not. Pick one that is right for you, practice with it, and you'll get those presentations to jump!

Chapter 11

Technology and Training

At first glance, when you look at corporate training, you would not think that the profession would be affected much by changes in technology. Let's face it: The most important tool a presenter owns is located in the human body. It's called the voice.

Since I first wrote this book, there have been few advances in vocal technology. However, that is not true of the other technologies that have filled the world of training.

In this chapter, I take a look at some of these new tools and measure the pros and cons of each. Please keep in mind that, like many of my other tips and techniques, what might be right for one presenter might be completely inappropriate for another.

The Technical Revolution

Oh, I know what you're thinking. "Where the heck has Jolles been? The technical revolution started years ago!" Well, that might be true, but its impact on the training world has been a much more recent development.

It's not that presenters didn't try to incorporate computers and other technology tools years ago; the tools just didn't work well and weren't very efficient. I can see a Xerox parallel to the emergence of technology in the world of training.

Few people actually know that Xerox credits itself as the real inventor of many items we depend on, such as the computer mouse, the windows operating system, email, and even the fax features you'll find in the most of the printers you buy to this day. Facsimile is a particularly interesting invention because once discovered it took another 30 years for us to use it as a way to transmit documents.

There were a number of problems. The first, and perhaps the most significant, dealt with perceptions. The public's perception was that a fax machine wasn't reliable. After all, how could a document really travel through the phone lines and reappear somewhere else? Study after study showed that people refused to believe it actually worked. They would double the costs of each transmission by calling the receivers on the other end to hear if their fax transmissions actually made it to their destinations. Ten years went by.

The second problem dealt with an ease-of-use problem. Nothing about the equipment that was being produced was intuitive to the user. The machines were difficult to understand and operate. Once again, fear of change got in the way, reared its ugly head, and 10 more years went by.

Another problem with the fax machines of the past was their size—what the office supply business calls "footprint." If you wanted to buy a fax, you needed a massive area in the office to place the monstrosity of a machine. For many, space requirements were a significant drawback to the world of faxing. Ten more years went by.

Yet the biggest obstacle of all was simply fear of change. The mail, courier, and phone seemed adequate. Why mess with what was already working? Fear of change reinforced all other objections to the fax machine.

Finally, times changed. The technology responded to its short-comings and improved. Thirty years of technology had passed, and finally our society was ready for fax technology to change our lives.

In the late 1980s, the sales of fax equipment not only broke through into our lives but represented one of the biggest automation booms in the history of technology. We were finally ready. Email had a faster ramp-up time but followed the same sort of technological crawl.

So now you're probably wondering, "What does all this have to do with seminars and workshops?" The parallels are similar. You've just read the computer revolution story in corporate training.

Actually, one of the most significant advances in training technology, the original PowerPoint software, has been around for quite some time too. It certainly was around in 1993 when I first wrote this book. The problem was, it was much like waiting for the birth of fax. It didn't take 30 years, but it did take about seven years before it was truly accepted.

To begin with, many had negative perceptions of this technology. Not only had we heard of reliability problems, but we had witnessed it firsthand. How many times can you remember watching someone have problems with LCD projectors in the middle of the presentation? Those images of fumbling around waiting for help are difficult to get out of our minds. Two years went by.

Fax technology had ease-of-use problems and so did the incoming training technology. We weren't facing the hook-up of a cable or two. We were facing a task that seemed as complex as the rewiring of an airplane cockpit. Two more years went by.

The fax had footprint problems, and so did the budding training technology. If you had a dolly to transport some of the projectors of the past, you could have some chance of keeping your back intact. "Large," "heavy," and "awkward" summed up products that were designed to impress audiences with the wonders of technology. Two more years went by.

Finally, as professionals facing fear of change, corporate trainers like me had no interest in using this technology. We laughed at its unpredictability, scoffed at the predictions of its use, and sneered at its claims of invincibility. We were terrified.

I had made a living using a variety of presentation aids as I bounced through my seminars. Of course, that variety included overhead projectors, slide projectors, flip charts, and an occasional videotape. As a matter of fact, when I left Xerox and went out on my own, I thought I really jumped on the technology bandwagon when I converted my flimsy little transparencies to 35mm slides. I had hit the big time. What more would a trainer need?

In other words, I would be a hypocrite if I didn't admit to you, my reader, that I struggled with my conversion to the array of training technology that is available to us. Ah, I might have been a little slow to convert, but it didn't take me long to begin to chant the immortal words that fill the minds of all who successfully go through change: "How in the world did I live without it?"

With that spirit in mind, let's look at the good, the bad, and the ugly when it comes to incorporating into your presentation the training technology that is available to you.

Presentation Software

When it comes to laptops, projectors, and other peripherals, I will present you with multiple choices and recommendations. When it comes to presentation software, you won't be as lucky. In my opinion, there are two real names to consider for presentation software, and those names are PowerPoint and Keynote.

In the presentation arena, both are dominant and deserve to be. 'Fessing up with full disclosure, I was a PowerPoint client when it was the only show in town, but I converted over to Keynote a number of years ago. Keynote follows the theme of most other Apple products. It has the unlikely combination of power and simplicity. If you want to build a presentation on your laptop computer, Keynote or PowerPoint is the answer.

Using the software to put together a presentation can be a difficult job for even the most seasoned, grizzled veteran of training. The documentation that supports the software package can be intimidating. I have no interest in trying to reproduce those fine pages of documentation, but I would like to provide you with a page or two of my own.

Step 1. Create the Presentation   The first thing you must accomplish is to write the words for your presentation. My suggestion is to forget all the bells and whistles of transitions and backgrounds and, quite simply, gut out your presentation. What do you want to say? How long do you have to say it in?

Remember the idea here is to keep it as simple as possible. Three or four lines per slide and a half dozen words per line are all that are necessary.

Figure 11.1 is a very simple example of a slide that follows the rules I just outlined.

Step 2. Select a Background   Once the information has been outlined in your presentation, the fun part begins. Whichever program you use, find the template you like, and you will be on your way.

Despite what many others say, with the power of projectors increasing dramatically by the day, just about any color you select will be seen clearly. Therefore, it becomes more a matter of taste than of anything else when you're making your choices. It stands to reason that

---

THREE RULES FOR USING
BACKGROUND PROBES

- **Use Open Questions**
- **Avoid Problems**
- **Play To Your Strengths**

FIGURE **11.1** Slide

you will want to stay away from yellow colors, but again, these decisions are fairly obvious.

Figure 11.2 is the same slide with a background added. As I've said many times before, it's not always *what* you say, but *how* you say it.

Step 3. Apply Slide Transitions Slide transitions are the program's way of saying, "How do you want the slides to follow each other?" This is a classic case of an easy question with a few too many answers. You can pick from blinds, box, checkerboard, and a host of other options. My suggestion is not to get too cute here. Experiment, find an effect you like, and stick with it. It's always easy to spot the presenters who are new to these programs. They are the ones who use multiple approaches to slides transitions.

To apply transitions to your slides, my suggestion would be to click on Edit in the pull-down menus and choose Select All.

Next, select the slide transition you prefer. The rest is self-explanatory.

Step 4. Text Animation Text animation is the program's way of saying, "How do you want the words to flow within the presentation?"

FIGURE **11.2**   Slide with added background

Once again, you will not be disappointed by the number of ideas that are available, but keep it simple.

To apply animation to your slides, my suggestion would be to click on Edit in the pull-down menus and choose Select All.

However, if you want to work on one slide at a time, just highlight the slide you want to work on, select the animation you like, and have a ball!

Step 5. It's Showtime!   Finally, it's time to look at your handiwork. Select Slide Show from the PowerPoint menus, or Play from Keynote. Each time you hit your spacebar, you will be advancing your show.

Step 6. Create a Notes Page   Many speakers don't do what I'm about to teach you, but it's my book, and I'm going to teach it! I feel that the notes page is one of the best features of presentation software, and it isn't used frequently enough.

The name may be one reason why it isn't used. The programs have an option for you to capture your notes to assist you in delivering your presentations. No speaker I know uses this feature to assist in the presentation; the notes are too small to read. Speakers usually overlook Notes pages.

Now let me tell you why I think you should use them. Notes pages are ideal as handouts for your participants. How often have you had a participant ask for a copy of your slides? Why not exceed expectations? How about a copy of your slides along with the text that supports those slides?

If your participants have a workbook, you will not need Notes pages, but if you have a shot at speaking engagements in front of large groups, as I do, they are perfect. I'm not giving a large group of participants a workbook for a one-hour talk. I can, however, offer them my notes. Figure 11.3 is a slide page with notes added.

Now you've killed two birds with one stone. First, you are appeasing those in the audience who want a copy of your slides. Second, you are providing your audience with a guide that should direct and clarify the nice-to-know information from the need-to-know information.

One other benefit to using the Notes page technique is a more attentive audience. If you have ever worked in front of an audience that appears lost in their note taking, this might be just the cure. In your opening overview, tell your audience what you have planned for them as a handout, then they and you can enjoy your talk. Now you will have an audience that is focusing on you and your message, not on taking notes on slides that keep zipping by.

That's a simplistic view of presentation software. Yes, you can insert pictures, animation, and your own voice, or put the presentation on an autotimer. The list goes on and on. What I've outlined here will not only help get your feet wet but will probably answer 90 percent of the questions you might have along the way.

Laptop Computers

Now that we have appropriate software to create your presentation, we need equipment on which to create and display it. When I was preparing to leave Xerox years ago, I read a lot of books to help me prepare . . . or so I thought. Many of the books seemed to contradict one another, *except* for one piece of information.

Simply put, *don't skimp on the computer.* There are many other areas in your profession where you can cut corners, but not with the computer.

■ **Delivery: The Art of Making Great Presentations** ■

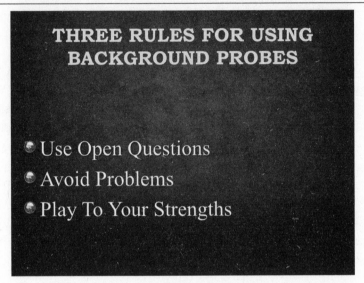

THREE RULES FOR USING
BACKGROUND PROBES

● Use Open Questions
● Avoid Problems
● Play To Your Strengths

Three Rules for Using Background Probes

The Research Stage has been called the easiest part of the selling process. Unfortunately, if this stage is not handled properly, the rest of the process becomes much more difficult. With this in mind, here are three rules that apply to the Background Probes that should make this stage a bit easier.

1. Use open questions. The whole idea behind this first stage of selling is for the customer to become comfortable with the seller and begin trusting that relationship. Remember, the more the customer speaks, the more he or she likes you.
2. Avoid problems. Too many salespeople begin to look for problems far too early in the selling process. Avoiding problems will help to continue to earn trust between seller and customer. Problems will come . . . in due time.
3. Play to your strengths. What do you hope the customer will want? This is a safe time to position many of your strengths to see if there is a potential for your customer to want some of these items.

FIGURE **11.3**　Slide page with notes added

For instance, many people are skeptical about the massive hard drives that come with most of the newer computers. My suggestion? Get the larger hard drive. As you develop your presentation skills, you may want to insert pictures or video clips. These items are space hogs, and you will be shocked at how quickly your massive hard drive will fill up.

This goes for speed, RAM, the works. I'm not saying you need to buy the biggest, baddest laptop that ever walked the face of the earth. What I am saying is, unless you want to replace this laptop in 12 months, don't take a shortcut. As your neighborhood Xeroid would say, "You get what you pay for." The problem is, you don't want to be in front of a large audience with a lot on the line when the truth hits home.

If you are not a computer nerd, do not worry. Most top-rated systems are ready to go, and these will provide you with more than enough speed, memory, and space to accomplish any presentation task.

Projectors

The laptop combined with presentation software might be dominating the training industry, but they are useless without something to project those images to the audience. The ease of importing pictures, adding graphs, and entertaining people with animations has changed a presenter's approach, and projectors are an essential piece of the puzzle.

When I first came out with my seminar book in 1993, I chose not to write about LCD technology. I wasn't being stubborn; the technology just wasn't ready yet. Four significant problems dogged the entire industry.

First, the equipment was very fickle. I watched presenter after presenter work with equipment that would not operate correctly during an important presentation. Companies like InFocus pioneered a number of approaches to simplify the setup of their projectors. Others followed, and the problems were pretty much eliminated.

Second, the equipment was very expensive. It's not exactly cheap now but, like the rest of the technology, the prices have come down and the products have improved dramatically.

Third, the products were big—very big. If you were working in a training facility, you were okay, but if you were training on the road, you had a problem. Now product size and weight has been cut dramatically, eliminating that objection.

Size is a critical issue to Road Warriors, because most of us who train on the road will not be parted with our projectors. I'm not giving an expensive projector to Baggage Claim to be tossed under the plane. That projector is staying with me. Today's projectors not only fit overhead, but they will fit right in your laptop bag.

Finally, and perhaps most critically, LCDs had to fix their resolution problems—and they did. In the mid-1990s, companies spent tens of thousands of dollars to be on the cutting edge of training technology. They paid a lot, fussed a lot while setting up the presentations, and hurt a lot while carrying the massive weights around. Companies put up with all of that and were rewarded with presentations that no one could see.

Projection technology has greatly improved over the past years, as the projectors have gotten brighter and smaller and offer higher resolution. We have more choices available to us today than ever before. This equipment is not just for corporate training. Projectors have found their way into more and more companies, schools, associations, government agencies, churches, and the home market.

Three types of projection technology are available today. The first is the more established LCD. The second is LED and the third is DLP technology by Texas Instruments. All compete within the portable and high-end markets.

The key to finding the right product comes down to a few important issues:

1. How much portability do you need? I happen to be a speaker who delivers over 90 percent of my seminars on the road. Size and weight are critical to me. If I were purchasing for a training center, this feature would not matter.

2. How bright do you need the lighting to be? This is a tough one.

   Once again, if you are working from a standard location that doesn't fluctuate, you will not have to worry about it as much. You could create an environment that would allow you to control the lighting.

   Projectors measure their resolution and brightness by what are referred to as "lumens." A few years ago, some projectors struggled to be seen with lumens in the 300–400 category, but not anymore. Now, even the least expensive and smallest projectors start at around 3,000 lumens.

The worst enemy of a projector is natural sunlight and fluorescent lights. All projectors with even a low number of lumens look good in the dark. As ambient light fills the room, it competes with the projector and causes the image to wash out.

As we pass the 1,500-lumen mark, ambient light begins to have almost no effect on image quality. Dark pictures and backgrounds also tend to show up better with a bright machine. The best compromise environment for projection allows the lights to be on at the back of the room while the front area over the screen is kept dark.

The problem is what happens when you take your training on the road. Often you will not see the facility where you are training until a few hours before the session begins. The real irony is that many hotel ballrooms and training rooms, which may have more training sessions a year than an average training center, have the worst lighting.

Frequently, all the lights are controlled by one switch. To bring one light down, you bring them all down. What's worse, often fluorescent lights are positioned right over the projector screen. You would think hotel managers had never seen a presentation in their high-priced meeting rooms!

3. Finally, how much are you willing to pay for this technology? The more lumens, the higher the price. The lighter the equipment, the higher the price.

Higher-resolution systems generally command a higher price. The average presentation does not require higher resolution. Explore the graphic video card in your laptop; it may allow you to create a lower-resolution image than the one shown on the laptop display. Many newer laptops have greater control and allow for this flexibility. If serious compatibility problems occur, you can just turn off the LCD laptop display; then you can display any resolution from the projector.

Prices vary for all of the many different types of units that are available. The best rule of thumb is simply to buy a projector based on the degree of portability and light desired. New systems on the market command a higher price, while the older level of technology may do the job within your budget.

Used systems are always desired, but you give up warranty support. This is the most significant drawback. This technology seems to mirror the trends of the personal computer, where at some point, it just is too dim, too big, and offers none of the newer features and electronic capability. Nobody wants an IBM 286 computer today.

Additional Projector Technology

Once you've decided on projector size, weight, and brightness, you're still not ready to make a purchasing decision. The additional technology available in today's projectors is really quite amazing.

Let's start with the air mouse. An "air mouse" is projector talk for a remote control. Nobody wants to run back and forth to the computer every time he or she has to advance a slide. The air mouse takes care of this problem.

When it comes to selecting an air mouse, you have two choices. The first is to work with the projector's air mouse. Most projectors come with one, so the choice appears rather obvious . . . or is it?

I own an InFocus projector that came with an air mouse. I rarely use that particular feature. One of the problems is the way it connects. When you start your presentation, you actually need to follow a sequence. Once all the wires are set—and never underestimate the number of wires necessary—you need to turn on the projector, then turn on the laptop.

That's not a suggestion; that's a *requirement*. If you turn on the laptop and then the projector, the air mouse will not work. The air mouse needs to read its requirements from an active projector. If I see 20 presentations incorporating presentation software a year fail, 15 fail because of the air mouse connection.

Another problem with the air mouse can occur once the presentation is under way. If the wires are bumped and the mouse cable is loosened, it's all over. The laptop will not be able to read the air mouse or its own mouse. "Houston, you have a problem."

Finally, many air mouse units that come with a projector use an infrared system. Projectors typically have a little infrared panel installed in the front and in the back. Users must aim the air mouse to hit one of the infrared panels. It looks silly to see a speaker pressing and pressing to advance a slide and then see a few slides or unwanted words come shooting across the screen. Unless you are good at hitting small targets while under pressure, the infrared system is not for you!

For that reason, I'm going to recommend you dig into your wallet for another air mouse choice. Let's face it, if you own a projector, you've already shelled out a lot of money. Come up with about $50 more, and I'll tell you how to spend it.

Put the projector air mouse away and buy a separate air mouse. My recommendation is to buy a product from a company called Logitech.

These separate air mice connect directly to your laptop and have no relationship to your projector. It could not care less what the projector is doing. You don't have to follow any set sequence for the setup routine. You can hook the mouse up while the laptop is already on, and it will operate immediately. You can take the cable out, and the laptop will resume its regular mouse operation. That means no more panic if the cable gets knocked loose.

Perhaps the best thing about this air mouse is that it is not controlled by an infrared signal. It is controlled by a radio signal, which means you can point your air mouse out the window in the opposite direction of your laptop, and the laptop will read the signal. Quite simply, you don't have to worry about aiming this air mouse and hoping for a connection.

The air mouse might dominate the peripheral technology available for projectors, but there are other options you might want to consider. For instance, many of the air mouse units have laser pointers installed in the handheld unit. I've never been a big fan of laser pointers, but they are an available option.

Some projectors offer what's called "picture expansion." This feature allows you to zoom in on details displayed on the screen. Ask yourself how often you will need that feature within your presentations.

Want to travel *real* light? How about getting a projector with a PC flashcard system? This particular feature eliminates the need for your laptop computer altogether. If you go around the country delivering the same presentation over and over again, this feature might appeal to you. There is some room for editing the presentation within the system, but it isn't easy.

Troubleshooting

Unfortunately, the more technology you use, the greater your chances of a malfunction of some sort. Well, having a *chance* of a problem occurring is no excuse to avoid the most important technological advance in corporate training. With that in mind, Figure 11.4 is a quick troubleshooting chart that might help you out of some of the more common problems that might occur.

Other Considerations

Now that you have a better idea of projectors and features, there are just a few other things you might want to consider when you're working with LCD projectors. Screens can make a big difference in how a projected image looks. With the new high-gain screens on the market, older and weaker projectors can hold their own on almost any stage.

The viewing angles of these screens tend to be narrow, so room design must be taken into account. Most of the high gain is down the middle and reflects back down toward the projector.

Let's talk about color for a moment. The hue of the white and color saturation can also have an effect on the quality of the image. Different lamp technology produces light at different frequencies that can appear to be bluish or more yellowish. Blue images tend to appear brighter and cleaner than the yellow. Lower-watt lamps tend to produce this yellow tint, although it all depends on the lamp.

Lamp life is another issue, although most people will change a lamp only once or twice during the projector's life. Believe me, that's good news, because the cost to replace these bulbs can be expensive.

This might shock you, but I don't actually carry a spare. Between the risks of having the bulb stolen or broken, I still present with a flip chart in the corner to cover emergencies. People who plan on using this unit for eight hours a day, every day, should have a spare; but as for me, I'll pass.

Music

As you know if you've read this book, I am a big fan of using music in my seminars. The problem is, it becomes extremely difficult to include this critical element of training when you are on the road.

Problem	Solution
LCD air mouse not working	Check all connections. If any cables are loose, reattach cables and reboot laptop.
	Look for a power saver button on handheld unit. The unit may have moved to an automatic Power Save function. If so, hold down a designated key for 3–5 seconds.
	Make sure you are aiming mouse at infrared port.
	If that does not work, check batteries of handheld unit.
Separate air mouse not working	Check all connections. If any cables are loose, reattach them but do not reboot laptop.
	Make sure unit is turned on. Look for separate switch.
	If that does not work, check batteries of handheld unit.
LCD not working	Check all cords and connections.
	Check to make sure unit is not running on Power Save mode. Look for a power save button or lamp button and activate it.
	If there is power, but no light, check lamp.
Laptop not projecting	Check all cords and connections. If a cord is loose, there is no need to reboot; simply reattach it.
	Check laptop Function key. For some computers it is the F5 key, but this is not consistent. This key allows you to toggle among three settings: computer only, computer and LCD, and LCD only. Hit appropriate function key.
Presentation image not fitting on screen	Go to Control Panel on laptop. Then double click Display icon. Move to Settings option. Increase pixels by sliding Screen Area bar to the right.
	If that doesn't work, go back to the Display icon, move to Settings, and *decrease* pixel to the minimum. Then, depress Function key and turn off laptop screen. As crazy as this sounds, it usually works!

FIGURE 11.4   Troubleshooting chart

If you are conducting your training in a corporate facility, your chances of having access to music systems are remote. If you are in the hotels, your chances are better, but you will pay a price. The price that concerns me is not from the AV company that is contracting to the hotel to support your training efforts. You won't have to worry about paying these companies extra because they have nothing to rent to you.

No, the cost I'm referring to is the cost of your damaged training. The hotels that will be able to support you will have a form of elevator music piped into the room with a separate dial. Yuk! I don't believe this will set the tone you are looking for. The idea is to use music to support your training, not to take away from it.

Well, with advances in training technology, we are all saved.

As the audience grows, the effectiveness of a laptop's speakers fades. Not to worry though, because Bose comes to the rescue. The Bose SoundLink Mini Bluetooth Speaker will do the trick. Weighing in at a paltry 1.5 pounds and only 2 inches high by 7.1 inches wide by 2.3 inches deep, this little speaker packs a powerful punch while taking up a small amount of suitcase space.

If you are presenting to a group of over 100 and you need music, the Bose Wave Radio/CD is the best product on the planet. (See Figure 11.5 for examples of both speakers.) For the sounds it produces, it's amazingly small. I have carried this radio, which weighs less than 7.52 pounds and is 4.375 inches high by 14 inches wide by 8.5 inches deep, to training sessions in my laptop bag. Amazingly enough, I have used it with audiences of close to 1,000 and have had no problems having my music heard.

Using a handheld remote control the size of a credit card, I have moved groups to breaks by gradually bringing up the music from across the room. From every presenter who takes to the road, thank you, Bose.

Electronic Whiteboards and Copy Boards

Another communication tool that is available to today's presenter is the interactive whiteboard. The interactive whiteboard allows for a person to print and save the work and give copies to people who might have missed the meeting. Not that this will ever happen to you, but it will also help to bring up to speed people who are walking out during your

FIGURE 11.5   Bose Wave Radio/CD for larger rooms, and the Bose SoundLink Mini Bluetooth Speaker for smaller rooms

presentation. Prices range from around $1,000 to $20,000, depending on the size and quality of the board. A number of key players are competing in this space, but Google and Microsoft appear to be the leaders here.

The interactive whiteboard includes a CD-ROM with interactive software, digital pens, digital eraser, and electronic dry-erase markers.

Other whiteboard applications allow two people to run each other's computer system and work on a project together. This can be accomplished on a central secure computer server.

A new portable interactive whiteboard concept is also available. This highly portable device fits onto any existing conventional white-board with suction. Using sound waves, this device provides some of the interactive features mentioned previously for a fraction of the cost.

Copyboards work much like the whiteboards but function inde-pendent of a computer. Without getting too technical, copyboards usually give a heat thermal printout of what was written. The copy-board is a lot like a whiteboard, but unlike a whiteboard you are able to retain your work and have the option of printing or electronically storing what has been created.

This image can be saved and printed from the computer during the meeting without interrupting the board's function. In addition, with a projector, the interactive design can become virtual and can function as a whiteboard without ink. Besides functioning like a whiteboard, the device also can control the computer and can serve as a touch screen at the forward part of the classroom.

Document Cameras

Document cameras have evolved over the past few years. Their primary purpose is to allow a presenter to put a hard-copy visual aid into a presentation without having to digitize the object.

Here's how these cameras work. Using standard video imaging, the document is transmitted through the projector's RCA video input to produce a larger-than-life image for review by the audience.

These units have been miniaturized over the years as well. Today's 1.8-pound cameras from Epson, Ipevo, and Elmo fold down to almost nothing and allow for the open road traveler to consider this format in a presentation.

Summary

Just like the changes in visual aids, the technology that supports the presentation industry continues to change and evolve. There's no value in turning a blind eye and demonstrating your lack of interest in technology. For the most part, this ever-changing world of technology continues to support and improve the training process. You don't need to jump at every new, shiny piece of technology that comes onto the market, but keep your eyes, ears, and checkbook open because the right fit can make a huge difference in the programs you are working on.

Chapter 12

Taking Your Training Online

D id you ever wake up one day, and realize you had become the old man standing in front of his yard shouting, "Get off my lawn!" That old man is set in his ways, and he's not tolerant of new ideas. When it comes to online training, I understand this man all too well. It's never too late to try new things, nor is it too late to recognize that there is a time and a place for online training.

I want to be emphatic when I say this: I have never been a fan of online training. This form of training has been knocking at my door for years, and I've done a magnificent job of hiding under my sheets, hoping the knocking would stop. I have been bred to present information in a certain way, and I wish the intruder would stop knocking at my door and just go away. However, if I'm going to be a thought leader on training, I need to learn about new forms of training and point out the strengths and weaknesses of each innovation that comes along.

I have a vivid memory of being 22 years old and selling life insurance and of watching the changes occur within the insurance industry. I actually consider myself fortunate to have sold when there were no laptop computers. You didn't show up at a client meeting with stacks of illustrations under your arm, you showed up with a rate book and a yellow pad of paper. But technology has a persistent way of not going away because it does one thing that many of us forget to do; it evolves. It gets better. It conforms to its surroundings, and forces us to adapt right alone with it.

It was tragic to see so many of our most talented and tenured salespeople become casualties during the computer revolution of the late 1970s because they refused to change; they refused to give up that human interaction. They became obsolete overnight, and, unwilling to change their ways, they quietly faded away. My father, Lee Jolles, was one of them; I was not. I was one of those young whippersnappers standing on his lawn, not just embracing change but flaunting it.

And so I find myself at a crossroads. I don't want to give up that human interaction, but I have to acknowledge and appreciate how far online training and the technology that supports it has come. I need to listen to these changes, point out their shortcomings, and acknowledge their strengths. That said, let me get a few things off my chest and start with the challenges that still persist. Then we'll see what we can do to fix them because if we're going to embrace the online approach to delivering presentations, we need to do it right.

The Challenges of Online Training

One of the most fundamental challenges of online training has to do with one of the most important principles of any actual presentation, training event, or performance; it has to inspire. Online training has struggled, and always will struggle, to inspire those who watch it. To truly reach into someone's heart and make a lasting impression, you have to do more than just dispense information.

I never wanted to write a book to teach people how to perform at an average level that meets expectations. I wanted to write a book that helped people perform at an extraordinary level and far exceed expectations. To dispense information is to meet expectations. To inspire an audience requires a whole lot more work. To truly reach into someone's heart and get his or her buy-in and mindshare requires far more than just dispensing information.

I'd love to tell you that we can just fight harder in front of that camera, reach down deeper, and deliver the presentation of our lives, and that will surely help us win the day. Well, we're going to do all that and more . . . but the challenge still exists.

Don't believe me? Go to the theater and watch a good play. The energy is amazing, and the acting is captivating. There's a kind of exciting danger in watching a live performance knowing almost anything can happen and that, if it does, those performers will just have to work with it.

Recently some networks decided that not enough people were able to see live plays, so they filmed some and brought them to network television. These were the same great plays, with the same great casts, performing the same great lines on film. Yet the ratings were a disaster. So the networks thought maybe having these plays performed live would help. Doing so added an element of danger but little else. Interestingly enough, the ratings indicated that showing live perform-ances of these plays did in fact draw a bigger audience. However, the ratings also indicated that although more people watched initially, these plays could not hold their audiences, as viewers quickly lost interest and left.

Another challenge to online presenting lies in the inability to actually see who it is you are speaking to. Yes, the technology certainly exists for two-way viewership and is easily available, but think of the last five times you attended an online presentation. How many times did you actually see the speaker and the audience you were a virtual part of?

The larger the program, the greater the risk of not seeing a whole lot more than a running participant count typically located on the side of the screen showing how many people are actually dropping in and out of the presentation you are delivering. It happens to be a weakness of mine, but I am no fan of anyone walking out on a presentation I deliver, and when it happens it, I'm not a happy camper. When I do online programs, the shuffling of participants dropping in and out distracts the heck out of me! I'm quite sure that if those leaving an online session had the actual eyes of the presenter and audience on them, there would be far fewer defections.

This brings me to my third and final rant about what's wrong with online training. It is difficult to engage the audience and actually get them to participate. I will always believe the more the audience talks, the more they enjoy who it is who's talking to them. Online presenting by nature just doesn't allow for significant interaction.

I live to engage audiences. I like to watch them tackle various problems in small-group exercises. I like to watch them work through case studies, engage in role-plays, navigate their way through simula-tions, and interact with each other.

I can't tell you how many times I've conducted programs for clients to regional teams who are located all over the country, paused to ask a simple question, and waited over 20 seconds for the first response.

Want to know why it takes 20 seconds? The audio of every participant has been muted to mask the noise of the breakfast being cooked and other household tasks that are being done. I even had a person once proudly tell me, "I loved your session. I was able to vacuum my entire house while you were speaking!"

What's more, I like and appreciate the interaction that takes place between participants when the training is not being conducted. I'm referring to the conversations with the presenter during breaks, the conversations among participants during breaks, the dinners that allow for a type of bonding that can never be achieved in an online format.

Grrrrrr. Okay, I needed to vent and in full disclosure let you know I will *always* prefer a live training event to a program delivered online. But that doesn't mean we can't embrace what is here, because online delivery has some impressive strengths, and it's only going to continue to evolve.

The Strengths of Online Training

One of the first and most obvious strengths of online training centers on the bottom line. Budgets are tight, particularly in the training world, and conducting a presentation online can save a staggering amount of money compared to an in-person session. Taxi fares, airfares, meals, hotel expenses, and more are eliminated.

Online training also provides significant time savings. Almost all professional speakers will fly in the day before the actual training event is to begin. That means some significant downtime away from the office. Oh sure, many of us have established routines that allow us to maximize productivity and sneak in work here and there, but the fact remains that even a one-hour keynote presentation represents two days on the road. Online training eliminates the need for travel for both the presenters and the trainees.

Another key strength of online training centers on the actual length of the training itself. We live in a world a limited characters . . . and attention spans. The younger generations don't want to sit for long periods of time or listen to long presentations. Six- to eight-minute professionally produced videos seem to be seems to be their sweet spot. Imagine jumping on a plane and flying out to deliver a six-minute presentation. But online you can create a river of six- to eight-minute presentations.

Yet another strength of online training is the ability to self-pace the program being attended. When conducting a live training event, we try to pull that audience with us every step of the way. Well, we have all kind of learners, and sometimes varied training paces can create nightmares for trainers. Online video training, for example, is self-paced and can be completed by different participants at different speeds.

No, online presentations and training aren't going anywhere for a number of good reasons. That means if we're going to embrace the online world, let's figure out how to do so in a remarkable way.

Natural Fits for Online Delivery

Although I have fought my own online demons, I have, in fact, embraced online delivery for certain uses for quite some time. I've dedicated a lot of this book, and my life, to the critical nature of implementation. When a presentation is delivered that inspires a roomful of participants, we all hope that what has been taught will be implemented. You'll have no argument from anyone . . . for the first week or two. But we all know how difficult change actually is.

Follow-up training is a natural for online delivery. The live delivery creates a condition for change by inspiring those who attend. Online training can help sustain that initial training. Often this follow-up training doesn't require the level of change that needs to be embraced in the initial training, or the motivation to follow it.

Additionally, online training can be ideal for those who are struggling with the initial training. Due to fiscal concerns, most companies will not pay to have struggling trainees go through initial training twice. Online deliveries create a much more affordable opportunity to help those who are having problems.

Finally, online opportunities allow for a more intimate experience between a trainer and a participant. It is monetarily challenging to provide training and coaching to people one on one, but online, it's a completely different story. As a matter of fact, when I conduct my live online coaching sessions, I have my camera on and have a cup of coffee. I encourage those I'm working with to have a cup also. The coffee really does create a relaxed atmosphere.

Tips for Successful Online Delivery

A lot has been written regarding how to "perform" when conducting online training. You'll hear things like "be mentally present" or "establish clear expectations" or "encourage feedback." The list goes on and on. Personally, although I know pundits feel they are helping by laying these ideas out, I believe they are overthinking things, and that's not something I want you to do.

The fact is, very little needs to change at all when you are in front of a camera. I'm hoping you normally face your audience, speak clearly, are mentally present, establish clear expectations, practice your presentation . . . Do I really need to go on?

I've worked for years with clients who conduct all their business on the phone. Sometimes these are customer service departments and internal sales departments, and initially they are looking for some kind of magic process that pertains only to those who cannot see or be seen by their clients. Although we work on sound communication skills, we change very little in their actual delivery, right down to their smile. Yes, by golly, you *can* hear a smile! That said, unlike departments that interact only with a phone, online deliveries do possess some unique challenges, and you're going to need to adjust to them.

It may sound strange, but if you're on camera, one of the first delivery techniques you're going to have to learn is how to present in front of the camera. That certainly sounds simple enough, but if you're using your actual desktop or laptop computer, it can be a little trickier than it sounds.

Often a picture of the person we are working with appears on the screen, and it's natural to look at him or her. The problem is, when you are looking at the person, you are not looking at the camera! The fact is, if you're making eye contact on the screen, you are actually *not* making eye contact with the individual you are talking to. Pretty strange, but true.

You'll want to train yourself to look into that (often) little green light up top and pretend it is the individual you are speaking with. It takes a little practice. I've actually worked with clients who struggle with this so much, I ended up making a big paper face, cutting out a hole for the camera right between the eyes, and taping it up as a reminder. The problem was solved!

Just as you can learn how to speak to a camera by putting a face on it, you need to deliver a presentation as if there is an audience in front of you. No, I don't put a collage of faces up around my office when I'm conducting online presentations, but I work hard to imagine that audience is in my office. One way I recommend you do this is to think like an actor and get in character.

Watch a great actor like Daniel Day-Lewis. I can assure you, he'll make you believe in whatever character he is playing. Coincidently, he's famous for the intensity with which he studies each of the characters he is going to portray. Here are a handful of examples:

- *Lincoln* (2012). As he filmed the role, Day-Lewis demanded that everyone, including Director Spielberg, refer to him as "Mr. President." He wouldn't let English cast members speak to him in their own accents while trying to get Abe's voice right, for fear that it might throw him off.
- *Gangs of New York* (2002). For his role as Bill the Butcher, Day-Lewis took lessons as a butcher. He was so into the role that he refused to wear a warm jacket because, according to him, it wasn't in keeping with the period. He caught pneumonia but rejected modern medicine when it was offered to him.
- *In the Name of the Father* (1993). To accurately portray a wrongly convicted prisoner, Day-Lewis spent several nights at a time, in solitary confinement in the abandoned prison that was being filmed in. He even kept himself awake for three days in preparation for an interrogation scene.
- *Last of the Mohicans* (1992). To prepare for his role, Day-Lewis taught himself how to live as a survivalist and learned how to hunt animals for food. He refused to eat anything that he hadn't killed with either his flintlock rifle or his tomahawk, both of which he could use very well.
- *My Left Foot* (1989). While playing the paralyzed poet Christy Brown, Day-Lewis refused to leave his wheelchair and had crew members carry him around the set during the entire shoot. He also insisted that he be spoon-fed all of his meals.

Daniel Day-Lewis does far more than just learn his lines; he immerses himself into the life and behaviors of each character he plays. He becomes 100 percent believable by not just learning his lines but by becoming the characters he represents. What about you?

I'm asking you to play the role of a phenomenal speaker with an audience that is filing in to see you. They've heard great things about you, your ability to clearly communicate information, sustain interest, and inspire audiences. Now look at that green dot and let them have it! Let that green dot see you emote, gesture, shout, laugh, and basically do everything you would normally do if the audience were in front of you.

One of the only things you can't do is move around . . . but you can surely stand up! If you haven't done so already, it's probably time to invest in a good stand-up desk. They say sitting is the new smoking so you'll be doing a great thing from a health standpoint if you get standing. From a delivery standpoint, I believe it's imperative. Remember, you're in character. How many times did your "presenter character" sit down in a chair when delivering a presentation to a live audience?

Not to worry, you don't need to go out and replace all your furniture, although you can if you'd like. I happen to own a Winston Sit-Stand desk and love it. This is a steel piece that sits on top of my desk. With a push of a button, I can lift my monitor along with a steel shelf my keyboard and mouse rest on with room for a pad of paper. With a stand-up desk, you'll have no difficulty really getting in to character and firing away at our friend the camera.

One last point. Sometimes there is no camera. Perhaps it's a podcast, or a presentation that does not allow you to see the audience or have that audience see you. Feel free to reread every delivery tip you just went over. I wouldn't change a thing!

Tips for Successful Online Videos

A subset of online training is online video training. Once again, I resisted this form of training . . . until I had lunch with a fellow professional speaker. I knew he had embraced putting a lot of his content online. We talked about the year he was having and he told me his onsite delivery was down, but he was more than happy with the online revenue he was receiving. When I stepped a bit out of line and asked him how much revenue we were talking about, he coolly said, "A little under half a million dollars." Once I stopped choking on my sandwich, I made a note to myself: "Take this online training seriously!"

Now, before you start choking on your sandwich, let me tell you that a lot of his success lies in his ability to drive traffic to his website where these videos can be found. It's also safe to say that with strong content, there is the potential for some strong revenue.

One tip to making better videos is to start reducing the length of those points you've been making or those modules you've been delivering. That's because in the world of online video training, the length of the videos has come way down. Typically, online video training clips are between four to eight minutes long. If you put your training videos online, because the length of the clips you are producing are short, the cost to produce these videos is normally pretty low. You can easily recoup these costs and then some by monetizing this form of training on your website.

However, when you look at the number of clips that are potentially involved, monetizing these clips can be lucrative. If you were to take a typical one-day program and break it into small clips, you could be looking at 60 to 80 separate clips.

Developing a repeatable online style is another way of maximizing your effectiveness. My wife and I have been watching *Survivor* since it first came on the air. It's a reality show that has no script, yet there is a definite formula for every single episode. The host seems so unscripted, and yet my wife and I know 90 percent of what he is going to say, because he says it the same way each time. Things like:

- ♦ "Once again immunity is up for grabs."
- ♦ "Survivors ready? Go!"
- ♦ "You need to bring me your torch."
- ♦ "The tribe has spoken."

Those phrases do not change, and that's only a list of phrases for what's called "The Immunity Challenge." The show feels new each week, yet there's something familiar about it. That's because although the show is unscripted, it's littered with familiar phrases. When you produce what could amount to 60 to 80 separate clips, you want each to feel new yet there be something familiar to them. Your opening, your closing, the support materials, and more should follow a recognizable pattern.

The more comfortable you are, the more comfortable your online audience will be. The easiest way to gain that level of comfort is for you to become comfortable with the technology. The first time I ever shot something online was for a company that had secured my services through my publisher. I had been asked to come in and let the group film me doing four three-minute online programs. "Piece of cake," I thought to myself. I've been recorded doing many of my keynotes, and this didn't intimidate me in the least.

I do not get nervous when the camera goes on, but I was shocked at how clumsy my first take was. When you're shooting a short, tight video, there really isn't a lot of room for hemming and hawing. There also isn't a lot of room for you to use notes either. You can use a teleprompter, but much like reading from a lectern, it's an all-or-nothing proposition. It's nearly impossible to kind-of use a teleprompter so you've got to ask yourself if it's really worth it. The bottom line is practice, practice, practice!

Another tip is to try to create and follow a reasonable, step-by-step process. Needless to say, this makes the program you are putting online a whole lot easier to understand for the participants who are watching. What's more, if you are building information while following a logical sequence, you will reduce the chances of participants jumping around. Remember, unlike a live session that allows the presenter to control the flow of information, online clips, and the participants who watch them, offer the presenter no such control, and participants don't always want to watch clips in the order they were designed to be viewed. If you are teaching a program that is based on a repeatable process, it will be a whole lot easier for your audience not only to understand what you are teaching but to be in a position to measure success as well.

If you are going to use graphics that are embedded in your video, keep them simple, and that goes for any text you might want to use. Like those short videos, if you are using text, use short one- or two-words bullets.

Finally, if you really want to create an online program that stands out from the others, you need to go above and beyond in how you engage those who are watching. Some ideas might include:

◆ Pretest surveys.
◆ A participant guide that can be downloaded for each participant.

♦ Various assignments to complete either during or after the observed program.

♦ Interactive options within the clip itself. Clips can be created with filmed responses based on participant choices.

♦ Posttest assessments.

♦ Implementation exercises that allow participants to put into practice what has been learned.

Notice that each of the ideas just listed has one thing in common—each possesses an interactive quality. Upon even closer inspection, you'll also notice that almost every suggestion mimics what would be recommended if you were delivering your presentation live. Coincidence? I think not!

Letting Others Know about Your Online Presence

Once your online program has been created and filmed, you'll need to market these clips. Sometimes I worry that so much attention is focused on the creation of the clips themselves that little attention is given to actually driving traffic to these clips. Instead of BITS (butts in the seats), you need to focus on BOTL (butts on the line). It reminds me of the first Halloween party I ever threw. I produced a nice mix of music, brought in a keg, adjusted the lighting, put out some great food, bought trophies for costume contests, and more. I did everything except put time and effort into actually bringing people to the party.

I don't want you to make that same mistake. I leave you to your Google optimization techniques and the consultants for hire to drive traffic to your site. That doesn't mean you can't do your part to help. Make sure you are using your social media platform to announce what you are up to, tap into any and all sites that will help you broadcast to their followers, and continuously remind folks what you are doing.

Make sure participants who are attending your live deliveries know what you are doing as well. Tuck information in your participant guides, create announcement cards that can be passed out after you've presented, put information on your business cards for after you've presented and more; so much more! We all have amazing outlets to trumpet what we're up to. Unfortunately, so does the rest of the world. It takes creativity, discipline, determination, and persistence to build an audience. People are mildly impressed with the BLArticle® following I have amassed (www.jolles.com/blarticle). Of course, they're not quite as impressed when I tell them how many years I've been plugging away at this. Again, building an audience takes creativity, discipline, determination, and *persistence*.

There are also companies popping up that may be willing to help. Geniecast, for example, operates as an online speaker's bureau connecting online deliveries with clients who want a virtual presenter as opposed to a live presentation. Companies like this provide all the infrastructure needed to connect you to your client, allowing you to deliver your presentation in a virtual environment. Be prepared for a speaker's fee that will be a fraction of your typical fee, but then again, be prepared not to have to catch a cab, catch a flight, sit in a hotel room, get up and deliver a presentation, get in a cab, get in a plane, and fight your way home. The fee you will receive is much lower, but then again, so is the wear and tear on your body, and stress you will feel delivering it.

Publishers are also beginning to get into the act. This form of training is a natural fit for publishers because unlike an online bureau that could have thousands of speakers available, a publisher may have only a few hundred. Rather than overwhelm a prospective client with too many options, a publisher can provide a shorter list of subject matter experts who have, in a sense, been more carefully vetted.

Change is often inevitable, and ultimately we adjust our ways to allow technology to enhance what we do. Used properly, online technology should mean better service and improved efficiency. Those who are careful to blend technology with old-school delivery techniques should do well.

And so, standing by my door, watching you walk by my lawn, I leave you with this one last reminder: The next online program you put on live or the next session you record, don't forget the great equalizers: energy and enthusiasm. They serve you well in the pit, and they serve you just as well online.

Although I've resisted the idea of online training, if it helps my clients, I'm willing to open the door and see who's knocking, and encourage you to join me. It may very well be opportunity knocking and the direction a lot of our training is going.

Summary

When considering your approach to taking your programs online, there are a lot of moving parts to be examined. My suggestion is, don't jump into the online water alone. There are plenty of pros out there who will be happy to help you out. My suggestion is to visit as many websites as you can to help you determine the look and feel you're after. Whether it's producing your own podcasts, or your own online programs, do your homework, get started now, and don't get left behind.

Chapter 13

Giving Feedback and Coaching

Probably one of the most emotional issues that any presenter must deal with, on a regular basis, is giving feedback to students. On the surface, this may appear to be a rather insignificant issue, but be assured, it most certainly is not.

To begin with, it is extremely difficult to judge just how well a student will receive the feedback you intend to give. This uncertainty regarding how feedback will be received can be one of the major pitfalls that awaits a new presenter. On the outside, most students appear to accept feedback readily. It is socially and professionally unacceptable to act any other way. The problem is, students do not internalize such rules.

Pitfalls to Avoid

The first trap a new presenter can fall prey to involves working with a student whose learning pace falls behind the pace of the seminar. Often, in an attempt to catch this student up, the instructor creates an overload of negative feedback. Not only can this demoralize the student, but it can also confuse the major items that need repair from the minor items. Once again, the old saying "If you emphasize everything, you emphasize nothing" comes true in this scenario. The student typically tries to fix everything and therefore ends up fixing nothing. Now the presenter is faced with a demoralized student who most likely will continue to drop further and further behind and will resent your feedback as well.

The second mistake a new presenter can make involves working with a student whose learning pace is ahead of the rest of the trainees. This trainee could also be referred to as the superstar. Everything this trainee typically touches turns to gold. He or she is good at whatever you are teaching. You know it; the trainee knows it; and the rest of the trainees know it. From the outside, his or her ego appears hard as a rock. With the constant showering of praise and respect, the trainee's ego seems indestructible. This is where the problem lies. The typical approach to evaluating this student can be a quick and frivolous brush with the positives and a more extensive look at the negatives. This approach can have disastrous effects on a seemingly strong and confident student. Once again, internally, the student's ego may very well not be as strong as he or she leads everyone to believe. Even the most seasoned superstar can become depressed and unsure when showered with negatives. To make matters worse, often these are the students who tell the presenter they really are looking forward to the constructive criticism they will be receiving and to please lay it on them. Many presenters will fall prey to that trap. Probably only once.

The final consideration in giving feedback relates to careful control of any public feedback. By "public feedback," I am referring to an old trick of allowing trainees to give feedback to another student in front of the group. In theory it sounds like a good idea to involve the rest of the trainees and gain increased participation, but the problems created by the process outweigh its strengths. Trainees are not schooled in giving feedback professionally. They do not possess the discipline that you do in trying to be objective and fair. How would you like it if everyone raved about the presentation *before* yours and looked rather blank when you finished your presentation? The nonverbal communication alone can be more than some trainees can take. It may be the one trainee you have been working with and whose confidence you have been trying to build up for the past week who gets shot down publicly. Your efforts were in vain. It just is not worth the risk.

Giving Feedback without Intimidating Trainees

How do you give feedback to trainees without suffering through these frightening problems? The approach I recommend is a five-step process that should alleviate all these fears.

Step 1. Ask students for two areas that *they* felt they did well.
It is human nature for students to be overly critical of their own performances.

Additionally, because of inappropriate past feedback sessions or even to avoid appearing arrogant, 90 percent of the time a student will focus only on the points that he or she did not like. By asking for feedback on issues the student felt good about, you move this performance to a conscious competent level and stand a greater chance of having the student repeat these strengths in the future.

Allowing the student to go first eliminates the risk of a student simply repeating the feedback received from you, the presenter. You are in a better position to identify unconscious incompetence when your feedback follows that of the student's. If a student identifies an area that you do not agree with, simply probe the student for more information. Usually it is simply a misunderstanding by the student, and he or she will take the item off his or her list. Make sure, however, that if you do question a strength and it is removed, you ask the student for another.

Step 2. Ask students for two areas that *they* felt they could improve in. Nothing is gained by allowing a student to ramble on and on unfocused. Force the student to clearly define these two deficiencies and probe for suggestions on how he or she intends to fix them. Sometimes a good way to get this step started is to ask students what two things they would do differently if they could do the observed task again.

Step 3. Tell students two areas that you observed as strengths within their performance. Model the same rules that you established for the student. Remember, these are areas of strength and not an opportunity to fix what has already been done better. Often good feedback is wasted when a presenter says, "This was really good, if only you had . . ." There will be other opportunities to make something good even better. If this is one of the only two areas that you are identifying as good, leave it at that!

Step 4. Tell students two areas that you observed as weaknesses within their performance. Words that work better here are "alternatives" or "suggestions." Be direct and not apologetic. Try using words such as "I saw" or "I heard." Avoid feelings and stick to facts. Try not to use words such as "I feel" or "I think." If you feel it is vital to bring out a third point to be worked on, make sure you capture a third strength as well, and vice versa.

Step 5. End the session with one last encouraging remark.
This allows the student to leave the session motivated with a
positive, upbeat feeling. This might be something like "I am really
encouraged by the improvement you are showing," or "I really
think this process is going to become second nature to you soon.
Keep up the good work."

What should you have accomplished when this process is over?
First, by limiting students and yourself to two points for each step, there
is just enough to feel good about and just enough to work on. Taking a
student through every point on your evaluation form complicates
everything. The old saying fits here again: "If you emphasize everything, you emphasize nothing."

The second strength of this process is that in an area of extreme
sensitivity, it ensures fairness. Some students (and presenters for that
matter) do not take criticism very well. When they know what to expect
and know others around them are being evaluated in the same manner,
criticism is much easier to accept.

Finally, in a relatively short period of time, the process becomes
second nature to all involved. Feedback becomes so natural that the
presenter need only monitor the process. Typically, after two or three
times with the same student, the presenter need only sit back and listen
as the student methodically lays out what he or she did well, what he or
she needs to improve on, and how he or she intends to make that
improvement. Feedback is no longer feared, and egos are set aside.

To assist you in the use of this coaching technique, see Figure 13.1.
It shows a worksheet to use as a guideline until the process becomes
second nature.

Coaching Using the Three Ss

Giving feedback to a trainee is similar to coaching the trainee. I am
saddened that most of the trainees I work with initially react to the
word "coach" with "Have I done something wrong?" I believe this is
caused by most of our experiences of being coached. Most of us in
business have learned to relate coaching to a problem behavior.
Management often steps in to coach when an employee needs to be
disciplined.

Feedback and Coaching Notes

Step 1—Ask Student . . .

1. Area of Strength _____

_____

2. Area of Strength _____

_____

Step 2—Ask Student . . .

1. Area to Improve _____

_____

2. Area to Improve _____

_____

Step 3—Provide Student . . .

1. Area of Strength _____

_____

2. Area of Strength _____

_____

Step 4—Provide Student . . .

1. Area to Improve _____

_____

2. Area to Improve _____

_____

Step 5—Positive Finish

Figure 13.1 Worksheet for feedback and coaching notes

In corporate training, there is a different mind-set. In the training room, coaching should conjure up other words, such as "opportunity" and "inspiration." The old school of thought was to show and tell someone how to accomplish a task, prompt the person along, and then release the person to accomplish that task on his or her own. Somewhat productive, but not what I would call inspirational.

The keys to good coaching are similar to those of giving effective feedback. I like to refer to my own model using the Three Ss: situation, support, and solution.

SITUATION

To begin with, there must be two-way communication throughout. This point is especially critical when discussing the first "S": *situation*, or the issue in question. Coaching cannot be the presenter dictating what the problem is and what it is the student needs to do. There must be a mutual acceptance of the situation, or we are wasting our time. Open probes relating to the subject and active listening are helpful here.

SUPPORT

The next "S" in effective coaching is *support*. Not all situations are negative. Coaching often can center around a task that is being successfully accomplished but possibly can be done better. "If it ain't broke, don't fix it" is thankfully a dying sentiment. Too many companies subscribing to that theory have been caught flat-footed by other companies that believe "If it ain't broke, try to fix it better." A critical factor to any coaching session revolves around support. Regardless of the task, positive or negative, individuals deserve and need your support. Maybe it is a reference to a previous success, or perhaps it is a mention of another area of strength. Sometimes it may even be an expression of confidence by you and a willingness to help if help is needed. Coaching often treads on egos, and support is a way to soothe those egos.

SOLUTION

The final "S" stands for *solution*. This is the "S" that so many presenters want to leap toward in a hurry. As with the description of the situation, once again this must involve two-way communication. If the trainee accepts the situation and feels the sincerity of your support, he or she may very well be able to offer realistic solutions. Once again, your ability to probe in the areas where you wish the trainee to look for solutions can help you in getting the trainee to focus on necessary issues. Work with the trainee in making the solutions tangible and realistic. If possible, try to finish your coaching session with some kind of follow-up strategy to measure effectiveness.

Summary

Coaching and giving feedback have the potential to be highly emotional tasks. They are, nonetheless, critical skills for all presenters. My hope is that my suggestions for handling these processes will give you the support you will need to carry out these vital skills. Many times, feedback and coaching may feel more like having to give your trainees a shot of medicine. Remember this: A lot of people can stick a needle in another person's arm and give a shot. There are, however, only a skilled few who can give that same shot but, through their people skills and their empathy, can make acceptance of the pain easier. That is the real goal behind giving feedback and coaching. Perhaps the real pain we are avoiding is in our minds.

Chapter 14

Tricks of the Trade

Up to now, I have attempted to show you some solid, conventional approaches to corporate training. As with most professions, once you master the technical aspects of your position, you need to learn certain tricks of the trade. In this chapter, I present you with a number of these tricks. Depending on your style, topic, and trainees, some may be appropriate for you. Tricks that do not seem helpful now may be of use to you someday down the road when you are a presenter with your career on the line.

1. Avoid Too Much Material

We need to start here, because you are looking at the single biggest mistake made by 95 percent of the presenters you see today. Why does this phenomenon exist? It's a combination of two issues that permeate the seminar business. It's all about timing.

The first issue is about timing. When a company wants to train its employees internally, timing never seems to be an issue. This is because the costs are relatively low, and the logistics are fairly simple. However, once a company engages the services of a consultant to conduct a seminar or workshop, timing becomes an obsession. Consultants typically bill based on time, and clients want to keep this timing to a minimum. So the material is condensed, and the program is delivered . . . quickly.

When I conducted internal sales programs for Xerox, the length of the program for a typical new hire consisted of two two-week classes conducted in the first two months of employment. Xerox had sold its external sales training program to another company with a five-year noncompete clause that expired in 1987. Once we were legally allowed to approach clients, when we approached them with our new external four-week program we could not attract one single client to the Xerox Document University for training.

There wasn't a lot of fluff in the program, but there were a lot of individually filmed role-plays. With some cutting and tweaking, we were able to cut the program down to one week, and in came the customers.

Within a couple of years, the number of clients attending classes began to fade, so the program was cut to 2.5 days. This time the tweaking was not quite as easy, but removing some small-group activities and personal coaching sessions allowed us to meet customer demands for shorter training. In came the customers again. Well, in fairness, in came the customers for a while, but the program was not nearly as effective. Word reached the streets, and today Xerox doesn't even offer sales training to its customers.

So, what's the moral of the story? I won't take the easy way out and tell you to convince your clients that you need more time to do the work properly—that's too obvious. The fact is, some clients simply can't afford the time or money for longer seminars and workshops. The moral of the story is to work intelligently within the time frame provided.

Don't fall prey to the temptation to speak faster or to cram in too much information. When you are given three days to conduct a seminar, do a great job with those three days. When those three days become three hours, do a great job with those three hours. That means take a smaller piece of the pie, and do a wonderful job with it. That also means don't ever sacrifice the interaction you must incorporate within your seminars to truly do a wonderful job. Ultimately, you will be judged on how much your participants can retain and use, not on how much information you can cram into a seminar.

2. Avoid Too Many Visuals

Have you ever attended a seminar only to have the wind knocked out of you by seeing the pile of visual aids? Transparencies and slides used to be the most common culprits; however, a careless projection of all your presentation software slides can create panic in the trainees as well.

If you are required to show a lot of visuals, what is the solution? *Hide* your excess visuals. If you are still showing transparencies, take enough to get you to the first break and stow the rest away. You might want to keep the rest of the morning's supply inside your lectern or close by just in case you run fast. Every time the trainees leave for a break, replenish. For slides, I would recommend you invest in extra trays and fill each one about one-third of the way. Each tray may represent a half day to a day of training.

This idea even works for curriculum. Some presenters will bring in enormous notebooks stuffed to the gills. If that is not enough to turn trainees' stomachs, presenters also typically travel through the curriculum slowly during housekeeping and introductions. Seeing a presenter take 20 minutes to turn the first page of a 400-page book may be too much for some people to bear. Strategically break the instructor guide into less intimidating, manageable books, and keep those not in use out of sight.

3. BUILD A SEQUENCE OF INFORMATION

Here is an idea to help trainees who like to write down everything that appears on a visual aid. No matter how many times you tell trainees not to do so, they try anyway. You can plead with them that everything that appears visually is located in their participant guides, and they will still write it down. Having to wait for those trainees who are not listening but copying the visual aid down often can break the rhythm a presenter is trying to establish. (As an aside, this form of learning never appealed to me. However, I appreciate that this is a proven learning method for certain types of people.)

To work with these trainees and keep your pace up as well, try building sequence by ghosting information into your visual aid. This can be easily accomplished using just about any type of visual aid. Each visual should have what was on the previous visual plus a new item or line. The only difference between this and a typical list is that the previous information should be faded back and the new information should jump out at you. This will allow those who wish to copy everything down an opportunity to do so while allowing you to move along.

4. KNOW THE VALUE OF A NICKEL

When delivering training seminars, sometimes it truly is the little things that can pull a presenter through. Consider the nickel. It makes not one but two contributions to your training. First, as I mentioned in Chapter 8, it provides you enough collateral to pay for answers to questions that get trainees involved in your presentation.

Second, if you are still using an overhead projector, it allows you to focus on the screen. When you are following a previous speaker or walking into a room where trainees are already waiting for you, you need to make a decision. Do you want to project a transparency on the screen to center and focus your overhead? Admittedly, this does not sound like a question that should keep you up at night, but we are talking about tricks of the trade and we are talking about looking polished. Often I do not want my trainees to see certain visuals until a strategic time. In such cases, pull out a nickel, lay it on the overhead, center, and focus your projector on the nickel. Once you do this, put your nickel away, turn off the projector, lay your transparency on the glass, and you are ready to go.

5. CREATE PROFESSIONAL FLIP CHARTS

They say a picture is worth a thousand words. Well, a professional-looking picture on a flip chart might be just the answer you are looking for to create the right kind of mood in the training you conduct. I know, I know . . . you are not artistically inclined. I have heard all the excuses before because I used most of them until I learned this technique.

Start by looking for a picture that relates to your topic. You might find it in a magazine, newspaper, or book. Next, make a Xerox copy of it (sorry, it's the Xeroid in me) on a transparency. Focus your transparency onto a flip chart from close range and begin tracing. Instant artist! You can trace your lettering as well.

For a real professional look, do not stop here. Put some color into it. The problem with markers is they typically come in basic colors: red, black, blue, and green. To get the pastels that are necessary for skin tones and other more realistic looks, try using colored chalk. The final piece to the puzzle that will keep the chalk in place is hair spray. Lightly spray your artistry three to five times, and you will lock in your masterpiece.

6. ASK A TRAINEE TO ACT AS SCRIBE

One of the most frustrating positions to be in as a presenter is to be at the flip chart scribing with one hand while twisting around trying to make eye contact. It is enough to give even the best of us a headache. Try selecting a trainee to scribe for you while you stay in the pit and work. I usually quietly scout out who has clear handwriting by looking at notes that have been taken. Sometimes you can strategically rotate trainees, which allows you to work more effectively with more of your trainees. With a scribe at the flip chart, you can stay in control of the room, involve trainees in the presentation, and perhaps even be let off the hook if your own handwriting or spelling is not what it should be.

7. Focus on That Screen

This recommendation goes out to presenters who are projecting visual aids onto a screen, specifically, those who are projecting from an area below the screen. What happens in this case when a visual is nearly impossible to focus on? If you focus on the top, the bottom is blurry; if you focus on the bottom, the top is blurry. The solution is rather simple. Try matching the pitch of the projector by taping or pinning the bottom of the screen to the wall behind it. Most screens are hung a few feet away from the wall. Bringing the bottom of the screen to the wall compensates for the pitch of the projector.

8. K.I.S.S.

It is an old saying, but a good saying just the same: "Keep It Simple, Stupid." This saying pertains not only to the written word but to the spoken word as well. You must be careful with the language you choose. Start by determining the knowledge level of your audience. Do they share the same company terms? Do they share the same business terms? In no way am I recommending you talk down to your audience. You must determine where their knowledge level is, use terms they are familiar with, and try to keep the words simple.

9. Avoid the Ache of Acronyms

When I taught flood insurance for the government, I used to start the course this way. "Hi, . . . I'm Rob Jolles. I work for CSC, which administers the NFIP for FEMA." I was not out of my introduction, and I had worked in three acronyms! No one likes them. People are intimidated by them. Trainees get demotivated by them. Although we might wish we could avoid acronyms, unfortunately, often that is not an option. As presenters, your job is to teach trainees everything, and if they will be exposed to acronyms once they leave the seminar, you must prepare the trainees by teaching them.

There are a number of approaches to working with acronyms, and each has its strengths. The problem for presenters is that they not only have to use the acronyms, they have to teach them. The most effective technique I ever used was to keep a separate Acronym Chart off to the side; each time I used an acronym, I would write it down in acronym form. Before and after each break, I would walk over to the Acronym Chart and have the trainees recite their meanings.

I recommend that you avoid using acronyms whenever possible. Acronyms have the potential to get you into trouble. The flood program had many acronyms; one was BFD, standing for base flood depth. This was a rating term used often in the program. Once while routinely testing the National Flood Insurance Program's hotline, a government monitor had her son call up to test the system. The customer service rep routinely asked, "What's the BFD?" The monitor's son was of an age that made another interpretation very clear. When the son told his monitor parent his interpretation of the acronym, memos went flying, meetings were held, and that acronym was stricken from document and dialogue at an expensive cost. Moral of the story? Watch out for those acronyms!

10. TRY PARKING TOPICS FOR DISCUSSION LATER

Here is the situation. You are teaching a group of trainees, and you are on a roll. The trainees are just beginning to warm up so you want to be extra careful to respond to questions appropriately. A hand goes up. You call out the trainee's name and receive your question. The only problem is that the question pertains to something that you do not cover for two more days. What's worse, once you enter that topic, it will probably be extremely difficult to get back to your original topic without eliciting more questions. The stage is set. If you avoid the question, you might send out signals that discourage your most precious ally: participation. Answer the question, and you run the risk of throwing the seminar into an illogical, confusing tailspin. This is the real world. This is another situation that places you under fire.

So, what's the solution? Park the question. In a remote section of your room, set up a flip chart pad or sheet with the words "Parking Lot" on it. Every time a trainee has a question that would be better answered later, use this approach:

TRAINEE: I was wondering if you could tell us how to handle a situation that required the computer and the administrator.

Presenter: That is an excellent question. We are learning about the computer's role in policy handling, but what about the administrator? Tomorrow afternoon we discuss the administrator's responsibilities. I think it might be a good idea to revisit and answer the question at that time. Let me write it down over here in the "Parking Lot" so we do not forget to answer it at that time.

You could just tell the trainees that you will answer the question at the appropriate time, but often when the appropriate time comes, all we remember is that someone had a question relating to this topic. When you write it down, you give credibility to the trainee who asked it and assurances that you will not forget to answer it. The responsibility becomes yours to keep an eye on the "Parking Lot" and answer the questions at the appropriate time. You might even want to check the answers off as you address them to alert trainees that you are actively answering their questions.

11. Use Post-its to Remind Yourself of Problem Areas

All presenters typically have a few habits they are trying to break, no matter how proficient they may appear. Just as with a strong round of golf, you can always do better. The first task is to determine what you want to work on. A lesson can be learned from Vilfredo Pareto, father of Pareto analysis. In the late nineteenth century, Pareto became interested in the distribution of wealth and determined that a significant few people, 20 percent, were controlling a vast majority of the wealth, 80 percent. It is certainly more profitable to fix a significant few problems than some of what Pareto called "the trivial many." This goes for training as well. Do you have a significant few problems that would be more profitable to fix than the trivial many? Dropping a marker on the floor once would be considered a "trivial many" problem. Rocking back and forth constantly would be considered a "vital few" problem.

Once you have determined which important areas you want to work on, try using Post-its to help you. If you want to smile more, post the word "smile" on the lectern. Even though you may be turning pages in the curriculum, the word "smile" remains in place. Often, correcting problems starts by becoming more conscious of them. The note will make you conscious throughout, allowing you to start correcting even the most difficult problems. One last point. Do not overdo it and clutter your lectern with these notes, or you will be back at square one. Two or three notes at a time should be sufficient to correct even some of the most stubborn problems.

12. USE A LECTERN

Time once again for a little bit of controversy. Arguments have been made for and against the use of lecterns for some time now. The key argument against the use of a lectern is that nervous presenters have a tendency to hold onto them. Without question, that is a habit you need to avoid; however, when you look at the advantages of using a lectern, that problem becomes somewhat trivial.

The lectern's most important advantage is that it actually allows you more mobility. There are those who say using a lectern will cause a presenter to remain stationary behind the lectern, but in reality, the opposite is true. Let me explain why. Let's begin with the assumption that you need to look at your notes or some sort of guide. With a lectern, you can actually get comfortable strolling back and forth, in and out of the pit, working your way back to the lectern when you need to glance at your notes. The key here is *glance*. A lectern is typically higher than a desk or table, allowing you to subtly peek at your notes. That ability to sneak a little peek makes the lectern worth its weight in gold. It gives you the confidence to leave your notes, knowing that help is a few steps and a glance away. If the material is located on a desk, unless you have super vision, you will have to bend over to take a look. Through my years as a professional speaker and many, many subtle glances as I have strolled by the lectern, I have developed super vision. The only side effect is that now I truly can read my notes better when they are alongside me than when they are straight ahead of me.

Another advantage the lectern provides is the ability to conceal strategic materials from the trainees. As I mentioned in item 2, when you are saddled with too many overheads or slides, the lectern becomes an excellent place to hide them. If you are planning a competition with some prizes, once again the lectern is a place to store the prizes. You name it, and often it can fit inside a lectern. As a matter of fact, without seeing a presenter speak, I can learn an enormous amount of information about that presenter from what is inside the lectern.

One last little point that I would like to clear up. People often confuse the words "podium" and "lectern." Ninety-nine percent of the people you meet will call what a presenter stands behind a podium. For the record, *Webster's New World Dictionary* defines podium this way:

A low platform, esp. for the conductor of an orchestra.

To my knowledge, although presenters can perform many exciting tasks in a seminar, none has conducted an orchestra. Lectern is defined this way:

A stand for holding the notes, written speech, etc., as of a lecturer.

Used properly, a lectern can be one of the most helpful training tools available to you in the seminar. You can even purchase portable lecterns that fold up and can be carried like a briefcase. So, when it comes to using a lectern, my recommendation is, don't leave home without it. As for the habit of holding onto the lectern, leave yourself a note on the lectern and stop doing it!

13. STAY IN CHARACTER

As you can tell from reading this book, I am quite a fan of mobility and training from inside the pit. One major fear many presenters have is forgetting where they are in the curriculum and having to take that long, long silent walk back to the lectern to look at their notes. Take a tip from the acting profession and stay in character.

When I got involved in theater and landed my first sizable role, I learned an unforgettable lesson from a fantastic director. This lesson has helped me as a professional speaker and is one that I pass on to all my Presentation Skills programs. I was dutifully studying my lines night and day. At rehearsal, the director began asking me some nagging, rather silly questions about the character I was playing. "What is his favorite television show?" "What beer does he drink?" "What is his favorite breakfast food?" How ridiculous! I was learning my lines; why not just leave it at that! No wonder acting is perceived as such a strange profession, or is it? One of the theories behind what that director was doing was preparing me not only for success but for failure. I began to know my character better and became a better actor. I also later realized how this technique saved my life when there were problems on stage. No words can describe the terror an actor feels when he or she or someone else on stage forgets his or her lines. It is very similar to the terror presenters feel when they forget where they are in the curriculum. There is an audience, and there is fear. Learning all about my character in theater allowed me to stay in character. Now, for a few precious seconds, I may have been confused as to what line was next. If, however, I stayed in character, it was impossible to forget what my character was doing. In other words, I was still acting as the character I was playing, although I might not be delivering what was written in the script.

As a professional speaker, I can guarantee two things. One is that you will occasionally forget what comes next in your curriculum. The second is that you will not forget the basics. The basics are who you are and what topic you are talking about. That is really all you need. Stay in character (which means you do not have to announce to the trainees that you are hopelessly lost) and ask a question that pertains to your subject. "What do you think so far?" "Has this ever happened to you?" "Do you think this information will be of help to you?" These are not deep questions, but they can help stall. Your next move is to appear interested, backpedal your way to the lectern, nod, smile, and find out where you are. Following this technique allows you the confidence to prowl the pit where you belong. By the way, what does a presenter eat for breakfast?

14. BE ON TIME

This next suggestion may be more of a reminder than a training tip. When it comes to actually conducting your training, be on time. By the way, "on time" means get to your training early. Your best bet is to take no chances. I am not necessarily a superstitious person, but I would not tempt fate. As you are learning, you must deal with a number of variables before you actually begin teaching. Is the air conditioning or heating working? Are the projectors working? Did the materials that you were expecting get delivered? The list can go on and on. (Chapter 6 provides suggestions for what you should check out *before* your trainees arrive.) Arriving early allows you to accomplish all these tasks without that frazzled appearance. Get to your seminar early, relax, collect your thoughts, and enjoy the day. With that type of start for you, I know your trainees will enjoy the day as well.

15. Watch Out for Those Filler Words

Presenters do not like to talk about it. Trainees get distracted by it. Observers can get obsessed by it. What is it? you ask. Little words known as "filler words." These words can take on many forms, such as "um," "ah," or, one of the most common found in the training profession, "okay." They are used in place of pauses and can be a real headache for many presenters.

One way around this difficulty is to use the old Post-it trick. Unfortunately, some presenters actually increase rather than decrease their use of filler words if they spot them in writing. An approach that worked for me was to join an organization called Toastmasters. Toastmasters specializes in the development of those who wish to improve their communication skills. At a typical Toastmasters' meeting, roles are assigned to a number of participants. The role I so fondly remember is one called an Um Counter. This person's job is to spend the entire meeting counting every single filler word that is spoken. At the end of the meeting, the Um Counter calls off the names of all the speakers and the number of filler words each one had used. When it comes right down to it, the best way to correct the problem with filler words is to be conscious of using them and discipline yourself to correct the habit. Toastmasters provided an excellent opportunity for me to correct this habit and simply pause instead of jamming my sentence with filler words. If you are interested, there are Toastmasters chapters in most metropolitan areas, nationally and internationally.

16. Don't Put Trainees on the Spot

One simple fact of life is that due to our slow rate of speech (about 175 words per minute) and our high rate of hearing (about 310 words per minute), students have a natural tendency to mentally check in and check out. This is often referred to as "leapfrogging" and occasionally can frustrate a presenter whose course material requires a lot of questioning and facilitation. Relax. This leapfrogging is natural and, to a limited extent, to be expected. The real danger is to the student who has been asked a question about material he or she has missed. All of us have been in that embarrassing situation before, blankly looking for an answer that will not come. Try a Leap Chip.

At the beginning of each day, I give each student a round two-inch disk to keep on his or her desk. Its use is a simple one. Once a day, for any reason (be it leapfrogging, daydreaming, or simply not knowing), the student may hand the instructor the Leap Chip when called on for an answer. It is important that the instructor does not break stride when receiving a Leap Chip and in no way calls attention to this incident. The instructor simply moves to another student and carries on. The student is now left without a Leap Chip for the rest of the day, which will force the student to work a little harder at tuning in.

17. REWARD TRAINEES

When teaching a class that requires participants to role-play or do any task frequently, friendly competition can sure liven things up. At the beginning of the session, lay out ground rules. Each day, one participant will be selected as a winner based on any of the following criteria: most improved, best overall, best implementation of a new tactic taught, and so on. The award? Try a Frisbee or card hung on Velcro in front of the participant's seat, or even a mug that reads "For today, I'm as good as Rob!" Needless to say, the award name can be whatever you choose (although I am partial to Rob), but I recommend the award not be too serious in nature. The idea is to create friendly competition. Cash prizes may be just the wrong idea here. Make it silly and fun!

For the rest of the day, the winner receives minor privileges, such as determining when the class should take breaks, announcing how long to spend on reading assignments, and making other simple class decisions. At the beginning of the next day, another winner is chosen. The amazing thing about this simple idea is that rarely, if ever, will a student abuse these privileges. In addition, because the criteria for selection are left wide open, the award can be spread around to all the individuals. As the class becomes closer, the students begin to root for and assist those who have not won. Now, that's what training is all about!

18. GET A LOOK AT THOSE EVALUATIONS

The next idea is a simple but effective one. Most presenters I know (including myself early on) avoid looking at the evaluations that will be used following the training. Sometimes the organization that conducts the evaluations is almost secretive about the content of these forms. I used to become frustrated after I finished a seminar and then found out what it was the trainees were evaluating me on. I would then vow to fix it for the next seminar. What about this seminar? If I look at what it is I am to be evaluated on before I speak, I benefit in two ways. First, looking at the evaluations reminds me of what I need to be doing to be successful. Second, it gives me confidence when I know I am ready to comply with what is on the form. Take the mystery out of your training and address the evaluation criteria before you speak.

19. Watch Those Transitions

Once you have studied and learned your UPPOPPR and final review, there is one last piece of the puzzle that I recommend you work with. Most presentations cover three to five major points. What becomes key for you is your ability to move smoothly from point to point. These moves are referred to as "transitions." When watching a presentation, you will notice that an unskilled presenter bumps his or her way from major point to major point. That transition might sound something like this:

Presenter: . . . and that is how the entire process began. Uh, if, um systems are important too. You see, when a system is hooked up correctly. . . . Now, processes are all well and good in theory, but the system you create will be the true signal of your success. You see, when a system is hooked up correctly . . .

20. Start and Finish Strongly

As I have already stated, you get only one chance to make a good impression. You get only one chance to leave a lasting impression as well. A lot can be forgiven when you start your presentation smoothly and end it just as smoothly. Chapter 7, on creating process-driven presentations, discusses the tools you need. Make it a priority, regardless of the condition of your curriculum, to start and finish strongly. That means right before you are scheduled to speak, do not study the entire presentation. If you do, you will be as confused as you were before you started. Look over the curriculum, but five minutes before you begin teaching, study the UPPOPPR. During your last break, look over your closing review. After that, it's practice, practice, practice.

21. Learn Your Trainees' Names

Life just is not fair sometimes. Here you are, with another week of 10 new trainees. Their responsibility is to remember your name and maybe the name of a classmate or two. Your responsibility? To remember the names of the entire class (within reason), and to do it as quickly as possible. It comes with the territory. Nothing says more or less about you in trainees' minds than your ability to remember and use their names. We like to hear our names. Remembering them demonstrates you care and want to get to know participants. Forgetting them can be taken as a slap in the face.

Name tags help a lot. Actually studying the names and committing them to memory help even more. If this is difficult for you, try associating the trainees' names with something or someone that will help you remember. You might even want to take a memory course yourself, but if you make learning your trainees' names a priority, you will be perceived as a more caring presenter.

22. Watch Your Timing

In my humble opinion, I would not say that timing is everything . . . but it is pretty close. Ultimately, many groups will remember you more by your timing than anything else. Think about it.

In this book, I have attempted to illustrate key points by relating them to some of my successes and my failures. Let me now present a doozy of a failure. Many years ago, as a consultant, I was asked to conduct a one-hour motivational seminar to Farmer's Home Administration employees in upstate New York. What did I know about motivational seminars? I was a trainer, not a dinner speaker, so I turned them down. I do not like to bring money into this, but when they offered me $1,350 for the hour and expenses, I changed my mind. One hour, $1,350. I became obsessed by that figure. I had never spoken in front of more than 50 trainees, but what was another 450? I began making little jokes about the money. I would make obnoxious statements to my wife like, "I'd like to talk to you about that, honey, but I'm not sure you could afford it."

The presentation? A piece of cake. I usually can speak for hours off a dinner napkin, but for this presentation, I took no chances. I prepared about eight pages of material, from poems to stories, to help motivate the listeners. I even, rather smugly, prepared two more emergency pages just in case. I had the world by the tail. Big-shot motivational trainer at a resort speaking for one hour to motivate. I took my golf clubs, arrived a day early, and got set for the easiest money of my life.

As I approached the lectern, after being introduced, I was greeted with my first surprise. Five hundred people are *not* fifty people! I was experiencing unaccustomed butterflies. Then came the big surprise. I began to ask my usual barrage of questions only to be greeted by a room full of blank stares. No one ever told me that 500 people do not talk back to the speaker. It was quiet, too quiet. I panicked and began to churn through my material at an absurd pace. I now knew this was not training. There was no real topic. At 16 minutes, I finished my material. At 29 minutes, after slowing to a crawl, I finished my emergency pages. In my mind I kept thinking "$1,350 for one hour."

I began pacing back and forth, sweating profusely, offering a word or two about a message I had already delivered and demanding the audience "think about it." Over and over again I told them, "It could happen to you . . . think about it," followed by a profound "because it has already happened to others . . . think about it." From there, I went into a number of "it might just happen to me . . . think about it!" At 44 minutes, and for the first time in my life, I had nothing left for an audience to think about. I walked off, in a daze, 10 pounds lighter, to polite applause. I was thanked and paid. I was also never invited back.

What did I learn from that experience? Like a good fighter, I needed to be beaten to really grow within my profession. It was a tremendous experience (easier to say years later) and one that I have benefited from immeasurably. When it is all said and done, timing is one of the most critical criteria on which you will be judged. The presentation is the routine. Perfecting your timing is like sticking a good landing. It is a true measure of your professional ability. If you are running short, ask more thought-provoking questions and facilitate some discussions. If you are running long, trim away those discussions and net out what you need to say. Keep a watch inside your lectern and work your glances in subtly. Do not wait until the last five minutes to begin making decisions regarding timing. Remember, whether it is one hour, one day, or one week, that is what the customer requires and that is what you are under fire to deliver. Think about it. . . .

23. Start with an Activity

For many presenters, one of the hardest aspects of training is simply getting started. Time and time again, you will hear someone say, "If I can just get past the first five minutes, I will be fine." Here is an idea that might help. Plan an activity, such as a small-group exercise relating to your subject. It could be as simple as splitting the room in half and allowing the trainees to come up with five benefits that they could receive from attending your seminar. With an exercise like that, you will not only have a head start on building one of the most critical pieces of your presentation, your utility, you will get a good indication of trainees' attitudes as well.

The key to this idea is the time that a well-placed exercise will take will allow you to get your emotions under control. Once the exercise is over, chances are, you will have worked through a lot of your nervousness and will be in better position to nail down a solid UPPOPPR.

24. Cover Up and Shut Up

Why is it that when presenters make mistakes, there is such a great need to inform all those around? Perhaps it is nervousness, or maybe the perfectionist in all of us. In any case, it is unnecessary. Nobody is keeping score so just keep moving forward. How many times have you taken a course where the instructor seems to keep up a steady chatter every time he makes the slightest mistake, mumbling to the trainees and himself. Most of the time the trainees are neither aware nor interested. Keep moving on and roll with the punches. It is nice to have a presenter who is not perfect.

25. Check Your Spelling

You know, I'm going to tell you a little secret. My spelling really isn't that bad. This is a secret because many participants in my training programs wouldn't believe it, and for good reason. Frequently in the programs I put on, as I'm writing something on the flip chart, I casually ask the group how to spell a certain word.

The truth of the matter is, I really do know how to spell most of the words I am asking them to spell. I just want to nudge the people behind me, and asking them to clarify the spelling of a word does the trick. Swallow your pride a bit, ask for help, and watch your quiet room jump to your aid.

26. USE A SEPARATE AIR MOUSE

As any trainer or presenter has seen, there has been a revolution in the way presentations are given today. With the help of presentation software and LCD projectors, a presenter can create crisp, vibrant slides, animations, graphs, and charts. Most of the projectors come with a handheld device called an air mouse that advances slides. Unfortunately, with the air mouse has come trouble.

In this book, I have included tips on how to troubleshoot some of these problems, but let me provide you with a trick of the trade to bypass the problem altogether. Buy a separate air mouse that isn't run by the projector. If you do this, you won't have to worry about rebooting your computer or checking for bad connections. You can walk up to any laptop, plug in the air mouse while the laptop is running, and, within seconds, your air mouse is activated.

This sure beats the alternative of shutting both systems down, rebooting the projector, and rebooting the laptop. If that isn't enough to scare you off, remember, after all of this, you are still not guaranteed that this projector's air mouse will work properly.

When you finish using an air mouse that hooks directly into the laptop, simply unplug the air mouse, and the regular mouse takes over again in seconds. When there are multiple speakers piggybacking off one laptop, this solution is a must.

27. USE A HUMAN AIR MOUSE

Now that you have a basic idea of how to bypass the projector's air mouse with one of your own, let's look at another idea that will bypass the air mouse altogether. I discovered this idea one day when my air mouse stopped working.

Rather than run back to the laptop every time I had to advance a slide, I asked one of the participants to do it for me. I must admit I hammed it up a bit by working out a signal system to let my participant know when it was time to advance the slide.

We started innocently enough with me pointing or nodding at the participant who was helping. Of course, soon I was pointing the dead mouse at him, pointing my elbow at him, pointing a pen at him, standing on one leg and pointing my other leg at him, and then I got a little silly. In any case, too much hamming can take away from what you are doing, but suffice it to say, there were a lot of people who not only stayed awake but enjoyed the presentation quite a bit.

28. CARRY A POWER STRIP
Let's stay on that theme of technology for a moment. Years ago presenters carried a bunch of overheads or slides for one visual aid. Times have changed, and so have the power requirements. Hotels or meeting rooms might offer you a screen, a cart, and an extension cord, but the rest is up to you.

When you use your laptop for a presentation, you now have two plugs, one for the laptop and another plug for the LCD projector. But wait. If you are really trying to jazz up that presentation, there is more.

How about some music? The device is going to have another plug. Will you be incorporating any video to be run through your projector? You're going to have another plug. All of a sudden, you are out of outlet space.

I'm not saying you should carry an eight-plug power strip, but I would recommend a four-plug power strip. They are fairly small and easy to carry. In addition, most power strips come with their own fuses to protect against power surges. If you are plugging in a laptop, LCD projector, music, and video, you may very well be plugging in $10,000 worth of equipment. Shell out the $10 for a small power strip and sleep well.

29. PICK UP SOME SIDE SPEAKERS
As projectors get lighter and brighter, one small problem can arise. Something had to go when the size of projectors shrank, and in this case, it was the projector's speakers. That means if you are playing a video or perhaps even running some music off your laptop, you are in a little trouble. For larger seminars, you can get your local AV professional to wire the sound into the house speakers, but what about the small ones?

Go to your local electronics store and purchase your own speakers. They can be very inexpensive ($20 to $40), but make sure they are amplified. That means they will electronically project the sound to your audience. It also means they will either plug in or need batteries, so plan accordingly.

30. Be Vulnerable

I suppose it's a little unusual to hear a professional speaker who has spent the majority of his time encouraging you to stay in control while presenting to give up a little bit of that control, but that's just what I'm saying. Sometimes we can be so in control it intimidates an audience. Sharing a story that shows a softer side or humbles you can bond you with an audience. Given the nature of presentations, for most professionals, there are plenty of stories to pick from.

31. Dress for Success

An often-overlooked aspect of delivering like a pro is looking like a pro. Many I work with will boast of their favorite tie, or suit, or shoes. Well, that's terrific, but the fact is, this isn't about your favorite clothes but rather matching the audience in their appearance. One logistical question that always needs to be asked is "What's the attire for this meeting?" Perhaps it's business suits, or business casual. Whatever it is, your job is to match that request and then dress it up slightly from there. You are the presenter, but you don't want to call attention to yourself but dressing below your audience or too high above it.

32. Address Implementation with more than Words

The 600-pound gorilla in the room after any presentation centers on implementation. Can the group you just worked with implement what you just taught them? Why leave the answer to this question to chance? Try putting in exercises that can be accomplished after the training has been completed and done without an instructor present. Based on what you are presenting on, try to utilize templates, job aids, implementation guides, and more to show your audience you are serious about implementation.

33. Get Help for Those Role-Plays, Case Studies, and Simulations

Creating the perfect exercise from the participant's perspective is imperative. If what's written doesn't mirror the real world from the participant's perspective, a lot of good work just went down the drain. For years I tried to write exercises myself until one day I realized I had subject matter experts on call: my clients. Let your client create a real-world scenario and then pop it inside the exercise you are developing. You and your client will be awfully glad you did.

34. Learn How to Say Thank You

Thanking a participant certainly sounds easy enough, doesn't it? My father-in-law taught me a simple approach to handle compliments. Every time I finished a seminar, a few people would come up and slip a compliment my way. I would respond with a typical "Oh, that really wasn't my best" or "Normally, I'm a little sharper during my Q&A sessions." My father-in-law encouraged me to look at the situation from a different angle: from the angle of the person who was complimenting me.

He also reminded me that when someone pays you a compliment, it's a very important moment for that person. Someone has been so moved by something you did that he or she felt a need to step forward, move past his or her own fear, and tell you something that is somewhat personal. With this knowledge, are you still sure you want to reward this leap of faith by another person with the phrase "That really wasn't my best today?"

The solution is an easy one. It requires a few moments of placing your hands on your computer keyboard, or grabbing a pen and paper, and writing out a phrase or two that feels comfortable for you. My phrase goes something like this:

"That means a great deal to me, and I can't thank you enough for those kind words."

This is usually greeted with a smile, a handshake, and a look of satisfaction on the face of the person who had the courage to offer those thoughtful words. Oh, and it will make you feel pretty good about yourself as well.

35. Try Using a Bell

The last suggestion I would like to make treads dangerously close to a style issue, but you might want to give it a try. For many years, I have kept a small call bell on the desk that my lectern sits on and have found it to be helpful. When do I use it? Obviously, I can use it to regain control when necessary, but there are other uses as well. I find myself using it to start and stop seminar breaks. I find myself ringing it when something funny is said or a good idea is mentioned. I also use it when something exciting happens in the seminar or when the trainees are competing and want to signal a good response. In other words, there are endless opportunities to use a bell. Coincidentally, about 35 Xerox trainers have call bells perched next to their lecterns. Put one in front of your lectern, and I guarantee you will be amazed at how often you find yourself ringing the bell.

Summary
My intent in presenting these ideas to you was to spare you from some of the harder lessons that can be learned under fire. Also, I hope that maybe I have inspired some of you to try a couple of ideas of your own. There is no risk in trying, only in complacency.

Part III

Improving the Training Process

Chapter 15

Inside the Mind of a Professional Speaker

How to Present Your Best Self

Few jobs can match the role of presenter in the number of skills that must be displayed publicly by one individual. Presenting is one of those rare professions that is nearly impossible to understand unless you have actually done it yourself. As I mentioned before, there are no real simulations for firsthand action under fire in the pit. The ultimate irony in most training departments, unfortunately, is that these departments typically are managed by individuals who have never conducted a day of training themselves. Empathizing with the feelings a presenter is experiencing is difficult, to say the least. It is my intent to take a stab at giving you a tour inside the mind of a presenter to help you better understand some of the unique aspects of professional speaking.

Always Present a Positive and Enthusiastic Attitude

Let's start with a presenter's attitude for the programs he or she delivers. To illustrate a point, I will be more than happy to tell you my attitude toward conducting a Presentation Skills program. Usually the anticipation starts on about the Wednesday before the week I am to teach the course. It is only a little stir, but it counts. Thursday morning that little stir becomes more of an anxious hum anticipating next week's fantastic class. For some reason on Friday, I walk around with a kind of silly grin. It looks as if I just pulled off a practical joke on my coworkers when, in fact, I am already looking forward to Monday's start. Saturday I try to avoid thinking about what is to come, but it is usually no use. I find myself happily daydreaming about the first five minutes of the course.

By Sunday, my daydreaming takes me well beyond the first five minutes, with sleep not coming easily that night. I am always up well before my alarm clock goes off on the Monday morning of a Presentation Skills program, anxiously looking forward to the start of what I am expecting to be a cohesive group of trainees coming to town for what I consider the best course ever written.

Do you think that is a true story? If you asked me to answer that question, I would tell you quite simply: What does it matter as long as *you* believe it is true? That is the bottom line when it comes to a presenters' attitudes toward their curriculum. They have no choice; they must fall in love with what it is they are teaching. They must acquire this love affair for two reasons. First, when presenters do not like the curriculum they are teaching, it flat out shortens their life span. Once again, think of a salesperson. Most good salespeople will tell you that they can overcome just about any obstacle you put in front of them to make the sale if, and only if, they truly believe in their product. If salespeople do not believe in the product they are selling, no matter how they try to deny it, those feelings eventually act as a cancer ending their career. It soon becomes nearly impossible for them to get up day after day and sell ideas that are poorly put together or that they do not agree with. It becomes imperative that a presenter sit down with the supervisor, manager, or whoever is responsible for the curriculum and work out a solution he or she is comfortable with. This is by no means a time for management to adopt a "my way or the highway" approach. For the sake of the presenter, both parties must use patience until they can reach a compromise. Remember, you are looking inside the mind of a presenter, and nothing shortens the career of a presenter faster than bad curriculum with no compromise.

The second reason a presenter must sell to the seminar his or her love for the curriculum is a little more selfish. The presenter's attitude plays a major role in the participant's attitude toward the curriculum. That goes for every module as well. When a presenter stands in front of the trainees and says, "This next module is a little on the slow side, but we are supposed to teach it, so hang in there," the presenter does a terrible disservice to the trainees. This happens often. Next time it does, look around. I will tell you what you see. You will see an entire audience tune out everything that is taught for the duration of this "slow" module. If that does not scare you, let me try this one on you. As you now know, I believe it is quite rare for a trainee to come to training prepared to snipe the presenter. It is not rare, however, for trainees to come to a seminar discouraged, depressed, frustrated, or unhappy about training. Most presenters learn the hard way that a bad attitude on their part acts as a catalyst to trainees who are one step away from acting as snipers. For presenters' own well-being, it is imperative that they adopt a healthy attitude toward what they are teaching.

Don't Advertise Any Lack of Experience

In most professions, it is absolutely normal for a person to tell fellow workers information that affects him or her on a day-to-day basis. In training, for a presenter, nothing could be further from the truth. A presenter's personal life, health, and job satisfaction are irrelevant. Training is a position that does not afford you with that type of closeness to your trainees.

For instance, if you were to teach a course you had never taught before, would you tell your trainees it was your first time? Better think this one over for a second. Let's get the reasons in favor out of the way first. Most presenters who inform their trainees that they have never taught the course before are looking for a crutch. They may not word it quite that way, but that is what they are counting on: "Well, it is his first time"; "He was pretty good for his first time." The thinking here is if you want some empathy and understanding, you will probably get it if you inform your trainees you are teaching their course for the first time. Sounds pretty good to me, if it were not for the word "probably."

You see, you probably will get a lot of empathy if you announce you are teaching a seminar for the first time. The downside to this sudden dose of honesty is you may get just the opposite. If you have trainees in your seminar who are disgruntled or potential snipers, you have just given them a loaded pistol and asked them to aim it at your head. To that handicap, add the difficulties some trainees who are natural skeptics may bring to the training seminar. Also add the probability of being constantly challenged on practically every point you attempt to make. Your disclosure to these individuals may represent a serious challenge to your credibility as a presenter.

The risks involved with disclosing this type of information just are not worth it. So what is the answer, lie? Absolutely not! I would never suggest such a thing. How does selective disclosure grab you? In the example we just looked at, I would assume most presenters would at least have had an opportunity either to see the course taught or to work with the developers if the course has never been taught. How does this sound to you:

PRESENTER: As for my experience with this course, I have been working in various capacities with the course for some time now and have a good knowledge of the program from both a presenter and trainee perspective.

In other words, "Don't mess with me; I know my stuff!" So many presenters get themselves in hot water disclosing information that not only is no business of the trainees but also is of no value.

I worked to cross-train an individual once on a program I used to teach for Xerox, which was an insurance-type sales course for property and casualty agents. Although the individual I was cross-training had a tremendous amount of knowledge about the curriculum and the topic, she had no experience selling the actual product the trainees sold. Certainly it would have been preferable to have some specific product experience, but contrary to popular belief, it is not that critical. Selling is selling, and although product experience may represent added credibility in the trainees' eyes, it can and must often be worked around when forced to train under fire. In this situation, I begged the individual I was cross-training simply to tell the trainees that she had a lot of experience in their field, from home office duties to work in the field (she had gone on numerous sales calls with salespeople). What the trainees did not know would not hurt them. I do want to emphasize here, if the trainees asked directly about sales training experience, this individual was prepared to respond "None." As the three-day training was to begin, I sat back like a proud father waiting to see the fruits of my labor. Instead, the individual I was cross-training decided to toss out what we had discussed and informed the group the only experience she had within the area they sold in was as an underwriter. The trainees became so agitated with her and her lack of "real" experience that the woman called it quits by lunchtime. The proud father was then forced to conduct the training for the duration of the course, and the woman never attempted to teach the course again.

You see, when all is said and done, the precious credibility that every presenter strives for is not given; it is *earned*. Selective disclosure only allows you the opportunity to gain enough listening time with your students to earn that respect. The rest is up to you. As a footnote, I taught that course to property and casualty insurance agents for over three years, and the course received the highest marks it has ever received in the nine years that Xerox conducted it. I mention that simply to prove my point. I had no experience in nor had I ever sold property and casualty insurance in my life.

How to Handle Illness on the Job

Illness is another example of an issue presenters can be torn over regarding how much they want to share with trainees. As with the first-timer example, one side of telling an audience about your condition is the feeling that trainees will be sensitive and supportive. True enough. These same trainees will also scrutinize your performance and every action you take: "Not bad, considering the presenter was sick," they will say. "Too bad, our presenter was sick. I wonder what this course is like with a healthy presenter." For someone who does not have a positive attitude coming into the seminar, the comments could be much harsher.

Let me give you a rather macho example of a trainer dealing with an illness. Once I flew to Madison, Wisconsin, to conduct a three-day sales training course for Xerox. Twelve trainees were flown in from all over Wisconsin and some of the bordering states. The night before the presentation was to begin, I began to feel strange. I say "strange" instead of sick because (please knock on wood as you read this), I seldom get sick and am never really sure when I am. As a child, I came down with no childhood illnesses despite my parents making me play with every child who was exposed to or was coming down with any of the classic childhood diseases. Well, at 5:00 p.m. I was feeling strange, and by 7:00 p.m. I was sick. As I lay alone in my hotel room sweating one minute, freezing the next, I began to wonder what I was going to do in the morning. After a couple of trips to the bathroom, I decided to try to sleep on it. After enduring a rather long night of discomfort, I made my decision. With so many participants coming from so far and clearing their schedules for these three days, I decided to go for it. In presenting, as in the theater, the show must go on. I would tell no one of my illness, try to not get too close to anyone, and give it my best.

My best was spending about 90 percent of the time I was teaching sitting in my chair in the middle of the pit, drinking fluids constantly and wheeling myself around to different trainees to answer their questions. Occasionally, I would summon up every ounce of strength and make a token move out of the chair to cross the room, shaking my fist in a pathetic attempt of enthusiasm, and then return to my chair. Remember, no one in the room had ever seen me train before, and they had no idea this was not exactly my style of teaching. The only other times I would get out of my chair would be to call a break, wait until the trainees left the room, and go throw up. I did a pretty good job coming up with excuses as to why I could not go out with the trainees at night, but I could not get out of the final dinner celebrating the conclusion of the program. Those who know me know that for a 160-pound man, I can put away a lot of food when I want to. That night I reverted back to my childhood days, ordered a shrimp and rice dish, and proceeded to push my rice around the perimeter of my plate, successfully hiding my shrimp. If my childhood dog, Brandy, had been there, I would have been funneling my scraps to him as well.

When the program was all over, I had gone almost three days without eating anything and had lost eight pounds. This I am not proud of. I had no real idea how sick I was, and if I had known I was not going to get any better during the program, I probably would have called it off. What I am proud of, however, is that I received 12 evaluations from trainees who raved about the training they had just received. A couple of the evaluations specifically made reference to the enthusiasm I displayed throughout. When all the trainees left, and only the person who coordinated the event remained, I told this man of my condition. He remarked, "I thought you were nervous. I saw your hand shaking some of the times you went to take a drink."

The point I am trying to make through this story is that presenters must keep their feelings and emotions to themselves to be successful. Presenters move. Presenters have fights with their spouses. Presenters have bad days. None of this information is relevant in a seminar environment. In reality, the decision at hand is not whether to tell trainees or not to tell trainees. The decision really becomes whether to teach the seminar or not teach the seminar. In my mind, barring a dire emergency, the show must go on.

Surviving with a Split Personality

In looking inside the mind of a presenter, I have attempted primarily to show you the public side of the presenter. I think that it is important to explain to you right here and now that anyone who conducts training on more than a casual basis is forced to acquire a split personality. There is a public side the trainees see and a private side friends and family see. The longer an individual remains a presenter, the more pronounced the split becomes. The more professional speakers I meet, the more I find this to be true.

The reasons for this splitting of personalities is really quite simple. When presenters are doing the job they are paid to do, they are putting everything they have into their work. Their attitude must be perfect, their control flawless, their focus acute. To carry this type of concentration out of the presentation environment would cause a trainer to burn out very quickly. It can also drive those working around the presenter a little wacky. Every now and then I will come home, forget where I am, and say things like, "I would like the salad, then the dressing. After the salad is served, everyone at the table may then eat the main course. Let's begin." Fortunately, I have an understanding wife who will basically tell me to join her in reality, and the episode ends rather abruptly.

Stay in Training Shape

Due to the energy required to properly conduct a seminar, it is rare to find a presenter with a substantial delivery schedule who has a weight problem. A presenter gets into training shape when he or she begins to teach courses. Maintaining the proper type of focus for eight hours a day, five days a week, is no easy matter. For a presenter to handle a typical schedule (four weeks on, one week developmental), it typically takes about three weeks to get in shape. The work can be so exhausting that often when presenters take off for as long as a month at a time, they will need to get back in speaking shape again.

Be Confident, Not Arrogant

Perhaps the most misunderstood aspect of a professional speaker involves the confidence this individual exudes. For many, this confidence appears more like arrogance. When looking inside the mind of a presenter, you begin to have a better understanding as to why.

Presenters who have been under fire in the pit know that the most dangerous mistake they can make is to appear unsure of themselves in front of the trainees. This lack of confidence can be detected in their voices, their facial expressions, and even in their physical movements. It is imperative, for the presenters' own survival, to learn to remove doubts or, at the very least, to mask them.

As with most sports, professional speaking is a profession that is actually very mental. Successful field goal kickers in the NFL all have their own strange little quirks and superstitions; however, they all share one common action. Listen to any kicker talk about his thoughts prior to kicking the ball, and he will tell you that he has a vision of actually seeing the ball going through the uprights. He must not let doubt sneak through.

One of my favorite sports heroes growing up was Joe Theismann. In my mind, Joe was one of the greatest quarterbacks who has ever played the game. When he played for the Washington Redskins, the press, fans, and even the coach frequently misunderstood him. George Allen, one of the most famous NFL coaches to ever roam the sidelines, was one of the many who misunderstood him.

You see, Joe liked to talk . . . a lot. One of the many quotes that made the rounds in Washington, D.C., was "Joe never met a microphone he didn't like." Many, particularly Coach Allen, perceived him as arrogant. He wanted to play so badly that when Coach Allen would not play him at quarterback, he lobbied to be played anywhere. In one of the most bizarre moves in the NFL, Coach Allen took him up on his offer and actually played him as the team's punt returner during one of his seasons on the bench. How many NFL quarterbacks who are playing now would volunteer, let alone be assigned by the coach, to return punts?

He returned punts because he told everyone he could. He led the Redskins to a Super Bowl victory, set team offensive records, became one of the greatest quarterbacks on the Redskins, and perhaps the NFL, and told everyone he could.

So what was holding Joe Theismann back? Certainly not his confidence! But he was considered undersized and did not possess the arm strength of the best quarterbacks. What he did possess was an immeasurable heart, and confidence—a lot of confidence.

He wasn't just a great quarterback for the Washington Redskins; he was a leader for that team. He would never respond to a question about his play by saying he might to do well with a little luck, or that his size might be a problem. He was so sure of his abilities that not only did he believe in them, but so did those who played with him. Without demeaning his opponent, he had faith his team wouldn't lose, he would tell you his team wouldn't lose, and coincidentally he rarely did lose.

When a presenter goes into a seminar believing he or she will absolutely positively be successful, that presenter will almost always succeed. Once, while working with Xerox, I was observed and then interviewed by a group that wanted a representative from the private sector to address about 700 participants. The purpose of the presentation was not only to speak for two hours on how we (as a company) negotiate with our customers but to be motivational as well. This was an annual event with a list of previous presenters that reads like a who's who of famous speakers. After watching me deliver a presentation, we sat down and they began to ask me some questions. I did not realize it, but every answer I gave them included statements such as "Without question I will do this" and "I can definitely make that happen."

Finally, one of the people conducting the interview stopped and said, "We have asked you 10 questions, and 10 times you have given us a definitive answer. How can you be so sure of yourself?" This was one of the first times I had ever stopped and consciously analyzed the behavior I was exhibiting. Still, the answer came out rather easily: "How can I get up and in two hours convince 700 people who have never heard of me that I am for real, my material is worthwhile, and they should be motivated and excited if I do not believe in myself?" Their search ended with that comment as the individual who asked the question smiled at me and told the others, "We've got our man."

I recently watched an interview with Joe Theismann who summed it up well. Theismann said, "I have been accused of being both egotistical and arrogant. To this I say 'Pshaw. I'm simply the best at what I do.'" As a lifetime Redskins fan and an admirer of Mr. Theismann, I must say I could not say it better.

Arrogance? No. Confidence? You bet. Presenters would look silly if they got up in front of a group of people and told them that they thought the ideas they was presenting might help them, but then again they might not. I want presenters who work for me to be team players. I also understand that a large ego comes with the territory. With that large ego comes the confidence to face even the most difficult situations courageously and without hesitation.

Coping with Doubt

I suppose the last aspect of the mind of presenters involves the five-letter word that frightens them the most. The word is "doubt." This word can haunt some presenters into early retirement from corporate training. There is no other profession that subjects an individual to as much scrutiny and judgment. The successful presenters do not remove doubt; they coexist with it. They know that doubt can actually inspire them to work harder and give more to a seminar. When these presenters are actually in front of trainees, thoughts of doubt are pushed away and confidence takes its place. Sometimes doubt remains dormant for a long time, but no matter how well it is hidden, it is often only a bad seminar away from surfacing. This point serves as a reminder to anyone who goes under fire that a presenter is only as good as his or her last seminar. Strangely, in retrospect, doubt actually becomes the catalyst that makes training so exciting to so many presenters.

Working with Anxiety

Anxiety regarding speaking in front of a group of people should not be taken lightly. It happens to be a very common fear among most people, as illustrated in this list of the 10 most common fears:

The Ten Most Common Fears[1]

1. Flying
2. Germs
3. Being closed in
4. Crowded spaces
5. Public speaking
6. Heights and falling
7. The dark
8. Snakes and spiders
9. Needles
10. Thunder and lightning

One of the biggest concerns most presenters or public speakers have to deal with when working is anxiety. You will notice that I do not

---

[1] John Hardy, https://healthversed.com/2016/09/10-most-common-fears

like to use the word "nervousness." I avoid using that word because it conjures up a lot of negative thoughts and fears. Anxiety, in contrast, is a better word and one that we all can live with. You see, anxiety is a natural occurrence that you can actually use to your advantage. Before a big presentation, I am often pacing about in another room attempting to channel my anxiety into energy. To this day, I still visualize a racehorse, loaded in and ready for the gate to open so it can be free to run. That is what anxiety can be directed to: energy and drive. The only time I actually do get nervous is when I am not feeling any anxiety. That is when you run the risk of being flat. Here are some other points you may wish to consider when coping with anxiety.

WELCOME TO THE CLUB

The first tip to remember is that everyone experiences the same anxiety that you do. True, sometimes it is to a greater or lesser degree, but everyone experiences it. Some of the most famous television and movie stars have documented their dealings with anxiety. We all experience it. It is natural and to be expected. Do not deny your feelings. Simply accept them and realize that we are all in the same boat.

THEY'RE ROOTING FOR YOU

Another point to remember when coping with anxiety is to realize that your trainees want you to do well. You don't believe me? Then I will prove it to you. Think back to the last time you were a trainee and attended a seminar. I refuse to believe you rocked back in your chair and whispered to the person sitting next to you, "I hope this seminar is terrible. I hope the presenter is boring and we get nothing out of our week here." You might not have been conscious of it, but I think you might have been saying just the opposite. If it were verbalized, I think it would have sounded a lot more like, "I hope this seminar is good. I hope we got a good presenter. I want to maximize my time out of the field and learn as much as possible." You see, I believe in a basic principle (please do not take this as being too cynical): People are greedy. We appeal to that greed by stating utilities that address "What's In It For Me" for the participants. Presenters are soothed by that greed, knowing most trainees would prefer not to waste their time in a seminar and want to maximize their experiences. Before you even speak, those trainees are rooting for you.

GET MOVING

One of the best techniques I know of to better control anxiety is movement. You already know that movement is a natural for helping maintain interest within your training. Now movement is back again as an aid to dealing with anxiety. Different circumstances will dictate just how much movement you can use. If you are teaching a new curriculum that you do not know well, obviously your mobility will be somewhat reduced. Questions, discussion, anecdotes, and presentation aids can still allow you to move in even the most difficult times. The bottom line is, if you want to cope with anxiety, get in that pit and move.

STUDY THE START

I mentioned it earlier and I will mention it again: Study the start of your presentation. If you put in the time to get comfortable with the first three or four minutes, your anxiety will come down. Think back on the presentations you have given in your life from grade school on, and one memory will most likely be constant. Those first couple of minutes were difficult and then things got easier. Study those first couple of minutes, and I assure you things will get easier and you will become more confident as well.

PREPARE, PREPARE, PREPARE

In real estate, they say the three most important factors in buying a house are location, location, and location. In coping with anxiety, some of the most important factors a presenter needs to deal with are preparation, preparation, and preparation. More than anything else, anxiety is a fear of the unknown. The more unknowns you can eliminate, the more confident you will become. Want to make sure you use your equipment properly? Prepare. Want to ask the right types of questions at the right time? Prepare. Want to deliver a meaningful UPPOPPR? Prepare. The list can go on and on. Want to thrive under fire? Prepare!

TAKE A BREATH . . . OR TWO

Everyone experiences anxiety, and on particular occasions, you may be fortunate enough to experience butterflies. That feeling in your stomach called "butterflies" is really nothing more than a lack of oxygen in the middle region of your body. This is caused by a stress response sending more oxygen to the larger muscles in your body. This feeling can be reduced by taking one or two deep breaths, holding them, and letting them out slowly. Remember, that is one or two deep breaths. I do not advocate hyperventilation as a technique to conquer anxiety. There is an old saying regarding the management of butterflies: "If you get butterflies, the trick is not necessarily to get rid of them but rather to just get them to fly in formation."

Put on Your Game Face

If all else fails, allow me to give one suggestion of what not to do. Try not to give in to the anxious feelings. Do not feel obligated to tell your audience how nervous you are. If I could report to you that I have seen this technique work, I would. You can let everyone in the seminar know how nervous and afraid you are and the reality is, the seminar will not be one bit easier for you. There are just too many trainees who will take advantage of that type of situation. So, you do not feel 100 percent confident. Welcome to the club. Put on your game face, which, by the way, is a confident, enthusiastic face, and have a ball.

Summary

Standing up, and speaking in front of others is far more complicated emotionally then most would think, and often underestimated until someone actually steps in the pit. Understanding the way professionals think, act, and survive can help you cope whether it's your turn to take to the pit, or your turn to support someone else who is. Most importantly, stay positive, stay in shape, stay healthy, and stay away from doubt, and you'll be sure to present your best self!

Chapter 16

The Value of Good Training

Hiring Effective Trainers

When was the last time you left a retail store thinking to yourself, "That is the last time I come back to this place"? Was it because the item you were considering buying was not up to par, or was it something else? Perhaps it was a futile search for an item that was no longer in stock. Maybe it was that it took so long to be waited on. Maybe it was a feeling of indifference by the individual waiting on you. All these possibilities add up to one thing: lost revenue.

Now let me ask you another question similar to the first. When was the last time you left a retail store thinking to yourself, "That was a pleasant experience; I really enjoyed that"? In this second scenario, perhaps it was the courtesy extended by the salesperson. Maybe it was the organization's ability to convince you that you were important. One thing is for sure. You will return.

I am not saying that every time you have a favorable experience, it is a direct result of good training . . . exactly. I am saying that statistics speak for themselves. A general rule of thumb used in business today is that when it is all said and done, about 15 percent of a company's problems relate to people and about 85 percent relate to process. I am a firm believer that one of the goals of good training is to teach repeatable, predictable processes to assist on the job. The sad truth that reinforces this point is that most people will actually tolerate a level of service that is subpar, as long as it is consistent. A lot of people really want no surprises. Often it is inconsistency that causes rejection from our customers.

Statistics also show a rather frustrating correlation to the impact of a less than favorable experience. Depending on your source, you will find the experts saying that a disappointed customer will tell anywhere between nine and 15 people about his or her dissatisfaction. The frustrating portion of these studies is that a satisfied customer will tell anywhere between two and five people about the experience. It would seem only fair for customers to tell an equal number of people about their experiences, good or bad, but it just does not work out that way. One way or another, after that first bad experience, the honeymoon is over.

With those numbers in mind, it is time to turn your attention to the training that is or is not up to par. Gone is the notion that an individual who does not have frontline contact with the customer is somehow insulated from responsibility to that customer. No matter how far down the line of internal customers or how removed from direct customer contact these individuals are, the results of their actions eventually affect the customer. Therefore, not only can the training that employees receive have a major effect on how these employees do their jobs, it can have a major effect on the customer as well.

Meet the New Breed of Presenters

With more and more companies beginning to realize the impact of good training, a revolution is occurring in corporate training departments. The old idea of the corporate trainer being a stuffed shirt who "could not do so he teaches" is evaporating.

Corporate trainers touch the company and customer more than any president or CEO. Who is the first employee most new hires are exposed to in a mentor position? It is seldom the manager, because new employees are usually too overwhelmed and intimidated with management. Coworkers send too many conflicting signals. Even early on in a new hire's career, there can be a sense of competition among employees or even just a lack of time to really show a new person the ropes. The only group aggressively approaching the new hire is one I like to refer to as the We Hate It Here and Think Anyone Who Likes It Here Is a Fool club. It consists of employees who for some reason or another are fed up with the company and want out. Like junkies, one way they make themselves feel better is to prey on the vulnerable and try to turn them to their way of thinking. As soon as a new employee joins the company, these club members go on a membership drive. Starting a new job is traumatic enough without aggravating the stress by doubting the decision to take the job in the first place. Often the person who can most quickly come to the rescue of the new employee is this new breed of presenter.

How about the more tenured employee who has been with the company for enough time performing at an acceptable level? Nothing flashy, you understand, just quietly doing his or her job. Do you realize how many people go about their lives quietly doing their jobs? In my management training experiences talking with many frontline managers, all seem to agree that in any given work situation, the numbers break down about like this:

- ♦ Ten percent of the employees are superstars. They do a wonderful job, receive constant recognition, and will continue to perform at that level.
- ♦ Ten percent of the employees are regarded as (for the lack of a better term) mistakes. Most likely they should never have been hired, are probably hanging on, and will eventually quit or be terminated.
- ♦ Eighty percent of the employees are competent. There is nothing flashy about these individuals; they are the ones who just seem to quietly do their jobs. The discouraging point is that so many managers simply forget about these employees. As a matter of fact, the vast majority of these employees end up quitting for that exact reason: a lack of recognition.

So here we have this silent mass within the workplace that to all intents and purposes remains untapped. What would happen if we made a point of recognizing their work? Nothing to recognize you say? Oh come now, look harder. Maybe they are not flashy and do not excel in some of the more obvious areas, but there must be something they are good at. For instance, maybe they simply come in on time every day. Do you think if they were recognized for it they would be late the next day? No way! Essentially, what you would be accomplishing is solidifying good habits. As a matter of fact, you may help to open the floodgates that will inspire the employee to do other jobs better as well. I want to be sure that I am sending out the correct message here regarding the intent of recognition. It is a way to inspire employee performance. It is not a way to have a discussion to improve performance in other areas. That is the quickest way to negate any positives that may come out of this experience.

You may be asking yourself, "What does giving recognition have to do with training?" Before I answer that, let me first tell you why most managers I have met do not give recognition. It is not because they feel there is not enough recognition to go around. It is because they feel that all employees want is more money, and there is not enough money to go around. This is where the possibility of training can come in. When training is truly effective and has the kind of reputation that it should have, it can be used as a reward. I count on the new breed of presenters not to let you down.

According to the Manager Foundation, when you consider wasted salary, recruitment costs, training, impact on the rest of the team, and missed or delayed business deliverables, the cost of hiring, and then firing an employee can be a minimum of 25 percent of their salary. The higher the salary the more expensive the costs, which could range between 20,000 to over 120,000. The stakes are high when it comes to making the correct decision regarding the hiring of new employees. It would be a crime not to do all you can to save employees on the edge of failure. The new breed of presenter can come through here too.

Let me now introduce you to the new breed of presenters. The new breed exhibits a number of unique qualities. To begin with, they are quick studies who can become subject matter experts, regardless of the curriculum, in a matter of one or two seminars. Add to that their enormous energy and enthusiasm for their curriculum and students, regardless of the topic. The new breed consists of risk takers who will stop at nothing to make their messages understood and retained. Their tremendous amount of empathy for their students sends trainees out motivated and ready to apply the principles learned.

Successful companies are now, finally, putting the same level of attention into who is teaching the material as they are into what material is being taught. The fact of the matter is, the curriculum is only as good as the presenter delivering it. The stakes are high, and the consequences are real. No one in the company directly affects as many individuals as most trainers. Hiring the right individual has become essential.

Whom to Hire

A question that is often asked of me by other training managers is, "What do I look for when hiring a trainer?" As with most mysteries of hiring, there is not a patent answer. If there were, I would dedicate this entire book to it, and I would be retired and wealthy as well. Different trainers have different styles that they make work for themselves, which complicates the answer even more. Let me instead answer the question by telling you some traits I would be most interested in spotting during an interview.

The first quality I would be looking for during my questioning would be the individual's ability to think quickly on his or her feet. The majority of my questions would be case study scenarios with many possible answers. As an experienced interviewer will tell you, the intent of these questions is not necessarily to spot the best response. There really should not be a best response but rather other less obvious areas to look at. First, watch the logic pattern the individual is following. Are you detecting good problem-solving skills? Good trainers are good problem solvers. Also, see just how well this individual can make you believe in his or her answer. It will be one of your best opportunities to judge how articulate and persuasive the individual is. It will also be an opportunity to get a sense of whether the individual can make you believe in his or her point of view. Sit back, and allow yourself to be swayed if the selling of the answer is a good one. This exercise, and watching for a candidate's ability to persuade, will demonstrate one of those rare skills that cannot easily be taught to a new trainer. Some skills you either have or you don't have. It is not imperative, but I sure would like to feel persuaded.

Another quality I look for is one I personally emphasize a great deal. A crucial quality that is a common link among the finest trainers in the world is "compassion." It shows up in the seminar room again and again as a sense of empathy for the trainees. This trait is not an easy one to spot in an interview. However, you may want to try this idea. To begin with, due to the unique nature of the position of trainer, a portion of the interview must consist of a presentation. Fifteen minutes should do the trick, with the subject a topic of the interviewee's choice. I like to see strong stand-up training skills incorporating good questioning, but they certainly are not imperative. Most of those skills can be taught to the trainer. They do not have to be instinctual. Compassion, though, is a difficult lesson to teach. To get a sense of how much your interviewee possesses, ask a question that intentionally makes you look a little foolish. Humor me for just a minute. This question may be about a point that was just covered or perhaps something that really does not relate to the subject. I look to see just what type of instincts this interviewee has for showing empathy to future students. Does the individual maintain his or her composure and attempt to find value in your question? Does he or she acknowledge the question as a good one to have been asked? How would you feel as a trainee in a room with 20 other strangers after this individual's response?

A third critical quality I look for and consider essential is a feeling of enthusiasm from the interviewee. I like to feel this enthusiasm during the presentation, during the question-and-answer period, before we start the interview, after we finish the interview, and in the hallway. As with compassion, it is difficult to teach enthusiasm.

There are some final qualities that I look for when hiring a trainer or seminar leader. Individually, however, these traits might fall in the category of nice to have as opposed to need to have. Flexibility is important, as is physical stamina, and sheer acting ability. This is not a position for a perfectionist simply because, in the pit as well as behind the scenes, things seldom go perfectly. Those who venture into that pit must bring with them many skills that are often taken for granted and, if possessed, are barely noticed. Presenters can be taught a great deal, but verbal skills, problem solving, and leadership are intangibles that some people possess and others do not. If you structure your interviews to include a glimpse of these traits, you will find the individual you are looking for.

Summary

To wrap this up, with regard to backgrounds conducive to training, I have seen enough stand-up trainers with diverse backgrounds to avoid making any definitive statements as to where the best trainers come from. Yet, with all due respect, I am convinced that the highest percentage of successful trainers typically have sales backgrounds. My own theory for this phenomenon is that these individuals have had to make a living by getting people to listen to and agree with their messages. When turned loose in the seminar room, their typical response is to do the same thing. What a marvelous quality these people bring into the room with them. They not only naturally teach their material, they unconsciously sell it to the trainees. However, I've seen amazing professional speakers who have never sold a thing in their lives. A desire to give your very best, all the time, and roll with the punches wherever they may come from is the ultimate trait found within this amazing profession.

Chapter 17

Avoiding the Training Trap
Problems with Relevance and Respect

Company training departments can take on many appearances. Some look strangely like personnel departments while others look more like marketing departments. Still other training departments appear so far removed from the rest of their organizations, they almost are separate entities. This would all be well and good, if it were not for the fact that the more removed a training department is from the rest of the company, the less credible it is in the eyes of those who depend on it.

How to Build Credibility and Gain Respect for Training

One of the biggest problems any training department must take on is the notion from those who are out doing their jobs as opposed to learning about it, that the training department is out of touch with what is really happening within the company. Therefore, we must confront problem one: *relevance* within a training department.

This lack of relevance issue is one of the first and often cheapest shots that a training department must contend with. At first glance, it appears to be a pretty good argument. How can this individual teach me something he or she is not currently doing? A particularly poignant example would be that of sales training. Products change, as do customers and their demands. How does an individual who has not been actively selling in the field effectively teach someone who is? There is an answer, albeit a somewhat disappointing one.

BUILD A QUALIFIED TRAINING STAFF
The training department must develop a staff where the majority of individuals have experience within the subject to be taught. This is a

rather basic principle, but often it is not adhered to. Experience will begin to establish the elusive credibility that is a "must have" in a good training department. You will notice I said a majority. I disagree that the department must consist entirely of successful field personnel. I firmly believe that a realistic combination of talents often can keep a department from tunnel-visioning ideas and techniques. With all due respect to the Smith family, who wants to live in a world where everybody's name is John Smith? Diversity breeds change and creativity, which are imperative within any department, especially a training department.

A formula that I have grown comfortable with is more like 75 percent out in the field teaching exactly what they have done previously and 25 percent who have had related experiences. Perhaps they have sold, but not that particular product, or they worked with systems, but not that particular system. The percentage would obviously change depending on the subject to be taught. The numbers I am speaking to reflect a "field, nonfield" environment.

MAKE SURE TRAINERS ARE KNOWLEDGEABLE AND UP-TO-DATE IN THEIR FIELDS

Next, to build this precious credibility, training departments should undertake a plan to keep the department relevant. Departments often try to do this by providing presenters with copies of all the literature, magazines, memos, and other correspondence involving their topics of expertise. Nice idea, and I would recommend it highly, except, unfortunately, that alone is not nearly enough. Presenters are faced with more pressures in a day than most people face in a month. Coping with the pressures of good delivery and eating and sleeping the subject matter on a daily basis make a lot of the correspondence placed in the presenter's mailbox meaningless, if that's the only source of information to keep the trainer up to speed. Even the most disciplined presenter has a poor chance of being able to absorb the information that is building on that poor, piled up paper holder once referred to as a desk. I am not for an instant saying this information is not important and need not be read. I just think if it is that critical, go over it in a team meeting or rotate individuals to summarize and redistribute the information. What I am also saying is to stick with the most successful approach to retaining relevance. Get that presenter out of the office on a regular basis and into the field where he or she belongs. One day of field observation or coaching will go a lot further than the out-of-control documentation disaster waiting for that presenter in his or her mailbox. Such fieldwork makes a strong statement to those who question the credibility and relevance of your department. It also does wonderful things for a presenter's confidence. A steady diet of fieldwork serves the entire company.

Training Can't Solve All Business Problems

Probably one of the most frustrating misconceptions that most training departments must contend with is the notion that practically anything that cannot be explained away must be a training issue. This brings us to problem two, hereby referred to as the "Dumpster Effect."

The ironies of training are astounding. First, this poor department, searching desperately for an identity, must work day and night to establish its own credibility. Then, almost as quickly as the department accomplishes this, it must begin to contend with the idea that everything can now be fixed with good training. Performance problem? Send them for training. Losing good personnel? Must be a training issue. Customers unhappy? Training. Apathy within another department? You guessed it, training. I could go on and on. The important point here is that, contrary to popular belief, not everything is a training issue. If the training department is not careful, though, it will find itself taking on issues it cannot and should not solve.

A series of four steps should accompany any request for training:

1. Consult.
2. Analyze.
3. Investigate.
4. Pilot.

CONSULT TO FIND OUT WHETHER TRAINING IS REALLY NEEDED

The idea of utilizing an outside consultant takes on a slight different connotation when you're reviewing a request for training. Here I simply mean that before you waste a tremendous amount of time and energy, you should ask some questions regarding the request for training. It is time to start questioning all those who are even remotely involved with the situation.

Let's look at a typical example. Let's say you are managing a telephone hotline and the director notifies you that there has been an increase in customer complaints about operator rudeness. This director immediately has the situation pegged as another training problem. Before wasting a lot of money on a problem that may not be, it's time to ask some questions of a lot of people. I would be most interested to hear from the customers—the dissatisfied ones and the satisfied ones. I would like to hear from the operators—those with a record of some complaints and those without, also tenured operators, and new hires. I want to hear from supervisors as well as management. Basically, I want to hear from just about anyone who has a relationship with this department and its duties. It is important to have a plan for this questioning. There are several questions I want answered:

+ How long has this been going on?
+ How often has this occurred?
+ How severe is this problem?
+ What are the repercussions of this problem?
+ What other actions, if any, have been taken in the past?

With this sampling of questions, I want to make sure, first, that the problem really exists and, second, that I am not reinventing the wheel. Often similar problems may have existed a generation ago (that's about two years in a typical training department), and those problems were dealt with in any number of successful or unsuccessful ways. I want to know about them.

Analyze the Potential Audience for the Training Program

It's not that I'm a skeptic . . . exactly. It's just that to be totally sure a problem exists and to add some real-world experiences to the potential training, it would be a good idea to observe and analyze the expected audience. Doing this should settle any last-minute doubts and begin to direct you to selecting the appropriate training package.

Investigate the Training Curriculum

Now that all involved have been consulted and the situation has been analyzed, it is time to research and select the curriculum. If time is an issue, benchmarking may help. Selecting the training format is almost as important as the curriculum itself. How long will your program be? How interactive and participative would you like to make it? Often you can answer questions like these by looking at the background of the audience and the size of your intended seminar.

Pilot a Test Training Program

Once the curriculum has been chosen, it is finally time to conduct the seminar. If the course is going to be taught more than once or twice, it is vital to take a look at its effectiveness. It is rare for restaurant chains to introduce new selections nationwide without setting up a few test sites first. Better to make a little mistake than a large one. Studying and reading a curriculum is one thing; teaching it is another. A pilot will allow you to test the curriculum and its effectiveness. Be warned: Pilots are not a whole lot of fun. There are a few rules that must be followed.

First, to make a fair observation, the curriculum must be delivered as written with little to no deviation by the instructor. No war stories, no analogies, and no embellishments. The idea is to see if the curriculum is strong enough as written. This is especially critical if more than one instructor is going to be teaching the seminar. The curriculum must be able to be handed off and still taught effectively. An addition that will complicate the evaluation is a presenter's style, which may not be duplicated by other presenters. In such scenarios, students are evaluating style and not curriculum. The fact of the matter is, a good presenter can make the art of paint drying an interesting topic, if allowed to embellish. The problem is, such presenters do not grow on trees, and it does not help with the evaluation of new training curriculum. Piloting means that curriculum is delivered word for word as written. That allows for a true test of the curriculum's potential success or failure. Not a lot of presenters will volunteer for this hazardous duty (this author included), but it is what is necessary to truly test the material.

Finally, when preparing to launch this new training campaign, it is important to set up some sort of measurement system to evaluate its effectiveness. Thinking positively, what are you going to use as evidence that the course is a success and the original problem has been fixed? Taking these measurements before the actual training takes place allows for a fair and unbiased appraisal once the program kicks off. For obvious reasons, whatever measurements are established before training must be taken after training. Nothing can be proven objectively without an apples-to-apples comparison.

Trying to solve all of life's problems through a Dumpster called "training" is a hazard that most training departments face. Be careful. Doing so will weaken the credibility of a training department as well as damage the morale of the presenters who represent it.

Validating Your Training Programs

One of many obstacles that a training department faces is proving its own validity. It seems that U.S. corporations either believe in the idea of training or they do not. Likewise, most individuals have a strong opinion supporting one side or the other. The unfortunate truth is that those who oppose training can make a fairly strong argument for their case as long as they are not pressed too hard. Their argument often involves a somewhat harmless, even insignificant little word. It is really all training foes have to do battle with, but for those who oppose training as a solution, this word is a battle cry. That word is "results." It's not that I am opposed to results. However, I often think individuals are looking in the wrong area for results. Let me provide you with a story that may help clear this up.

In high school and college, I had a passion for basketball. I loved to play the sport, and the sport liked me. I say liked, not loved, because although I had the desire to play with some of the best, my 5'10", 150-pound body took an enormous beating. After years of breaks, sprains, twists, and pains, I decided to hang up my high-tops and participate in a far less violent sport—running. After being dared into my first race, a half marathon no less, I realized I needed someone to help teach me the ropes. A friend of mine put me on a rather strict running program of about five miles a day. Same course, five miles a day. He preached to me that if I stuck with this course and this mileage, I would notice appreciable results after one week. That sure sounded good to me, so off we went on my first training run. When we finished, I was tired and panting as I checked my watch. About 35 minutes, and was I ever out of breath.

We drove home, and as I stood under the shower, still panting, I realized I had a long way to go. Night after night, I ran alone. The same course, the same five miles. What really frustrated me was that my time was not improving that dramatically, and I knew in my heart I was giving it my all. My panting at the finish line told me that! Finally, frustrated as I neared the end of my second week, I called my friend to voice my displeasure with his techniques (and my physical prowess). He seemed confused and promised a run together the next night. Together, again we ran the same course, the same five miles. Almost gloating with an "I told you so" sarcastic attitude, I pointed to my watch and showed him the time. It had not improved much at all. He was somewhat bewildered as he looked at me and said he never told me my time would improve dramatically in one or two weeks. He told me I would see results. He then suggested I look at my rate of breathing. We had finished the run one minute before, and I was breathing as if we had not even started. It was a classic case of looking in the wrong place for the wrong results.

The problem that most training departments must cope with is similar to that story. Those who fund and support training must show results. Those who are seeking this information often look in the wrong place.

Sometimes we look to see just how much more an employee is selling after training, and we do not see an appreciable difference. Certainly not enough to warrant the enormous expense of training! What we may fail to look at, however, is the immediate and major improvement in customer service with a salesperson who is perceived as polished and confident. Those are results that pay dividends for many years. Long term, that represents big bucks.

We may be automating an office environment and conducting technical training. Short term, it costs money to send a presenter out, and it costs even more in lost production. The argument is made that these employees could learn from each other, or on their own time. After training, the speed of those who participated has not gone up. Maybe the error rate has dropped, however. Certainly, if nothing else, morale has improved with good, effective training. As mentioned in the previous chapter, the cost to hire and fire an employee is astronomical. If you were looking for short term, there it is. Long term, it is no contest.

Remember, long term means you are going to have to wait for those results. This could potentially take years. Unfortunately, for those who do not enjoy a good mystery, tracking and measuring these results can cost more than the training itself. Regardless, let's at least make sure we are looking in the right place and taking the correct measurements.

Convincing those in your organization of the importance of training can be a challenge, to say the least. For the most part, we must be reminded over and over again that, as with a good stock, results are more accurately and more fairly measured long term than short term.

Summary

Understanding the true value of training and avoiding the training traps that can present themselves have never been more important than now. When budgets tighten it seems that training departments find themselves front and center to receive the first cuts. That means those of us in the training industry must fight even harder. You are as good as our last training program delivered, and that's why you must beware of what can and cannot be fixed through training, who to hire, and how to make sure that every program and delivery is your very best.

Chapter 18

Developing a Training Staff

Traditionally for most companies, a training department is born more out of necessity than careful planning. You can call it "budget problems," or you can call it "credibility problems." You can even call it "identity problems." Typically, when a training department really takes off, it is more for reactive reasons than proactive reasons. Assuming your decisions are based on the latter, here are a couple of thoughts you may want to consider.

Emphasize the Quality of Your Training Programs

As with any department (or corporation for that matter), the first emphasis should be on *quality*. I know that seems to be a buzzword for many businesses at this time, but it is a reality. As with any other customer-related business, word of lack of quality spreads at a much faster rate than word of quality. There is no reason to whine or complain about what is or is not fair about that statement; it is simply reality.

To establish a reputation for quality, the first thing a training department must do is make a statement to the other departments or outside organizations of its competence. There is really only one way to do this, and that is to start training. Most likely, this training will come from a request or need from another department. Once it is determined that, in fact, there is a need, be sure the department is not on the line to do too much. Training is not the end-all, cure-all. It exists simply to improve performance, not to solve world hunger. The sooner a training department and those around it realize this, the better.

Make Sure Trainers Work with the Curriculum Developers

Another important factor involving the creation of a training department is the function of its employees. One of the first things that managers seem eager to do, when running a training department, is to separate the presenters from the curriculum developers. Let me make one thing perfectly clear: This is a terrible mistake. It follows the same old logic that states we keep sales and service people apart. It seems many forget about the potential for one to teach the other, increasing both employees' value. Sadly, it remains an unwritten law in most companies. Suppose we keep those who work on your car's engine away from those who work on its chassis. I once owned a car where this was so much a reality that I actually had to stock two separate sets of tools—metric for the engine and linear for the chassis. Where the two connected, it was anybody's guess! This also explains why, for some cars, changing the oil filter is like heart bypass surgery. I guarantee, before that engine was placed inside that chassis, changing the filter was a piece of cake. So why is it so many training departments keep presenters away from developers? Certainly, the argument can be made that if presenters need only concentrate on delivery, the focus and presentation would be better. The problem is, I made that argument, and even I do not believe it.

The benefits of allowing the two departments to work hand in hand are many. If the presenter assists the curriculum developer, there is the potential for the presenter to master the curriculum and delivery faster. Next, not only does the pride factor give an instructor more confidence, it translates to the credibility that presenters and training departments are often seeking. Also, the potential for an out-of-touch curriculum developer missing out on real-world information is eliminated. Typically, presenters have experience in the fields they are teaching, and involved presenters can help monitor the relevance of a curriculum they work with on a daily basis. The chance of an attitude problem among presenters is also held in check when they have a say in the final project. Finally, once a program is up and running, the training department essentially has a sea of subject matter experts to draw on when needed. Keeping these channels of communication open can help ensure the curriculum is not becoming outdated. It can also help to ensure your training department is not wasting a valuable resource.

Promote Consistency in Course Content and Training Style

The last obstacle training departments must clear, once a program is up and running, is consistency. By "consistency," I am referring to multiple presenters teaching the same curriculum. This scenario is a pretty typical one. An instructor sits through a pilot with other instructors to learn how the curriculum is to be delivered. The students come to town and are bowled over by the training. (Perhaps I'm a little biased here.) The instructors celebrate those first couple of tough weeks, and each begins to settle into the curriculum . . . his or her own way. Now, I am an advocate of each presenter developing his or her own style. What worries me is when a presenter crosses the style line and begins to change the curriculum. This often occurs due to boredom. It is a lot like an actor who delivers his or her lines dutifully night after night. When the part is new, so too are the lines.

After weeks of the same lines, night after night, the words begin to sound stale. The actor changes the lines to freshen up the part a bit and is lulled into believing the lines are now better. Some actors truly believe that they have somehow improved their Shakespeare. Fortunately, there are directors whose main job is to act as the actor's eyes from the back of the theater and remind the actor that although the words do not change, the audiences do. For them, the actor is saying these words for the first time. Each audience deserves the best. In business, the actor's script is replaced by the presenter's curriculum. The director is replaced by either a manager or an observer. In either case, take comfort in knowing the students' reactions and questions will no doubt take the curriculum to new and exciting places.

If it were not for the fact that students talk to each other constantly, inconsistency among presenters would not be such a major problem. Students have egos also, and each wants to assure the other that he or she is attending the best seminar and has the best presenter. I have actually observed students involved in heated arguments over which presenter's interpretation of the curriculum was most accurate. Often the students are forced to pick sides because both interpretations cannot be right. The loser's morale can be adversely affected along with the corresponding presenter's reputation and that of the department.

To make matters worse, the most challenging task involving consistency is not curriculum. It is subjective evaluation by presenters.

Subjective evaluation involves interpretation by the presenter. In school, most of us were subjected to this type of interpretation when we wrote papers or completed essay exams. There is not a large call for this type of testing in corporate training. However, a number of courses involve role-play, demo, or case study evaluation. In this type of testing, the presenter interprets an action or series of skills and judges the student's effectiveness. Perhaps now you can see the potential difficulty when more than one instructor is evaluating this type of behavior.

The good news is there are solutions to both of these scenarios. The problem with curriculum is best solved with the proactive approach of establishing a benchmark right off the bat. This will often be served best by using your most tenured or senior presenter. The simple truth is that carrying out this task is not rocket science. Using a tenured instructor will, however, act as the final word involving gray areas of the curriculum and the presenter's interpretation. The only reason I suggest it be a tenured individual is that few fields hold higher egos than the training field, and this designation, handled fairly, may help to prevent a mutiny. Once this person has been put in place, it should be his or her further responsibility to assist in cross-training any new presenters, act as a contact for the curriculum developers, and, if possible, attend the various seminars to observe on a random, routine basis.

The more difficult of the two scenarios, expertise and consistency, involves achieving consistency in the subjective portions of the instructors' evaluations. The most effective approach I have ever used involves a few steps and a few late nights. To begin with, video- or audiotape a few samples of whatever you are evaluating. By "a few samples," I am referring to samples of what is considered excellent, good, and not so good. The next step is assemble your team of presenters, order in some pizzas, and prepare for a late evening. What you need to accomplish is a consensus among those in the room as to what to interpret as what. Just a reminder: Consensus does not mean everyone in the room must agree 100 percent with the group's interpretation, merely that everyone can support the actions of the group. Gone are the days (and thankfully so) when consensus meant those in the group could *live* with the decision. That one word led to a lot of "I told you so's" by disgruntled individuals who did not get their way.

The mark of any good training department is its ability to achieve and deliver consistency. With the early establishment of a bench-marked individual and group consensus on the interpretation of subjective portions of the curriculum, a training department can sell credibility and effectiveness to whomever it interacts with.

Summary

When training is conducted properly, everyone knows it; and when it's not conducted properly, everyone knows it. Establishing a strong relationship with whomever is developing the curriculum is critical. Sometimes these developers are from your own company, and sometimes these developers are your clients you have been contracted to deliver for. Working together to ensure that your content is relevant and accurate and that the material is being delivered in a consistent manner will go a long way to making sure that everything delivered will be done in a quality manner.

Chapter 19

Evaluation and Support

Let's assume that you have diligently studied a proposed problem and have decided that training is, in fact, necessary. It is now time to look at how you are going to evaluate your training. This is by no means an optional step. Without feedback, you are wasting a valuable resource to help assess your training. First, we examine the evaluation options that are available for your trainees.

Evaluating Trainees

When most of us think about student evaluation, often the first word that comes to mind is "test." Years of schooling condition most of us to fear the dreaded evaluation. In corporate training, thankfully, often a few more options are available. Certainly, written or verbal tests are viable alternatives to evaluate trainees' retention of information. I only have one question: Do you feel written or verbal tests enable you to evaluate trainees' performance? My answer to that question is no; these forms of evaluation usually do not give the presenter a true insight into performance. Corporate training typically is put in place to teach information that trainees need to apply on the job, so there is a bit of a disconnect between written or verbal tests and corporate training objectives.

Another form of evaluation used in corporate training is called "ability testing." This form of testing is commonly used in more technical situations and requires that trainees merely parrot the skills being taught. Demonstrating a technique on a computer or other piece of equipment would be examples of this form of evaluation.

When it comes to evaluation, the trend in corporate training seems to be toward implementation testing. Can trainees actually utilize the information being taught? This form of testing attempts to pit trainees with real-world situations requiring them to apply what has been taught. Often this form of testing even prods trainees to make decisions in areas that have not necessarily been taught but occur in the real world and relate to their tasks. Some common examples of implementation testing are role-plays and, my personal favorite, simulations. Now trainees must think on their feet using the skills that have been taught as well as their instincts for the topic.

Evaluating the Trainer

Let's turn our attention to another important evaluation topic: you. Most training evaluations attempt to separate course content from the evaluation of the presenter. Your interest in the content portion of the evaluation will most likely be dependent on your relationship with the curriculum development side of your training. Content is usually evaluated on a 5- to 10-point scale that attempts to measure not only the trainees' proficiency after the training but their levels of proficiency before the training. A sample question may look something like this:

Hardware Configuration Knowledge

Before Training	1	2	3	4	5	6	7	8	9	10
		(Poor)			(Average)				(Excellent)	
After Training	1	2	3	4	5	6	7	8	9	10
		(Poor)			(Average)				(Excellent)	

Using this technique to evaluate content allows you to measure the end result of your training, and in addition it gives you a more accurate accounting for the level of improvement your training is providing.

Evaluation of the presenter is often a more controversial subject. This controversy lies in two areas. The first centers around who should actually see the evaluation. Some say only the presenter. It is the presenter's seminar, and he or she is most affected by the results. Others say just about everyone should see the evaluation *except* the presenter. Once evaluations have been tabulated and logged, the presenter typically is given what amounts to a quarterly rundown of the numbers.

I see value in both methods, but neither exclusively. When evaluations are compiled, the presenter gets a better sense of possible trends. The fact of the matter is that some seminars are difficult. It could be a bad mix of trainees or a bad week for the presenter. These things happen. That is why it is so important to look for trends and not isolated occurrences. However, it is a big mistake not to allow a presenter immediate feedback as to how he or she is doing. Why wait two months to start fixing or adjusting? The solution must be a combination of the two feedback methods. It should not even be an option to look over the week's evaluations. Study them, learn from them. Then turn them over to be tabulated to get some perspective regarding trends.

Advance Preparation Using Preschools

Another form of evaluation of trainees can be made using preschools and pretests. Every presenter has his or her own fears. Mine happens to be preschools. I have grown to cower when I hear that term for a couple of reasons. Before I frighten anyone who happens to be reading these words, let me tell you some of the positive aspects of a preschool.

To begin with, preschools are designed with one very basic goal in mind—to allow trainees to do certain work ahead of time that they can easily do alone. The concept is a simple one. If trainees look over the materials, are responsible, and study hard, they can begin together at a more advanced level. "Hit the ground running" is a popular phrase for what you are attempting to accomplish with a preschool. No need to waste valuable time with certain basics that do not require a presenter's help. More can be accomplished in a shorter period, thus saving money and time. Sounds too good to be true? It just may be.

I have several concerns with preschools. First, they are a little tricky to administrate. Remember, preschools have to be timed so that those who are taking them have enough time to adequately complete them. It is easy to have one of the preschool packages fall between the cracks and not go out properly or at all, and with that one miss can come a boatload of trouble for the presenter. The seminar training pace can be knocked off stride, and it is certainly no fun to hit the ground running when one or two trainees are lagging behind.

Another concern with preschools is trainees' realistic ability to finish them. To this day, a reality of training is that although many companies are finally seeing the light about more quality training, the majority of seminars still consist of new hires. Ask yourself this question: "What was I doing for those first precious, memorable couple of months on the job?" I'll tell you what I was doing, along with most of you—sorting through file cabinets, closets, and any other neglected areas that needed to be cleaned up. Often there is not a whole lot of time for the new guy to study preschools. And now it really gets scary.

Problem: How do you get trainees to study preschools responsibly? You could use an honor system, but if you believe that, you probably believe you really can shave a whisker one more time before it snaps back. Sorry to break the bad news to you, but my experience with honor system preschools says if you get 75 percent of the trainees to complete the preschool, you are way ahead of the game. That still leaves 25 percent of the trainees not able to move ahead. Although the temptation is to leave those who did not complete the work behind, the potential difficulties that would cause makes it an impossibility. What most training courses are left with is a preschool with no credibility, which translates to fewer and fewer students completing it.

The most common solution to the preceding problem is a pretest. A positive side to pretests is that you can count on the rate of completed preschools rising dramatically. The negative side is that there must be a consequence for not passing.

Here is where I start getting squeamish. You see, it is not the preschool that I really object to. It is the *pretest* that so often accompanies it. The most common device used by corporate training departments is the practice of "send homes." Fail the preschool test, you go home. Sounds simple enough. The ramifications, however, are staggering. As a child, I always marveled at how wonderful it must have been to be a teacher and have the power to pass some youngsters and fail others. To give life or take it away. (I had some rather rocky years.) Teachers must love that control over their students' destinies. Little did I know what a real nightmare that kind of power can bring. I have seen students on a send-home pretest involving a typewriter demo forget how to shift to capitalize the first letters in their own names. A sleepless night of fear can bring out some very strange results in trainees. If they pass, you often can rule out any real learning due to emotional fatigue. If they do not pass, it gets even worse. Let me draw a rather emotional scenario. A student flies to your training facility and faces a send-home pretest to see how well he has studied the preschool. With so much riding on the exam, he tenses up, and although he really does know the information, he does not achieve the passing test score of 80 percent. Instead he receives a grade of 75 percent. With tears in his eyes, he approaches the presenter and begs to be allowed to stay. Rules are rules, however, and he is sent home . . . humiliated, discouraged, and suffering from an emotional blow he may never recover from. The presenter often is not doing that much better. In some ways, it actually takes on the feeling of a death in the seminar to those who remain.

If I did not frighten you emotionally, let me take a shot at it financially. Let's take the same scenario as before, but reexamine it from a legal angle. Let's suppose that same student fails the same test. He received a 75 percent and needed an 80 percent to stay in the course. On that long ride home, this student begins to ask some questions: "Who says an 80 percent indicates you know enough of the information to stay in town?" "Who says every question asked was a fair one?" "Who says every question asked related to the preschool that we were given to read?" By the way, that student goes home, is fired from his company, goes on unemployment, and loses his home and eventually his wife. Sorry to paint such a bleak picture, but it is of such stuff that massive lawsuits are made.

The only way to counteract such a suit is to have the preschool test legally validated before anyone is sent home. To do this is no easy chore. It typically requires the assistance of a couple of clinical psychologists employed by companies that study each question against the material given in the preschool. They then go through a procedure that can take months of testing the exam. A norm is established and the test is then blessed as legally validated. To administer a test that is not legally validated is the equivalent of playing Russian roulette with a major lawsuit.

Even after the test is legally validated, you still are not out of the woods. You are going to have to have a talk with all the presenters who are involved in this testing. You must explain that the conditions of the testing (i.e., time limits, use of additional materials) must be consistent. One other message must be delivered as well. There can be no exceptions to who stays and who goes. By this I mean that if 80 percent is established as the passing point, 79 percent is a send-home.

No case-by-case interpretation is allowed. I would also recommend that a senior presenter or manager oversee the entire operation. That also includes the individual who has become distraught and is pleading with the instructor to let him stay. As I said before, reinforcing this rule is one of the most difficult aspects of a presenter's job. It is often better for all involved if a third party can intervene and can make the necessary arrangements. Any deviation once again opens the door to potential lawsuits from those who did not receive these same considerations.

It may seem as if you are damned if you do and damned if you don't, but there is one compromise I have become comfortable with. Rather than send home the student who does not pass the preschool test, intensify his or her workload. By this, I mean allow the person to take another test the following day that requires additional work outside the regular seminar load. If the student does not pass the second test, perhaps an essay or paper might be in order. The idea is to bring the person up to speed as humanely as possible. By "humanely," I simply mean showing compassion while allowing a trainee to continue to work and try with dignity.

Another idea that is particularly effective for a one-day course is simply to put in the preschool a letter that states test results will be sent back to the individual's mentor. Sometimes lessons from academia do work in the training world!

Realistic Expectations

As training approaches, it is always a good idea to solicit expectations of those involved in the training. Often trainings cannot live up to some of the advanced billing they receive. Unrealistic expectations can be set both for and against training.

What comes to mind when I think of expectations that are unrealistically conservative is the old saying that I still hear in a lot of the courses I teach: "If I can learn one or two new ideas in this training, then it will have been worthwhile." Yuk! If, during the course of your seminar, the average individual learns only one or two new ideas, I would consider your training a failure. Recently I attended a one-day seminar dealing with managing different personality types. At the end of a disappointing day, I looked over my notes and handouts and determined I had only learned one new idea that I could use. I do not recall jumping up and down for joy thinking what a productive day I had. I do recall being disappointed and feeling I had been taken advantage of. I assure you, we *can* dream for more.

Now, the flip side to this expectation argument is to assume too much will come out of training. Good training will not move mountains; it will not cure the incurable. The human brain can withstand only so much; even with the best written curriculum delivered expertly, there will be nice-to-knows and need-to-knows. Realistic expectations for training should call for stimulating training, delivered professionally (implementing a host of ideas from this book) that leaves participants motivated and satisfied.

The realities of management support are a little like a fair-weather friend. When the money is there, often management will stand on soapboxes and preach the value of training. "Do what it takes; I want these people trained right!" they'll say, or "Money is no object; my people have to learn the right way!" Sadly, when budgets are cut and times are lean, what is the first to go? You guessed it, training.

Summary

This book's intention, is not to paint a doom-and-gloom picture of corporate training. As a matter of fact, it is quite the opposite. I want to point out the realities of expectations when you are preparing to train. My real intention is to explain how to make your training so unforgettable and effective, through good times or bad, that it and your trainees will thrive. Having a realistic view of how to prepare your audiences, how to evaluate your trainees, and, in turn, how you will be evaluated, and how to prepare for those evaluations will make the job you do a whole lot easier.

Chapter 20

Adventures in Cross-Training

Once presenters have mastered the necessary teaching tools, they then have to begin to learn the curriculum they will deliver. How much preparation time is enough? There are many theories and opinions as to what is the best method for teaching a presenter a new course. Frankly, I have to say that in all the courses I have learned and then taught, I cannot remember any two cross-training approaches being the same. I will be more than glad to offer some recommendations, but first let me tell you some of the factors involved.

Factors to Consider before Cross-Training Trainers

To begin with, a key determining factor is the material type. On courses that require extensive technical knowledge and training, I have witnessed cross-training of new presenters that takes over a year before presenters are ready to teach without assistance. Some less technical courses can have presenters ready to go in a week.

Another factor to consider is how frequently the course will be taught. If you plan to teach the course only a couple of times, it will not be very cost effective to spend months just learning the curriculum.

It is my intent to look at situations that represent more of the norm. Every course is different in its own way, but hopefully you will be able to adjust your timetables and techniques using some of the recommended ideas.

How to Cross-Train a New Presenter

Let's look at a classic course that requires little technical information. It is one week in duration and is taught on a consistent basis by four presenters. On most teams, there is a lead or senior presenter, who should be running the show. As I mentioned in Chapter 18, it is important that someone take responsibility for consistency, which is critical when cross-training new presenters.

The mistake many training departments make is to throw the new presenter into the back of a new course, have him or her watch the presenter conducting the seminar without telling him or her what to look for, and ask both presenters to debrief after each day. On paper, that seems to be a sound approach. The problem is that it just does not work effectively. To begin with, try sitting in the back of a seminar without saying a word for a week and see how much you get out of it. Add to that the fact that at the end of a day, the presenter teaching the seminar is not exactly fresh as a daisy and raring to go. The net effect is a new presenter absorbing little during the day and picking up even less during the debriefs.

The best approach I have ever used is a combination of ideas. To do the job in a quality fashion, you are going to have to free up more than one presenter to help. Having the new presenter sit in the back of the room watching is not a bad idea, but get the senior presenter to conduct the debriefs. This will benefit your cross-training in two ways. First, you will provide your new presenter with someone who is not totally exhausted, and, second, you will achieve the consistency you must strive for when multiple presenters are teaching the same course. Look over the curriculum carefully. See if there are any areas that would allow you to have the debrief sessions while the seminar is going on. Some classic spots that often can be used are seminar reviews, small-group exercises, lab work, and individual study. If at all possible, try to conduct your debriefs during one of those times. New presenters also get exhausted. Sometimes I can honestly say that I am more tired at the end of the day after watching a seminar than I am delivering a seminar. I cannot provide any logic as to why that is true, but it is. I have not met too many presenters who do not agree.

Another classic mistake of many training departments involves the preparation, or lack of, that new presenters receive before watching the seminar they have been assigned to teach. Giving a new presenter a copy of the instructor guide, a highlighter, and well wishes is not my idea of preparation. The new presenter must be prepped on just what to look for while watching the seminar being taught.

Start out by telling your new presenter to watch for areas of the curriculum that might be confusing or difficult to teach. If, while observing a portion of the curriculum, the presenter is confused, that material most likely will be confusing to the trainees he or she teaches. The frustrating part of cross-training is that if you do not make note of these areas, you probably will forget where some of them are. Remember, by the time you study your way through these areas and work with the individual who is conducting the cross-training, you will know far more than the trainees know about your subject. You have put in more time and effort than the trainees will ever put forth. Once you become familiar with those areas, you will have a natural tendency to fly through them. If you make notes of these areas, not only will you become more confident knowing you can answer the most likely questions, but you will have a permanent reminder to slow down and make sure everyone understands.

Other things to watch for when cross-training are areas in the curriculum that you find yourself daydreaming through. As with the areas that gave you difficulty, if you are losing interest, so are a number of other trainees. Look around sometime, and you will see what I mean. Almost all curricula have dead spots. These are areas that, for whatever reason, tend to lose their audiences.

A classic example of this phenomenon can be found in movies as well. When I was 16, the first job I ever had was as an usher at a movie theater. This is where I first noticed dead spots. During the movie, I would stand in the back of the theater and watch the backs of 200 heads remain totally riveted on the screen. At certain points in the movie, often when the action changed, about 90 percent of the people would move. It would often be just a stretch or a crossing of the legs, but almost everyone would move. Then they would settle back again and get drawn into the action. Curriculum is the same way. Not every part can be totally spellbinding, but you do not want to lose your trainees either. As you have already learned in Chapter 8 of this book, you can always come up with some interest-sustaining ideas that might provide some punch without changing the curriculum at all.

The final and most important area to focus in on when cross-training has to do with logistics. In most situations, new presenters bring with them a certain amount of experience in the topic they are to train in. Certainly, some degree of brush-up is required, but for the most part, the product knowledge is there. The real challenge becomes learning the logistics of the course in question. Here are some examples of logistical concerns:

- ◆ Timing (probably the most difficult of all), included in all the examples
- ◆ Small-group exercises
- ◆ Trainee materials
- ◆ Handout materials
- ◆ Visual aids needed

When a new presenter is cross-training, it is critical for him or her to focus on these issues. Nothing can take the place of experience, but achieving logistical competence sure can do wonders. To begin with, a new presenter who knows what is coming next and is prepared with all necessary materials avoids a lot of anxiety. This preparation and newfound confidence translate into the presenter leaving a more polished impression with the trainees.

With the importance of logistics in mind, here is a suggestion that might make your cross-training more effective. Try using two or three different color highlighters when following a curriculum in a cross-training environment. Set up a key and stick with it. Perhaps red will indicate movement, either group activity or breaks. Green may represent handouts or direct references from the trainee's participant guide. Yellow can signify the use of visual aids. This is by no means a new trick. The problem is that most presenters who start out with an idea of this concept in mind end up with so many colors and symbols, their highlighted notes wind up being no help at all. I can't say it enough: "If you emphasize everything, you emphasize nothing." Be selective in what you highlight and in the colors you use, and you should not have any difficulties.

Don't Be a Perfectionist

So we are now back to the first question asked: "How long is enough?" Hopefully, by using some of the ideas that were discussed, you now have a better idea of how to gauge your response. Let me leave you with this one friendly warning: Be on the lookout for the perfectionist part of your personality taking control over your actions early in your training. When I use the term "perfectionist," I am referring to the individual who insists that he or she must do everything perfectly and that he or she must know everything there is to know before training begins. It is hard to criticize an individual for this type of work ethic. The problem is that perfectionists age very quickly in the training profession. I have often referred to years in training as "dog years." The 7-to-1 ratio in years is about right when you look at a presenter going under fire with an active stand-up delivery schedule. Presenters who attempt to prepare for every potential situation in their training usually find the results sadly disappointing. Let me provide you with an analogy to illustrate to you why I say this.

As I mentioned earlier, for some time now I have been a runner. For various reasons, my running has slipped a bit now, but from time to time, I take my running quite seriously. I am not alone. One of the reasons I run is that, although I enjoy running for its own sake, I love racing. Each year I enter a certain number of races, and although I have not run a marathon in a few years, it still remains my favorite race. A lot can be learned about runners by the way they train for this distance. I do not exactly consider myself a maverick, but my training has always been considered a little bit unique. To this day, when I am getting ready for a race or working with someone else to help him or her get ready, I preach a straightforward philosophy: "Work hard, take good care of yourself, show up strong, and trust in your abilities." That may appear to be a whole lot of rhetoric, but the thinking is rather simple. If you work hard and do what you need to do to take care of yourself, you will find the strength to persevere.

What helped mold this theory was watching the complete opposite in those I would compete with. Many would put in more miles training, would make sacrifices that caused them to feel miserable, and basically would show up at race time looking like death. Certainly you have seen these people running along the side of the road looking as if they are ready to find a bridge, jump off, and end it all. Too bad. There are plenty of runners like myself who actually look as if we are somewhat enjoying ourselves. The most interesting news of all is despite all the training and neurotic behavior, these athletes often lose to knuckle-heads like me. Why? Because they are too tired, run down, and often injured to do their best. Their best efforts were spent weeks ago around some dark, lonely track.

The perfectionist personality runs the same risk. The ultimate irony is that as with the neurotic runner, often you reach a point where the more you prepare, the less prepared you become. Repeat after me: *You cannot prepare for everything.* Relax. Put in a reasonable amount of time in your preparation and show up for training sharp and ready to think on your feet. Ask a combat soldier, and he or she will tell you there is no way to truly simulate live-fire conditions. There also is no way for a presenter to simulate conditions under fire. Study your notes, feel confident about your logistical preparation, and trust your instincts.

Power and Its Many Misuses

The final lesson that needs to be discussed before you deposit this book on some dusty shelf (hopefully in a prominent location) deals with one of the by-products of being a presenter and finally becoming comfortable with the curriculum and delivery: *power.* Sadly, one of the first, and often most tragic, pitfalls a newer presenter experiences is the lure of power.

As a new presenter prepares, his or her eagerness is unmatched. Working with as many new presenters as I do (and even some grizzled vets who come in for a checkup), I see the same pattern repeating itself. Presenters leave with a win-at-all-costs attitude: a desire to tailor the message to the trainees, to be enthusiastic, and, without question or hesitation, to do what it takes and go the extra mile to make the trainees' experience a rewarding one.

When does that desire stop? When do we begin to doubt our own message?

After successfully coping with the pressure of those initial experiences, a kind of metamorphosis takes place. After reaping the rewards—the praise of our participants and peers—we begin to believe in our own immortality. We truly are talented! We truly are powerful! Coincidentally, about this same time, the trainees we are sent begin to lack the motivation and drive we were accustomed to. Or do they?

This addiction to power now takes on a more cruel appearance. If trainees cannot keep up, they are to be admonished for it. If classwork does not meet our expectations, there will be a serious price to pay. And there we stand, pathetically believing our own misguided feelings:

"Boy, trainees just aren't what they used to be. It's a good thing they have me to kick them in the pants!" *Don't do it.*

Summary

Effective cross-training is the key to consistent delivery. When it's done properly, the only real difference an audience can pick up from one instructor to another is the style of the presenter. There is no perfect delivery, but that doesn't mean we don't strive to do the very best we can. Allowing for and appreciating that every presenter brings his or her own unique style reminds us that we are not creating clones, but rather program consistency. Focusing on the actual material delivered by maintaining a uniformed approach regarding what is handed out, homework, program timing, program activities, and more will help create the consistency you seek. Empathy and compassion toward those you work with will help you avoid the trap power can create.

Epilogue: What's Next?

Well, that is about it. Putting all I know into this book has been both rewarding and a bit disconcerting. That's because there are certain things, like technology, that change almost weekly while other things, like how we actually win over a room of people with sound communication skills and hustle, do not change at all. It is my hope that after reading this book, you are better equipped to understand the realities of nailing presentations and workshops and perhaps are in a better position to get up and do your job under fire. With this, the fourth edition of this book, it has now been a 25-year journey to keep you and it up-to-date.

The appeal of presenting and performing in front of audiences centers on the fact that few other careers offer as much excitement or allow for as much creativity. No two days are the same. Countless variables affect what goes on in the pit. As a professional presenter, you can die from the pressure or thrive under it. I have attempted to give you as many different forms of ammunition as possible.

Experiment! If one idea does not work, try another. To this day, I keep a pad of paper inside the lectern dedicated to nothing else but possible changes to the Presentation Skills programs I teach. As a result of changes in curriculum and delivery techniques, this course currently has seen a roughly 900 percent increase in participants from before I rewrote it. As they say, "If it ain't broke . . . fix it better!"

The possible frustration that often goes along with fixing it better is the reality that while you are trying to implement new ideas and processes, for some period of time, you probably will get worse. For example, take the UPPOPPR process. It is not easy to master immediately, yet anyone who watches it in action will swear by it. The real problem is not being convinced to use it but being convinced to stick with it through the conscious competent blues. The first time you attempt to use a number of the ideas I have laid out for you, you will probably be worse, not better.

Before you lose your temper and swear off the name of Rob Jolles, let me leave you with one last story that may help clear all this up. When I was about 13 years old, I was watching some new tennis prodigy named Jimmy Connors on television . . . Because I was left-handed, extremely competitive, and somewhat obnoxious, I decided that Jimmy Connors (who is also left-handed) was my new sports hero and was inspired to play the game myself. I went on a begging spree that ended with the purchase of a Wilson T-2000 just like my hero's. I would not say that many sports came naturally to me, but for some reason, tennis did. Without taking any lessons, I was immediately able to beat all of my friends who also got into tennis at about the same time. Later, when I went out for my high school tennis team, the coach asked me if I had ever taken any lessons. I proudly told him, "No." He asked me to work with another teacher on my serve. What puzzled me was that my serve was fast and consistent. When I went to the other teacher, the first thing he did was twist the racquet in my hand to what amounted to a backhand grip. He went on to explain that although my serve was fast, it was too predictable. He wanted to teach me how to spin the ball and create what in tennis is known as a kick serve. It was extremely frustrating trying to hit the ball with one-tenth of the racquet, but I remember him patiently telling me not to worry where the ball was going, just to use the correct technique and the ball would eventually go right where I wanted it to go. Perhaps the toughest part of learning this serve was playing against my friends with it. I double-faulted constantly and lost to people I had never lost to in my life. I would constantly look down at my grip and dream about switching back. I could get the ball in that way, and it was fast. I also realized I could play tennis every day of my life and my serve would never improve. It took discipline, but I refused to change back to my old grip. Now serving is effortless. My serve is more accurate, better than it ever was in the past, and the more I practice, the better it gets.

What's the moral to that story? Using a number of the techniques that I have taught you will require you to leave your comfort zone, and most likely you will get a little worse before you get better. You will probably find yourself muttering under your breath reasons for going back to your old ways. I hope you don't change your grip back but instead pay the price for improvement.

Watch out for the unconscious incompetent spirits that prey on more tenured instructors. Keep pushing yourself to "fix it better," and read those evaluations. Those are your customers speaking, and as with any other business, they ultimately will determine your success or failure.

There is no greater joy in writing than to hear from those who have read my words and listened to my stories. I would love to hear from you, so fill out the reply card or drop me an email at Training@Jolles .com. Good luck, and may these ideas as well as your energy and enthusiasm serve you when you go into the pit, and under fire!

Index

Please rate this book using the scale below.
Enter the appropriate number under the Rating column.

Unsatisfactory	Fair	Satisfactory	Favorable	Very Favorable
1	2	3	4	5

Rating

1. How effective was this book in teaching you the
   fundamentals of corporate training?   _____

2. If you have used the UPPOPPR process, how would
   you rate its effectiveness?   _____

3. In what ways was the book most valuable to you?
   Comment: _____

   _____

4. What would you like to see improved about this book?
   Comment: _____

   _____

5. Please describe your relationship to training (type of
   training, frequency, etc.).
   Comment: _____

   _____

6. Can you share a success story based on any ideas
   implemented from this book?
   Comment: _____

   _____

   _____

Your name & address (optional): _____

   _____

   _____

Send your comments to: Jolles Associates, Inc.
                           P.O. Box 30009
                           Bethesda, MD 20824
                           1-703-759-7767
Or e-mail to: training@jolles.com

From keynotes to multi-day programs, Rob Jolles customizes his content and delivery to suit your organization's specific needs. To learn more about booking Rob for a meeting or conference, or to attend a program at the Jolles Academy in Washington, D.C.:

Visit: www.Jolles.com

Email: Training@Jolles.com

Sign up: to receive Rob's free biweekly BLArticle®. Part blog, part article, Rob's BLArticle® is a one-of-a-kind e-communication dedicated to inspiring, informing, and interacting. www.jolles.com/blarticle

Join: Rob on Facebook www.facebook.com/JollesAssociates/

Follow: Rob on Twitter @robjolles

Connect: with Rob on LinkedIn